T0245567

THE ABOLITIONIST'S JOURNAL

THE ~ James D. Richardson ~
ABOLITIONIST'S
JOURNAL MEMORIES OF AN
AMERICAN ANTISLAVERY FAMILY

High Road Books   Albuquerque

HIGH
ROAD

High Road Books is an imprint of the University of New Mexico Press

Library of Congress Cataloging-in-Publication Data

NAMES: Richardson, James, 1953– author.

TITLE: The abolitionist's journal : the memories of an American
antislavery family / James D. Richardson.

DESCRIPTION: Includes bibliographical references and index.

IDENTIFIERS: LCCN 2022013261 (print) |
LCCN 2022013262 (e-book) | ISBN 9780826364036 (cloth) | ISBN 9780826364043 (e-book)

SUBJECTS: LCSH: Richardson, George Warren, 1824–1911. | Richardson, James, 1953– |
Abolitionists—United States—Biography. | Antislavery movements—United States. |
BISAC: BIOGRAPHY & AUTOBIOGRAPHY / Personal Memoirs | SOCIAL SCIENCE /
Ethnic Studies / American / African American & Black Studies

Classification: LCC E449.R517 R53 2022 (print) | LCC E449.R517 (ebook) | DDC 326.8092—dc23

LC record available at https://lccn.loc.gov/2022013261

LC ebook record available at https://lccn.loc.gov/2022013262

Founded in 1889, the University of New Mexico sits on the traditional homelands of the Pueblo
of Sandia. The original peoples of New Mexico—Pueblo, Navajo, and Apache—since time
immemorial have deep connections to the land and have made significant contributions
to the broader community statewide. We honor the land itself and those who remain
stewards of this land throughout the generations and also acknowledge our committed
relationship to Indigenous peoples. We gratefully recognize our history.

"DARK TESTAMENT" © the Pauli Murray Foundation. From *Dark Testament and Other Poems*
by Pauli Murray. Used by permission of Liveright Publishing Corporation. UK/British
Commonwealth rights used by permission of the Charlotte Sheedy Literary Agency.

Fort Pickering, Memphis, Tennessee, garrisoned by Black Union soldiers. Sketch by Henri Lovie,
appearing in Frank Leslie's Illustrated Newspaper, November 22, 1862.

Cover images courtesy of the author | Designed by Mindy Basinger Hill
Composed in 10/14 pt Adobe Caslon Pro.

IN LOVING MEMORY of my mother, Jean;
my father, David; and his sister, Madge.

AND WITH DEEP ADMIRATION
for the courage and perseverance
of the Huston-Tillotson University community.

AND FOR LORI who lived this book with me.

He hath sent me

to heal the broken-hearted,

to preach deliverance to the captives,

and recovering of sight to the blind,

to set at liberty them that

are bruised.

THE GOSPEL ACCORDING
TO ST. LUKE: IV:18,
from an anonymous
Civil War soldier's pocket Bible

CONTENTS

PART I

$\rightsquigarrow I \rightsquigarrow$

THE JOURNAL

Let my vindication come forth from your presence;
let your eyes be fixed on justice.

PSALM 17: 2 | BOOK OF COMMON PRAYER

The black, slightly frayed, hardbound notebook sat on my father's bookshelf for decades. The binding was held together with masking tape, and the pages yellow and fragile. Growing up, I knew very little about the words inside. My father called it simply "the journal," and all I knew is it contained the life story of our ancestor, my great-great-grandfather, George. This oversized notebook was my father's most cherished possession, as he made clear by issuing "standing orders" that if the house caught fire, the journal was to be evacuated first. My father, David Richardson, was the skipper of a small Navy ship during World War II, and our household was run accordingly.

Looking back, I realize my father knew me better than anyone on earth, and maybe better than I knew myself. He knew exactly when I should read the journal. When I finally did—at a pivotal moment in my life—I wished I had read it years earlier.

"Recollections of My Lifework," as our ancestor had formally titled his book—all 334 pages written in neat cursive handwriting—describes the remarkable tale of George Warren Richardson and his life on the edges of nineteenth-century America. He was born on a farm in New York in 1824, immigrated as a young man to the upper Midwest territories, and became a circuit-riding "itinerant" Methodist preacher on the prairie frontier.

George and his wife, Caroline—his childhood sweetheart—were ardent antislavery abolitionists. They secretly—and dangerously—used their home as a stop on the Underground Railroad, spiriting at least one enslaved young woman to freedom, and he recorded how they did it in "Recollections of My Lifework."

During the Civil War, George Richardson volunteered as the white chaplain to a "colored" Union Army regiment posted in Memphis. He saw bloodshed and carnage in Tennessee and Mississippi. After the war, George and

Caroline, with two of six their children, founded a college for emancipated slaves that in the twentieth century grew into Huston-Tillotson University in Austin, Texas.

And that is just the start of the remarkable story revealed inside the pages of the journal—tales that I knew almost nothing about as a child. It was almost as if our ancestor's journal contained a hidden family secret, which in a way it did. Few in our family knew much about George and Caroline Richardson, or their children. My father and his sister Madge were the only people I know who had read his journal. Truthfully, as the decades unfolded into the twentieth century, not everyone who had grafted onto the Richardson family tree and bore his name would have viewed George and Caroline Richardson's work with Black people as heroic or politically correct.

My father gave me the journal in the mid-1990s when I felt the pull to become an Episcopal priest. I had been a newspaper reporter for two decades, covering two presidential campaigns, the 1984 Summer Olympics, the California Legislature, and more murders and criminal trials in Southern California than I can now remember. At the peak of my journalism career, I had written a critically acclaimed biography of Willie Brown, the most powerful politician in California in the 1980s and '90s, and at the time, the most powerful African American politician in the United States. I was at the top of my game as a journalist. But something else stirred within me and would not let go.

After an intense year of conversations with the people closest to me, reading a lot of books, prayers, and meeting with church ordination committees, I was accepted as a "postulant for holy orders." I quit my job as a reporter at *The Sacramento Bee,* collected my vacation pay, and took a monthlong break before entering the Church Divinity School of the Pacific, our Episcopal seminary in Berkeley, California.

With all that preparation, I still had no idea what I was getting into. Leaving journalism for the priesthood was the most radical thing I would ever do and left many of my friends scratching their heads. Truth be told, I wasn't so sure about this either.

Maybe that monthlong break before starting seminary was too long. What had I done? I was in my mid-forties. Going back to school, reading volumes of dense theology books, taking tests, and writing term papers seemed, well, absurd.

Sensing my struggle, my father handed me the journal and suggested that I read it before embarking upon my new vocation. I thanked him, but I felt too busy to read it. I did not look inside again until the weekend before the seminary academic year began—the very moment when I was figuring out how to beg for my job back.

I did little else that weekend but read George Richardson's "Recollections of My Lifework."

I discovered that my ancestor had a flair for storytelling. His prose came without frills, in sharp contrast to the bombastic style of his preaching contemporaries. He was a keen observer of detail and had an ear for dialogue. He could have been a journalist in any age. He filled his pages with stories of war, white vigilantes, Black schools, church politics, and frontier congregations. He wrote of adventures at Yellowstone in the early years of the national park. He recounted getting lost on horseback in Minnesota in the winter and the crushing devastation in the Mississippi countryside in the days after the Civil War. He wrote of life in Black shantytowns, Texas Panhandle cowboys, and Idaho Mormons. His is the story of our country.

George Richardson's "Recollections of My Lifework" was handwritten over many years in three or four stages, sometimes in dark ink, and in other places with ink so light it looks like pencil. Sections of the journal are written on both sides of the pages, while other sections are on a single side. Each page is beautifully scripted and easy to read more than a century after he laid down his pen. He made his last entry in 1907, his hand steady despite many injuries and infirmities of old age. The final entry was written by his daughter, Emma, describing his last days and funeral.

Throughout his journal, George Richardson made clear that his deepest passion was more than about winning a single battle in the Civil War or freeing a single slave. He saw his life mission as the salvation of African Americans from bondage, ignorance, poverty, sickness, and racial caste. "I am willing," he wrote an old friend eleven years after the close of the Civil War, "to let the Lord and the colored people of the South have the balance of my life; for this part of my life is so much clear gain."[1]

His motives grew from religious conviction: bodies that were enslaved and minds that were uneducated could not read the Bible, and to him, that was a terrible sin. But as he experienced firsthand the depravations of war, racism and poverty, his motives widened beyond abstract religious doctrine. Living and struggling among Black people, his work became deeply personal. He wrote about Pastor Jeremiah Webster, his African American partner in the Texas school: "I had learned to love him as a brother."[2]

The first time I read my ancestor's journal, I found myself filling my own notebook as if I were afraid his book would vanish from my sight. After closing the journal, I felt that I was somehow joining the family cause. The next day, I showed up for seminary despite my doubts and reservations, and his words were still reeling in my mind. I didn't know where this new road was leading me, but I knew my ancestor was somehow pointing the way. I still had many moments of doubt—even panic. I recorded in my own daily journal: "Someone told me to remember to pray; I replied I'm trying to remember to breathe."

In those first few months of seminary, I did something more than study—and breathe. I resolved to retrace my ancestor's footsteps and find the places he wrote about, no matter how long it would take. Indeed, it has taken twenty years, and there are still more places I have yet to go.

I would never claim that our paths are parallel. But there are moments when I feel resonance with his life. This book is partly an exploration of those moments and my evolving understanding of my life. The craft of memoir asks the question about why a memory has a hook in us. In a sense, this book is a memoir about a memoir: it asks why my ancestor's memory has a hook in me. Tracing his story has not only given me a better understanding of his life, but indelibly changed my life.

I was ordained an Episcopal priest in 2001 in Sacramento, California, where I have lived and worked most of my adult life. As a priest, I have led churches in Sacramento, Berkeley, and Santa Rosa, California, and short stints in small Central Valley and Sierra foothill churches. For seven years, I was the rector of a large church in Charlottesville, Virginia, a bucolic university town that was recently thrust into the national psyche as the site of white supremacist violence.

While serving these congregations, I took many trips searching for old houses, farms, battlefields, forts, churches, schools, and graveyards in Tennessee, Texas, Mississippi, Illinois, Colorado, California, Oregon, Wisconsin, and Minnesota—the many places where George and Caroline Richardson lived, worked, and wrote.

My wife, Lori, has accompanied me in nearly all these travels. She has been long-intrigued by genealogy, and so has enjoyed this hunt into my family's past. Though she might not express it this way, I suspect our travels gave her a better understanding of whom she had married and my vocational calling beyond journalism.

Sometimes all we found was a weathered cornerstone of an old church or a marker left by a state historical society. But that was enough to feel the presence of my ancestors.

And sometimes we found their words.

Many years into our search, Lori discovered—by accident—a diary kept by Caroline. The diary was sitting on a stairwell in my Aunt Madge's home. My ancestors were writers, beginning with George Richardson. They wrote letters—lots of letters—many of them still in cardboard boxes stashed away in garages and attics. Underneath a pile of papers, we found a folder with letters written by George during the Civil War. At least two of George's sons wrote their memoirs. My grandfather, Russell, started his but never finished. My father also wrote a memoir. Never one to quit anything, my father finished his.

In writing this book, I've drawn primarily from George Richardson's finished journal, supplemented by these other documents. We found a partially completed version that appears to be a first draft, titled "Journal and Recollections of my life," the likely origin of the book's moniker "the journal."[3] George wrote the draft inside unused pages in Caroline's diary. I have quoted from the draft but not extensively because he chose to polish his words into the full-length book handed down from father to son.

My primary aim is to let George and his family tell their story and tell it their way. They lived in a time not my own and faced challenges I can barely imagine. Their lens was their religion. They understood that the work of emancipation did not end with the Civil War. They fervently believed that if the formerly enslaved were illiterate and destitute, they could not be much freer than when they were enslaved. They dedicated their lives to doing something about it.

My ancestors were not entirely free of the racial and regional stereotypes of both Blacks and Southern whites prevalent in their culture. They were Northern white people traveling as outsiders into world brutally ruled by Southern whites—a world where slavery, and the color of a person's skin, dominated daily life. They saw clearly the moral bankruptcy of the white caste system and the cruelties perpetrated on Black people. But, George and Caroline also found themselves bending to it. They were not always sure of what to do next, or where to go. They could be naïve, overly optimistic, and trusting. They made mistakes. They had their blind spots. But they also grew in their understanding of how race impelled everything. They kept going in the certainty that God had given them a role, even when it meant putting themselves and their children at mortal risk.

>•◦•<

In 1883, the school founded by George and Caroline Richardson in Austin, Texas, was busily serving former slaves and their children. But many, if not most, Blacks in the region were tied down as sharecroppers and could not afford to move to Austin. So if they could not get to the school, the Richardsons would bring the school to them. While Caroline stayed in Austin running the school, George rode a circuit through the Texas Hill Country bringing books and lessons to impoverished rural Black settlements.

On one of these treks, George was tipped off that white vigilantes planned to ambush and kill him.[4] Fearing for his life, he hid in the thick woods near a river. A Black postal courier secretly stopped on his route to bring George food and news—the courier putting himself in mortal danger if he was caught. On one of his stops, the courier received a letter from George to Caroline explaining why he had gone missing. The words of George's letter were later recorded in the journal, describing how a gentle breeze blew open his Bible to Psalm 17: "Hear the right, O Lord, attend unto my cry, give ear unto my prayer," the psalm proclaims. "Deliver my soul from the wicked."[5]

My ancestor told of how the words of the psalm gave him unexpected strength.

"I read through it very carefully," George wrote to his wife, "and felt great comfort while reading, and great satisfaction in committing my ways to the Lord in prayer."

Years later, we drove through the Hill Country searching for where George might have been hiding. From his description, we looked along the banks of the Colorado River (not to be confused with the river of the same name that runs through Arizona) meandering across Texas to the Gulf of Mexico. We knew we had to be close. Stopping along the river, we walked into the woods. A few yards in, we were invisible from the road. Gazing at the ground, I thought of my ancestor's loneliness and fear hiding in these woods. I also thought of his courage as he read Psalm 17.

Back home, in the safety of my living room, I read Psalm 17 regularly, and usually the version in the Episcopal Book of Common Prayer. Whenever I read the psalm, I think of how the words so encapsulate my ancestor's life.

And the second verse grabs me every time: "Let your eyes be fixed on justice."

✒ 2 ✒

AWAKENINGS

We spend our years as a tale *that is told*.
PSALM 90: 9 | KING JAMES VERSION

Words came easily to George Warren Richardson.

Drawing from his copious volumes of letters, notebooks, and diaries—words compiled over a lifetime—he began telling his life story to his journal simply enough: "I was born in the Town of Concord Erie County New York November 25 1824, and lived at the same place till after I was 21 years old."[1]

George Richardson's journal continues with his description of how his father, Elijah, born in 1774, was a veteran of the War of 1812 and had settled in western New York as a blacksmith. He also owned a farm but "gave more time to his shop than to his farm."[2] The Richardson family lived on the farm for thirty years.

The region where George grew up had been colonized by European settlers in the 1680s, pushing out the Iroquois. By the early nineteenth century, when George was born, it was no longer frontier but was still far from centers of commerce, government, and education.

George had piercing brown eyes and red hair like his grandmother, Ruth.[3] He was the fourth of five children, with two older brothers, an older sister, and a younger sister. His "Recollections of My Lifework" hints at sibling rivalries and constant turmoil at home; the reasons are never explained. George especially did not get along with his oldest brother, Elijah Jr., with repercussions far into adulthood.

By his own account, George was stubborn, outspoken, and intense. He was in frequent conflict with his father. George describes himself at age eleven as "a rude and thoughtless boy"—so much so that his parents sent him to live with an older couple, the Phillips. He was expected to help on the Phillips' farm in return for his keep, and he did not expect to return home except for occasional visits. Little else is known about his experience working for the Phillips, but such arrangements for younger children in large families were not unusual in rural nineteenth-century America.

George did not write much in the journal about his mother, Margaret Payne—which he sometimes spelled "Paine"—but he mentioned she "always maintained her Christian integrity, even when others drifted into worldliness."[4] She had converted George's father, Elijah, to her evangelical Christian faith, and he was eventually licensed as a preacher in the Free Will Baptist Church. George described his first childhood memories as "religious impressions" and his father's preaching as filled with "earnestness." George professed his conversion to Christianity in the Free Will Baptist Church when he was seven years old, though did not record the details of how that came to be. "My father and Mother were very careful about the moral and religious training of their children."[5]

George described himself at an early age as especially fearful of God's wrath. "I would go to the woods or to the barn and struggle a long time in prayer for pardon and a new heart," he wrote. "I envied the animals their place for they were not immortal."[6]

The Free Will Baptists were more than just strictly pious but especially known for their fervent opposition to slavery. The sect's doctrine held that individuals should be able to freely choose salvation. By definition, the enslaved were stripped of their free will, and so could not freely choose salvation. To the Free Will Baptists that made slavery an especially heinous sin against God. Souls in darkness were at stake, not just bodies in bondage.

Years later, he remembered that his "cheeks were wet with tears and his whole frame quivered with indignation" while listening to his mother read newspaper accounts about the "outrages of slavery."[7]

George's opinion of slavery as evil would never waver. On little else father and son agreed.

><><

George Richardson was twelve when his father suddenly died; George was summoned home in time to see his father's corpse before it was buried. The sight filled the young boy with dread about his own mortality. "I knew I was not ready to go to heaven where my father had gone. I therefore resolved that I would make it the first business of my life to secure salvation."[8]

But the business of salvation would have to wait. He was needed at what was now his mother's farm and moved home in time for the spring planting.

He still managed to attend his first Christian revival meeting in the local schoolhouse, but he felt indifferent to the experience.

Religious revivals were catching fire throughout the country in the movement that came to be known as the "Second Great Awakening."

The First "Great Awakening" of the eighteenth-century spawned a Protestantism so intense it crossed denominational boundaries.[9] Charismatic leaders, most notably English evangelist George Whitefield, traveled the Eastern Seaboard in the 1740s, summoning converts. New denominations were born overnight. Old denominations splintered. Among the most successful were the Methodists, so named for their "method" of establishing small colonies, or "classes" of converts. "The results were spectacular, but posed new questions," writes Oxford University church historian Diarmaid MacCulloch. "By 1800, around a fifth of all Methodists were enslaved people—and enslaved they were still, despite being Methodists."[10]

The Second Great Awakening of George Richardson's youth was even more fervent and successful than the first. The revivals were held under large circus-style tents, hence were known as "tent revivals." The revivals would go all day and continue for several days. Preachers would tag-team, imploring the crowds to come to Jesus for salvation. The revivals culminated in "altar calls," with tearful converts coming forward to accept Jesus as their personal savior and the prayerful "laying on of hands" by the preachers. Their exhortations were sprinkled with threats of the hell that awaited those who did not convert.

Upstate New York had so many of these revivals that it became known as the "Burned-Over District," so named for the hellfire-and-brimstone sermons. The revivals inspired an explosion of preachers and prophets of every imaginable stripe. Joseph Smith and the Mormons were among the sects spawned in the Burned-Over District.

The tent preachers often referred to the revivals as "sieges" to defeat the devil—and doubtless the length of the revivals could feel like a siege.[11] The format was so successful that American political party conventions copied them, creating a political liturgy recognizable to this today.

In Erie County, New York, the Presbyterians, Methodists, and Free Will Baptists joined forces. Denominational differences were unimportant. George continued attending the tent revivals, and he began to catch the fervor. "I began to pray more earnestly that God would show me my situation, and light soon broke upon my soul. I loved Christians as I had never done before. I loved the prayer meeting and I loved to pray."[12]

He soon found a regular Saturday night meeting for young converts. "We knew no church distinctions." At the age of thirteen, he made an "adult confession" and was baptized into the Free Will Baptist Church.

As George Richardson was coming into adulthood in the 1840s, Frederick Douglass, the escaped slave who was the most eloquent abolitionist of the age, toured the "Burned-Over District."[13] George made no mention in his journal of Douglass, who was only six years his senior. But certainly the Black abolitionist's words were heard sympathetically by the Free Will Baptists who shaped George's attitudes toward slavery and his future vocation.

><><><

Faith gave life to young George Richardson. The farm did not.

After his father's death, tending to the Richardson farm fell to George's two older brothers, Elijah Jr. and Nehemiah. George was sent again to live with another family. But in 1840, Nehemiah died, and George was summoned home again, this time to work as a farmhand for his older brother, Elijah Jr. The forced arrangement did not go well.

Soon after, the older brother abandoned the family farm entirely and moved to Wisconsin. At age sixteen, George was the only male left on the New York farm. "The care of the little farm came entirely on me."[14]

Among George's responsibilities was leading worship at the family altar, and he began to feel a calling beyond the farm. "The new responsibility gave greater firmness to my religious character and habits, and was a great blessing to me."

With his elementary education completed, he made arrangements to supplement his income by teaching school in the nearby township of Collins. But, as a new teacher, George discovered he was not much better at basic subjects than his pupils, and so he resolved to obtain more education. "If I could arrange to have my mother and sisters provided for I would spend several years in school."

In the fall of 1844—he was now twenty years old—George was admitted to Oberlin College. The school even offered him a job. Seeing his way out, he wrote to his older brother, Elijah, in Wisconsin and offered to forgo his inheritance of the New York family farm if his brother would return to take care of his mother and sisters. It was not to be.

"My hope was doomed to a sad reverse," he wrote. His brother refused to return to New York. "After a terrible struggle with my inclinations I decided to remain at home on the farm and keep the family together."[15]

"I could see no way the family could be cared for if I left. My duty to my mother was first, and I did not see how she could spare me," he wrote. "I began to be resigned to the life of a farmer, but God had a way of changing my plans."

Farming nearly cost him his life.

During the harvest in November 1845, George caught his right hand in the cylinder of a wheat threshing machine. His hand was so badly mangled that his right forearm was amputated to three inches below his elbow. The excruciating surgery was done without anesthetic. "I was perfectly conscious of every move of the knife and saw."[16]

Astonishingly, George recovered in five weeks with no infections, but with only one good arm, it seemed clear he could no longer be a farmer. "By this apparent affliction, which I have often since counted a blessing, the whole course of my life was changed."

He would become a preacher.

DAISY

Whatever white people do not know about Negroes reveals, precisely
and inexorably, what they do not know about themselves.

JAMES BALDWIN | *THE FIRE NEXT TIME*, 1963

At first glance, my birth and upbringing in the 1950s and '60s could not
have been more different than my ancestor's, just a century earlier. I was
born not on a farm but in a hospital near the University of California campus in Berkeley where my parents earned college degrees. My parents had
met during World War II when my father was in the Navy. I grew up in
the postwar white suburbs, and we did not reside long in any one of them.
We moved six times before I was sixteen, from suburb to suburb, while my
father worked his way up the corporate ladder at what was then a large
multinational corporation, the American Can Company. My dad managed
factories that produced tin cans for fruit, coffee, soft drinks, and a lot of beer.

Jean, my mother, was born in Seattle. When she was young, her family
moved to the San Francisco Bay Area during the Great Depression. My
mother grew up in Oakland. Her father, Arthur, was a middle manager at a
coffee roaster on the Embarcadero in San Francisco, commuting daily from
the East Bay on the ferry before the construction of the Bay Bridge. He
died when I was five. I remember very little about him except that my older
cousins called him "Ba."

My mother's mother, Julia, was firmly in charge of everything and everyone, and endlessly resourceful. She boasted of how she could change a
flat tire on her annual trek from Oakland back to Seattle to visit family and
friends. She could jack up her Model A, pull the wheel off, and put on the
spare like an old auto mechanic, and all the while with her three daughters
in the car. My mother, Jean, was the youngest.

My grandmother was a woman of strong opinions. She proudly claimed
Southern ancestry, always referring to Black children as "pickaninnies," and
adult African Americans as "boys," "girls," or just "colored." She did not use

these words spitefully or hatefully. I never heard her use the n-word, but I got the message: we are better because we are white.

My father David was named for his grandfather, the second son of George and Caroline Richardson. My father also grew up in Oakland, but in the tony hills above the white middle class neighborhood where my mother grew up—and far from the poor neighborhoods on the "Flats" closer to the Bay where Blacks had settled during World War II to work in the shipyards. Though my parents grew up in the same town, they did not meet until a blind date during the war when my father was in the Navy.

He was a lifelong Republican, following in the footsteps of his father, grandfather—and great grandfather who had voted for Abraham Lincoln. For my father, the party of Lincoln was the party of honest government and equal opportunity. A political ideologue he was not.

My dad's father, Russell, grew up in Minnesota and as a child had his grandfather's reddish hair. He was something of a swashbuckler. Russell had dropped out of college after two years and became a lumberjack in the Northwest. He enlisted in the Navy in World War I, and when recruiters learned he had a few college credits, he was commissioned as an officer and served on destroyers in the Atlantic.

During Prohibition, my grandfather signed on as third mate on steamers plying the seas from California to Japan and China. His ship also carried bootleg alcohol up the Pacific Coast from Central America. Adhering to his parents' temperance pledge, he never touched a drop. "I stayed dry," he recalled. "I was brought up as a Methodist and prohibition against drinking liquors. My family didn't and I didn't."[1]

As a boy, I adored listening to the sea stories of my grandfather. But I never heard him speak of his grandfather, George. "I'm not accustomed to thinking about those years," he told me in a series of tape-recorded interviews I made with him in 1976. Knowing virtually nothing about George Richardson at the time, I did not think to explore further with my grandfather about his grandfather.

On one of his voyages, Russell met my grandmother, Jessie, who grew up Hawai'i. She came to the mainland to earn an art degree at California College of the Arts in Oakland and was a talented "plein air" landscape painter. She had a lifelong love of Japanese art and filled her house with traditional painted screens, woodblock prints, ink brush paintings, ceramics, and ivory carvings. Her embrace of ethnic diversity, however, did not extend to Black people.

Jessie enjoyed her nightly glass of sherry, the only alcohol I saw in my grandparents' house. Jessie was decidedly not a churchgoer, and Russell fell away from the Methodist Church. He inherited the journal and recorded in its back pages the births, marriages, and deaths of relatives. Russell recorded my birth in 1953.[2]

After my grandfather gave up his life at sea, he took a job as an accountant with Associated Oil Co., which merged with another oil company better known as Flying A, owned by J. Paul Getty. My father's childhood memories were mostly about living on an oil refinery in Martinez, northeast of Oakland. His family eventually settled in Oakland as Russell worked his way up the corporate ladder. Russell retired from his role as corporate vice president a wealthy man.

My grandparents had a Japanese American maid who was imprisoned in an internment camp in World War II—a fact we turned up years later in a letter she wrote to my grandmother pleading for help. We do not know how, or if, my grandmother replied. My grandmother never spoke of it.

I am the second of three children. Before I was born, my older brother, Donald, died suddenly of encephalitis, an inflammation of the brain probably contracted from a mosquito bite. He was three years old. He had large ears and looked like our dad. My parents rarely mentioned Donald's death. "I shall not discuss the matter," began my father's brief mention in his memoir: "The loss of a child is a shattering experience from which you never recover. Our love for each other was the only thing that kept us both from losing our minds."[3]

I learned more about my dead brother from relatives than I did from my parents. The topic of Donald's death felt like a bridge we could not cross with my parents. My mother never spoke of it, but she kept a framed photo of my brother on her bedroom wall. I cannot fathom what she went through but I could always sense the stone of grief that weighed on her.

My mother was pregnant with me soon after Donald's death. I was an only child until I was six; my sister, Janet, came along in 1959 in good health.

My earliest memories are of Daisy.

Daisy had large horn-rim glasses, wore a white uniform, and carried me from room to room. At age three, I still could not walk. I was born with partially formed hips and legs and curvature of my lower spine. I had casts around both legs for the first two years of my life and was wheeled around on a makeshift gurney my father built. When I was three, I was fitted with a steel brace on my right leg and a shoe with a steel riser on my left leg. I wore all of this gear until I was five.

The steel braces were held in place by leather straps around my waist, which made dressing myself all but impossible. When fully equipped, my lower body looked like an erector set, and I seemed to be walking on stubby stilts. Yet with all that metal on me, I scooted around quite well. My father remarked in his memoir, "It was simply amazing how quickly he adapted to this set of contraptions and was able to walk and climb stairs with only an occasional fall."[4]

My braces were removed at night. I slept with special shoes connected with a metal bar holding my feet together. I could not have gotten out of bed even to go to the bathroom. I wore these shoes every night until I was nearly six.

My disabilities overwhelmed my mother, who was in fragile health much of her life. Daisy took care of me during the day. She changed my diaper, dressed me, fed me, played with me, and held me. Daisy had a beautiful smile and was always ready with a hug. I was with Daisy more than with my own mother. Daisy's lap was the warmest place I knew.

My mother referred to Daisy as her "colored lady." I never learned her last name.

I was born into a world where race mattered. The rules of class, caste, and race were on full display in the polite chatter of grownups at the Thanksgiving Day dinner table. All of that was ahead of me. In my small world, Daisy was my first awareness that there were people with a different skin color than my own. I remember staring at the contrast between the light skin on the palms of her hands and the darkness of the back of her hands.

My first school was for kids with physical disabilities. The school rigged up a special tricycle for me in the yard. I propped up my braced right leg on a hook over the front wheel and peddled with my left leg. My school was the first place I felt at home with other kids, and it would be the last school where I would feel at home for many years.

I did not have a Forest Gump moment blasting out of my braces in a full sprint. That was pure movie fantasy. I was gradually weaned out of leg braces, learning to walk with a hobbling gait. When I finally could walk without the braces I was allowed to go to public schools. For a year or two, I had to wear the braces when I got home from school and the leg-binding shoes at night. I walked with a what turned out to be a permanent limp.

My legs were too weak to play sports, and the pecking order among boys was always about sports. I found myself gravitating to other boys chosen last on the teams or left on the sidelines because, like me, they were different. When I was ten, my right femur slipped out of my deformed right hip. I was not allowed to run or participate in outdoor activities, and that meant I was left watching other boys play at recess. I was an outcast even more than ever. But as hard as it was being grounded, if that didn't work, I would be back in steel braces and probably sent to a special school. Somehow my bones found their way into place, and the braces never returned.

I don't know what became of Daisy after we moved to the next suburb. But nearly everywhere we lived, my mother had a "colored lady." In time, my mother stopped using the phrase.

⌇

I have one other deeply embedded childhood memory: church.

When my parents married, my father joined my mother's Episcopal Church, never having grown up in any church. My father was baptized and confirmed as an adult. Like many converts, my father loved the Episcopal Church more than many who grew up in it.

I was baptized at age three at St. Mark's Episcopal Church in Berkeley where my parents had been students. Baptisms at the time were private affairs for family and friends. Years later, my mother said she waited to baptize me until my leg casts were removed. I now realize there was a social stigma to my physical disabilities. Photographs of me in those years often show me with the braces removed and seated, or from the waist up. In one photo, my mother stands behind a low driveway gate at my grandmother's house in Oakland. She is holding me with my legs hidden behind the gate.

My first memory of church was at the baptism of my infant sister, Janet, at an Episcopal church in Westchester County, New York. We had moved to

New York for a year so that my father could work at his company's corporate headquarters. I was six and only recently out of leg braces. I could not have told you what baptism was about in church language, but I knew it meant that my sister was special and loved by God and all the people surrounding her.

We rarely missed a Sunday in church in whatever town we lived. Each of the Episcopal churches we joined had their own character. Yet, even at a young age I could feel the sacredness in all of them. The Elizabethan cadence of the prayer book, with its "thee and thou" language, and the aroma of beeswax candles transported me into a place far removed from the social minefields and drudgery of school. I sang in a children's choir. I was captivated by the choreography of the clergy, dressed up in their long monkish cassocks, draped in flowing white surplices and colorful cloth stoles over their shoulders. Mystery permeated the air. Hellfire-and-brimstone preaching and heavy guilt trips were not in the lexicon of the Episcopal churches where I grew up. I had no clue about fundamentalist Christianity.

The man who taught our confirmation class at Good Shepherd Church in Belmont, California, was in a wheelchair with multiple sclerosis. We pulled for him as much as he pulled for us. Besides Daisy's lap, church was the one place I felt fully accepted just as I was, with all of my physical limitations.

Even then, I had an inkling that I might become a preacher one day.

✎ 4 ✎

DREAMS

Our life as a dream, our time as a stream
Glide swiftly away

METHODIST HYMN BY CHARLES WESLEY | 1750

In May 1846, the Richardson farm in New York was abandoned, and the family broken up. George's mother moved to Wisconsin to join her oldest son, Elijah Jr., and the move "almost broke her heart," George wrote.[1]

George, who was twenty-two years old, stayed in New York and got a teaching job to support himself and a younger sister. Living in Erie County had another advantage: he could easily attend revival meetings. As he did so, George was increasingly drawn to Methodism, a Christian sect that would grow to be the largest in the United States by the end of the nineteenth century. He was granted a "License to Exhort" by the Methodists on August 10, 1847. "I was a private [lay] member of the Methodist Church about ten minutes."[2]

Years later, George wrote a short exposition in the journal comparing the differences between Methodists and Free Will Baptists. He reflected that on the finer points of theology the Methodists were closer to his views than the Baptists, and therefore it was logical for him to make the switch.[3]

But there was another reason he felt the pull toward Methodism: his childhood sweetheart, Caroline Amelia Fay, who was also reared Free Will Baptist, had converted to Methodism.

Caroline Fay, a year younger than George, was the oldest of ten children. Her family was Free Will Baptist but had converted to Methodism for reasons now obscure. As a child, she was steeped in the antislavery cause. Years later, Caroline wrote how as a ten-year-old she had been mortified by the murder of abolitionist Owen Lovejoy's brother Elijah, killed by a white proslavery mob. "The murder of his brother when I was but a child, and in an eastern home, filled me with an indescribable horror."[4]

Caroline was a constant companion of George's two sisters. Her determined mettle was evident even as a child. Although younger than George, she had defended him from schoolyard taunts about his red hair.[5]

Caroline Fay had a knack for poetry, writing verse on scraps of paper and in composition books. She submitted poems to newspapers, often anonymously, and pasted the clippings into her diary. Her poetry reveals her faith—and a touch of melancholy. Perhaps echoing a Charles Wesley Methodist hymn— her students many years later thought so—she penned these verses in March 1846 in a poem titled *Life A Dream*.[6]

> This life is all an empty dream
> That shortly will be o'er
> And as we glide down its swift stream
> Look to the distant shore.

That year, Caroline Fay and her family joined the exodus of New York farmers to the open lands of Wisconsin. George Richardson would not be far behind.

><><

In the summer of 1847, George and his younger sister moved to Wisconsin to join their mother and older brother. He recorded in "Recollections of My Lifework" the reason: "I found it necessary to leave school for want of means."[7]

But the overriding reason was Caroline Fay.

George and his sister sold the family farm, and friends raised a purse of seven dollars to help them move. He wrote to his brother, Elijah Jr., announcing that he and their sister would arrive in late August 1847. He got no reply.

Not knowing if anyone would greet them in Wisconsin, the siblings took a stagecoach to Buffalo and then a paddle steamer across the Great Lakes to Milwaukee. Their ticket cost five dollars. They arrived on August 26, 1847, with only a few dollars to spare. Elijah Jr. did not show up to meet them, and they still had a long way to travel. They paid a wagon driver to ferry them another 130 miles to Hurricane, Wisconsin, and their family. "It was the first time we had ever seen a prairie."

It turned out that his brother had never bothered to tell their mother they were coming. "She burst into tears" when they arrived, he later wrote.[8]

George found employment as a teacher in Wisconsin and joined a Methodist prayer and study group. He taught about forty pupils and paid his mother for room and board. He was soon in touch with Caroline Fay. "March 30th I walked with Caroline A Fay to her sister's who lived about a mile from the Fay home. During this walk we talked of love affairs for the first time."[9]

George did not stay long in Wisconsin. He departed for Allegheny College, in Meadville, Pennsylvania, only a few miles from the New York state line where he grew up in Erie County. His courtship with Caroline Fay would take another three years, conducted mostly by mail.

The Reverend Timothy Alden, a graduate of the Harvard Divinity School, founded Allegheny College in 1815. By the 1830s the college had become affiliated with the Methodists and boasted one of the finest libraries in the nation. The college was well-suited to the maturing George Richardson. In his first term at Allegheny, in 1848, George studied English grammar, Latin, and algebra.[10]

Nearly half the students were like him: of limited financial means, living in boarding houses, and finding whatever income they could scrape up from odd jobs. George and his roommate, Lucius Wood, lived on twenty-five cents a week.[11] George boasted that he and Wood taught themselves how to bake bread.[12]

He and Wood wrote what they titled their "code of bylaws." They adopted rules for studying, eating, sleeping, exercise, and reading the Bible. The Great Awakening promoted self-discipline as the cornerstone of Christian living, and the two young men were enthusiastic adherents. George excelled in Latin, mathematics, and geometry. But like many ministry students before and since, he struggled with biblical Greek and its complicated grammar and unfamiliar alphabet.

George's first efforts as a Christian evangelist sputtered. He started a Sunday school for adults that flopped. "I found that the reason for the decline was that we taught the doctrine of future punishment [his underline]."[13] He admitted his preaching was off-putting. He had followed the formulas of others, but it was not a formula that worked for him. Hellfire and brimstone henceforth would not be a staple of his preaching.

In the summer of 1848, George was broke, and he had not seen Caroline Fay in almost two years. He may even have been worried about losing her to another suitor because her letters seemed to hedge about their relationship. He pressed his marriage proposal upon Caroline in one of his letters.

She accepted, acknowledging her initial indecision: "I have been undecided, and now I cannot express myself as I could wish," she wrote. "But why should I hesitate, for in you I trust I shall find a guide & protector that is worthy of all confidence that I can bestow."[14]

Writing in his journal years after the fact, George exuded his relief that her indecision was at an end. He quit school and took a teaching job. "We met now with the assurance that we belonged to each other."[15]

George packed up for Wisconsin. On his way, he stopped in Waukegan, Illinois, and visited the teachers' institute there. He got an idea: Caroline could study at the Waukegan Teachers Institute for a year while he worked to support her. She agreed. Her training would serve her well decades later at the school founded by the Richardsons in Austin.

While she studied, George found a job as a traveling salesman, selling books to schools from a horse-drawn carriage. He discovered he loved the road and life in the saddle, and in 1849 even flirted with the idea of following a cousin to the gold fields of California. "I was very fond of adventures."[16] He did not go to the gold fields, but he also never returned to Allegheny College.

After Caroline finished her studies, the two decided to find teaching jobs together in Minnesota. They also decided to elope for reasons not explained.[17] They rendezvoused at a hotel and then rode a carriage to Iowa County, Wisconsin, where a Methodist pastor married them on May 16, 1851. After a brief honeymoon, the newlyweds returned to George's mother's home to announce their marriage. How they were received, he did not say.

Not long after, George traveled to Minnesota to look for a teaching post. There he met Pastor Chauncey Hobart, the presiding elder in the Minnesota Methodist conference.[18] Their relationship would flower for more than three decades.

Hobart convinced George to forget about being a teacher and instead take up life in the saddle as a circuit-riding "itinerant" Methodist preacher. "I passed a hasty examination," George wrote, and he was appointed to the Methodist circuit in Stillwater, Minnesota.[19]

George returned to Wisconsin in July 1851 to gather his few belongings and his wife, and the two boarded a paddle wheeler for the journey up the Mississippi River to his first preaching post.

For her part, Caroline wrote in her diary: "It was all new and strange to me, and I never saw a face that I had ever seen before except my husband's."[20]

Awaiting them was a hard life on the vast American prairie—farming, teaching, ministry, rearing children, and just surviving. In the years ahead, George and Caroline would see the faces of complexions unknown to them in their upbringing. Up until then, if either had set eyes on the face of an African American—free or enslaved—neither mentioned it in their journals or letters. For the moment, slavery remained a faraway abstract moral issue.

But not for long.

5

JAMES CROW

The discovery of personal whiteness among the world's peoples is a
very modern thing,—a nineteenth and twentieth century matter, indeed.
The ancient world would have laughed at such a distinction.

W. E. B. DU BOIS | *DARKWATER*, 1920

I never saw a crude "white" or "colored" sign on a water fountain or toilet, but nonetheless I grew up in the strictly segregated suburban world of California. We were governed by a racial code dictating who lived where, who did what for a living, and who went to which school and what church. The color barriers were outwardly polite but were as rigid as in the South. Sociologist Irving Babow of the University of California, Berkeley, summed it up perfectly in 1962: "In San Francisco, it's James Crow, not Jim Crow."[1]

Historians have written extensively about the mass migration of Blacks to eastern and midwestern cities during the Great Depression and World War II, but less noted was the movement westward and its impact on California. In the years just before the turn of the twentieth century, 90 percent of all African Americans lived in the rural South; eighty years later, only slightly more than half still lived in the South. The San Francisco Bay Area became a major locus of this migration as Blacks found work in factories, shipyards, and on the docks. The migration of Blacks continued unabated after World War II, transforming Oakland and San Francisco as radically as the Gold Rush a century earlier.[2]

After my father's one-year assignment in New York, we had moved back to California and lived in a house next to a fruit orchard in San Jose. One by one, the orchards would give way to another strip of cookie-cutter tract houses. Those orchards are now gone. But in the early 1960s, American Can Company—my dad's employer—manufactured cans for the fruit and vegetable packers that were still major industries in the area.

When I was six or seven, I often accompanied my dad on Saturdays as he drove his company-issue station wagon to visit the growers of the Salinas

Valley. That was the first time I saw bronze-skinned Mexican *braceros* working in the fields and orchards and the first time I became aware that there were people who spoke a language different than mine. I had no awareness yet that our family livelihood depended on their labor.

The civil rights movement blew into our safely segregated suburbs like a hurricane. Both of my grandmothers seemed threatened by the civil rights marches, the lunch counter sit-ins, and especially Martin Luther King Jr., and his campaign to end segregation.

Especially with my Richardson grandparents, a thick veil of collective amnesia about our family history enveloped us and was not about to lift. My paternal grandmother, Jessie, made her opinions clear, holding forth at family gatherings that King and his followers were "communists," "fellow travelers," and "pinkos." I did not hear hate in her voice so much as I heard fear.

But my father thought of this differently.

Away from his parents, in our home, he made sure that my sister and I knew about the civil rights movement and what it meant. I distinctly recall how horrified he was at images on television of marchers being hosed and attacked by police on the Edmund Pettus Bridge in Selma, Alabama. As we watched television, he told us we were witnessing history. He praised the courage of Martin Luther King and his nonviolent resistance.

My father ordered us to never use the "n-word." Years later, he told me he had privately admonished his mother to never use that word in the presence of his children. Our own mother stopped using the phrase "colored." Whatever conversations she had with my father on this topic remained between them, but someone—or something—changed her.

It might have been church.

We heard firsthand about the events in Selma from the pulpit at our local Episcopal church. Bishop James Pike, who confirmed me, and our local priest, John Daley, had gone to Selma to march with King. As they described their experience, I could see my dad nodding his agreement in the pews.

There was something else that influenced his attitude about race, but I didn't realize it until decades later. My father wrote his life story in 1988 when he was sixty-six years old, soon after he retired. He began his memoir not at his own birth, but with our ancestor's journal.

"Several years ago," he wrote, "I had the opportunity of reading a journal written by my Great-grandfather, George Warren Richardson. In this journal he narrated his experiences over a lifetime from the 1830s through the early 1900s. I have never been much of a history student but reading the journal gave me a new perspective of the lifestyle and events of that period. As I read the journal, I kept thinking how fortunate our family was that he had made the effort to record permanently the highlights of his lifetime."[3]

I still wonder why my father had kept all that to himself until late in life. No doubt it was safer at family gatherings to say nothing about how our ancestor had worked to abolish slavery, or that he had served with a Black regiment in the Civil War, or that he had founded a Black college.

Yet offhand comments by my grandmother hinted that she, too, knew the secrets inside the journal. Whenever she met a Black person whose last name was "Richardson," she'd comment to Russell, her husband: "There goes another of your grandfather's colored people." She did not mean it as a compliment. There was something about George Richardson's life that was uncomfortable, awkward, and socially incorrect. The genealogy charts in the back of the journal were more interesting to our wider family than the story in front of it.

⋙⋘

In the Spring of 1967, Black people were more a topic of dread than sympathy at family gatherings. Eldridge Cleaver and Bobby Seale led a band of leather-jacketed, rifle-toting Black Panthers from Oakland into the state Capitol in Sacramento to protest a gun-control law, proposed by Governor Ronald Reagan. The Panthers believed Reagan's gun control bill was aimed primarily at disarming Blacks. Goaded by news photographers, the Panthers briefly carried their firearms onto the floor of the state Assembly. They soon departed, harming no one, and were arrested at a gas station on their way back to Oakland.[4]

The Panthers and their publicity stunts frightened white parents and grandparents in our Bay Area suburbs.

By now, race, protest, and the Vietnam War were unavoidable topics at the dinner table and in school. My ninth-grade school was almost entirely white with a handful of Asians. Blacks went to another school a few miles away. My best friend, Brian Steinstra, questioned school authorities about this reality. How were we different than the segregationists in Birmingham? Brian did not endear himself to the school authorities, but he pressed them relentlessly.

Brian loaned me his paperback copy of Martin Luther King's book *Strength to Love*. I still have it. We talked for hours about it, and then read another of King's books, *Why We Can't Wait*. We were only fourteen, but Brian and I were inspired by King's faith and how he had embraced nonviolence as a way of turning the hearts of oppressors and ending the systemic racism in our country. Those books expanded my world, but I still had no friends who were anything other than white.

Many years later, Brian would come out as a gay man and felt the calling to be a pastor or priest. The Lutheran Church of his upbringing and the Episcopal Church of my upbringing shunned him. Brian became a seminarian in the United Church of Christ but died of an HIV/AIDS-related illness before reaching ordination.

Not long after King's assassination, my father's company moved him to Brooklyn, New York, to manage a can factory. We left California, and my parents bought a house in suburban New Jersey. My new school, Scotch Plains-Fanwood High School, was the first racially integrated school I had ever attended, but whites and Blacks kept to their own cliques. Hallways were known as white or Black, depending on where students of which color hung out. But there were some students who could cross over. A few of the Black athletes seemed to be friends with everyone. I was a Californian, and didn't fit in with any of the cliques, so I could cross over.

My first Black friend—ever—was Jerald, and we came up with an idea to start an afterschool forum for students to share our perspectives on race. In the lingo of the late 1960s, we called it the "Rap Session."[5] The school administration was nervous and told us we needed a faculty adviser. We soon got Richard Call, who taught social studies, allowing us to launch the Rap Session, which proved hugely popular. Jerald and I co-moderated the conversations, with Mr. Call sitting in the back of the room pretending to grade papers. He did not interfere.

We did not solve the racial issues of our time, or even in our high school. But we learned how to talk to each other, and more importantly, how to listen. A few people even made friends they might not have made otherwise. Students could blow off steam about anything without coming to blows, and the wary school administration embraced our project.

After more than fifty years, while working on this book project, I reconnected with Jerald. As we caught up on the phone, Jerald reflected on how our Rap Sessions were life-giving. "We started a conversation that allowed people to freely express themselves without being judged," he told me. "There was no trashing."

He remembered these afterschool conversations as opening our eyes to the larger reality of life beyond our school walls. "We were fresh off '68—assassinations, bussing, hippies," he recalled. "What it did—and especially for myself—was to allow us to see beyond ourselves, and to know we had the ability to change things." He said these conversations have stayed with him all these years. "What we were talking about then we are still talking about."

On Sundays our family went to All Saints Episcopal Church in the center of Scotch Plains. All Saints was a small stone church built in the 1880s in the classic style of an English countryside parish. I learned that one of my parents' church friends, Carl Gracely, was ending his business career so he could go to seminary and become an Episcopal priest. He lit a spark within me. I somehow knew I would follow the same path, later in life, as he did. Years later, besides me, two of my high school classmates went onto to ordained ministry in the Episcopal Church—and another into ministry in the Presbyterian Church. And years later, Carl would preside at my wedding.

The Vietnam War was raging while I was in high school, and it was Topic A of nearly every conversation among young men of my age. We would soon be subject to the draft, a prospect few of us found enticing. The local Presbyterian Church sponsored a "teach-in" to talk about the issues of the war and air our anxieties. That gathering was successful, so several of us at All Saints asked if we could hold a similar "teach in" at our church. My father took our request to the vestry—the governing board of the parish—but the vestry refused. The senior warden sent me a letter explaining that the Vietnam War was too controversial for the church to be involved with.

That was the beginning of my alienation from the Episcopal Church and the start of a spiritual void that deepened for the next two decades.

My political awareness was about to begin.

After graduation from high school, I was admitted as a student at the

University of California, Los Angeles (UCLA), and moved back to California. There I met Cesar Chávez, the leader of the United Farm Workers and got involved in the grape boycott to leverage growers to agree to contracts with the union. I also got involved in George McGovern's presidential campaign and served as delegate to the Democratic National Convention representing the precincts surrounding the UCLA campus. The co-leaders of our delegation were Congressman Phil Burton, then the most powerful kingmaker in California liberal politics; Dolores Huerta, the United Farm Workers organizer; and Assemblyman Willie Brown, who would become the most powerful African American politician in the country in the 1990s.

This was my baptism into the rough-and-tumble world of politics, and Willie Brown would become more than a passing acquaintance.

><><

As a UCLA student, I went to church a few times, but it felt out of touch with the world. I also soured on political activism after the debacle of McGovern's campaign. It struck me that the journalists I met had a commitment to discovering the truth that was lacking among both the religious and the political communities. I volunteered at the *Daily Bruin* student newspaper and fell in love with reporting and writing. After graduation, I landed a reporting job with *The Riverside Press-Enterprise,* a no-nonsense, old-school newspaper on the eastern edge of the Los Angeles basin.

My job as a reporter gave me a front-row seat to slices of life few other people got to see. I knew the mayor of Riverside and I knew the leaders of street gangs. I witnessed a lot of life—and death. I hung out with reporters, cops, lawyers, and judges. I never went to church in all of those years except once—to the funeral of Jim Evans, a sheriff's deputy who was shot through the eye at the end of a car chase with a gang of survivalists who robbed a bank.

I am convinced to this day that the Almighty wanted me to see life from the gutter up. And at the age of thirty, I would not have wanted to be anywhere else in the world.

~ 6 ~

CHAUNCEY HOBART

We have not forgotten the market square—
Malignant commerce in our flesh—
Huddled like desolate sheep—
Tumult of boisterous haggling—
We waited the dreadful moment of dispersal.
One by one we climbed the auction block—
Naked in an alien land—

PAULI MURRAY | "DARK TESTAMENT, No. 6," 1970

In the summer of 1851, George and Caroline Richardson traveled by steamboat up the Mississippi River to their new life in Minnesota. They were twenty-seven and twenty-six years old, respectively, and had married quickly and without their families' approval—eloped. They were on their own for the first time in their lives. They brought all their worldly possessions—not much more than their clothes, a few books, and a Bible. Their most valuable asset also came aboard the riverboat: a horse named "Prince."[1]

Churning its way up the river, the paddle wheeler stopped in St. Paul to unload freight. George briefly got off the boat to get his missionary orders from Chauncey Hobart, the senior Methodist pastor who had recruited him for ministry in the Minnesota wilderness.

It is hard to overstate the importance of Hobart in the nineteenth century expansion of Methodism in the Upper Midwest. More than any other single individual, Hobart built the Methodist Church in Minnesota, Wisconsin, and the Dakota territories. It is also hard to overstate the importance of Hobart in the life of George and Caroline Richardson. They were in his gravitational pull for the next thirty-six years.

Hobart is mentioned by Minnesota chronicler T. M. Newson in an exhaustive 746-page compendium of biographical sketches of hundreds of frontier movers-and-shakers, including men and women, Indian, "colored" and white. Newson described Hobart thus: "He has a prominent forehead and decided features, which mark him as a man of great endurance and power."[2]

Hobart's ego was even larger than his cranium. He boasted of being descended from Norman kings and counted Abraham Lincoln as a personal friend.[3] How he knew Lincoln we are left to guess. Hobart collected his victories saving souls like warriors collect their victories by earning medals. "He is a gallant old soldier of the Cross of Christ," Newson concluded.

Born in Vermont in 1811, Hobart was thirteen years older than George Richardson. Hobart began evangelizing Minnesota in 1835 when George was ten years old. By the time they met, Hobart had been a missionary in Minnesota for sixteen years.

Hobart had two primary passions: saving souls and abolishing slavery. He was a force on the national stage of the Methodist Church, advocating the immediate excommunication of any Methodist pastor who owned slaves.[4] He castigated anyone in his church who remained timid on the issue, proclaiming: "None have, nor could, truly assert that they have ever fully antagonized the monster, Slavery, until the old giant was in his coffin."[5] Hobart would go on to serve as a chaplain with a Union regiment at the horrific Battle of Shiloh in Tennessee.[6]

Hobart was progressive on other issues as well, favoring giving women the vote because they bring "purer moral perceptions" to the tasks of government than men.[7]

With equal zeal, Hobart promoted "the Method" from which Methodism derives its name. The Method was a system for organizing small groups, or "classes," of converts into congregations. The official name of the denomination was the "Methodist Episcopal Church," with "Episcopal"—the Greek word for "bishop"—in the formal name, denoting it was organized under bishops. Methodism was an offshoot of the Church of England, not to be confused with another American offshoot, the Protestant Episcopal Church—the church of my upbringing.

Methodist bishops oversaw presiding elders in charge of regional districts, and Hobart was a presiding elder for nearly a half-century supervising his huge territory in the Upper Midwest.

Methodism came with no elaborate rituals, no fussiness, no frills. Methodist preachers dressed simply—no vestments like the Catholics or Episcopalians. Nor did Methodist missionaries on the frontier build elaborate church buildings; they met in cabins, saloons, flophouses, and anywhere they could draw a crowd. Methodist worship focused on biblical passages, long sermons, and hymn singing—especially singing. The Methodist hymnal was packed with music written by one of the church's founders, Charles Wesley, whose hundreds of hymns crossed denominational lines and reach into every corner of church life in America to this day. Among the most popular Wesley hymns of all time is the Christmas carol: "Hark! The Herald Angels Sing."

Methodism found fertile ground in the "Second Great Awakening" revival meetings in upstate New York where George and Caroline Richardson grew up. Revival preachers condemned three big sins: booze, sex, and slavery. Northern Protestant preachers especially held forth that salvation was available to all, including slaves. Preeminent Civil War historian James M. McPherson wrote of the Northern Protestants: "The most heinous social sin was slavery. All people were equal in God's sight; the souls of black folks were as valuable as those of whites; for one of God's children to enslave another was a violation of the Higher Law even if it was sanctioned by the Constitution."[8]

The chasm between Northern and Southern Protestants widened year-by-year and proved an irreparable gulf.

Inevitably, the conflict over religious morality spilled into the nation's politics. The "culture wars" of our age have a long pedigree in our national life. Contemporary historians have argued that without the Second Great Awakening, there might not have been the Civil War.

Harriet Beecher Stowe, the daughter of Henry Ward Beecher—the most popular preacher of the age—wrote the most popular book of the age: *Uncle Tom's Cabin,* which was an indictment of slavery. The first printing sold 300,000 copies, an unimaginably large run for its time.[9] One story—likely apocryphal—has it that when Abraham Lincoln met Stowe, he called her the "little woman who wrote the book that made this great war."[10]

While Stowe fought slavery with words, her father raised funds to purchase weapons to fight those who would expand slavery into the territories. The guns became known as "Beecher's Bibles." Among Beecher's converts was John Brown, who tried and spectacularly failed to incite a slave insurrection by seizing the federal armory at Harpers Ferry, Virginia. His raiders were crushed by marines led by Col. Robert E. Lee, and Brown was hung.

For the young missionaries George and Caroline Richardson, the sparks of war remained far away from the Minnesota frontier.

Chauncey Hobart met with George Richardson at the riverboat landing in St. Paul and gave him "whatever directions I could get about my work."[11]

George learned his biggest challenge in his preaching circuit would be getting from one remote settlement to the next. It would take more than fervent preaching to instill "the method" with farmers, miners, and loggers. He would need stamina, ingenuity, and not least, horsemanship.

Hobart considered his preachers like sons. But he showed no tolerance for lazy or drunken preachers, removing them quickly if they faltered. If his protégés were having a rough time with a congregation—and they frequently did—Hobart moved them to another. Even if a preacher was doing well, he could expect to be moved every two or three years, the standard practice for Methodists for decades.

Methodist preachers were typically assigned a circuit of six to a dozen congregations and were required to keep up a regular schedule of visits to each. That meant the preachers were frequently away from family and whatever congregation they considered home base. The Method did not do much for the family life, but it proved to be an enormously effective way of building a church in the farming, mining, and timber towns on the American prairie.

In his old age, Hobart wrote about the physical challenges he confronted as a preacher on horseback on the frontier. His colorful description is worth quoting in full:

Then we plunged into the wilderness, which we knew to be a vast, dense unbroken forest for the next one hundred miles, with nothing to guide us but the sun, the stars, and a pocket-compass; had food for three and a half days; four blankets, coffee pot, two tin cups, a hand-ax, a rifle, and a pair of saddle-bags. After having traveled about fifteen miles, we camped in a deep ravine in a choke-cherry thicket, just deserted by a company of bears. The next day we passed over a rough country, many hills being more than four hundred feet high. Found shelter in a friendly cave while a severe thunder-storm passed by, and then we camped that night in a deep ravine, and were thoroughly drenched about midnight, being then driven out of bed to find shelter behind the large trees around us. In the morning we dried our clothes by a rousing fire, ate our breakfast, offered up our morning prayer, and pursued our journey.[12]

After meeting with Hobart at the St. Paul landing, George climbed back aboard the riverboat. He and Caroline soon arrived at their first post: Stillwater, a mill town supplied with logs floated downriver from the northern forests. The town's population was about 500, making it a big town in Minnesota and the last stop for the riverboats. Stillwater was the gateway to the northern frontier, and not surprisingly, had an abundance of hotels, saloons, and brothels. The Richardsons were at the ends of the earth.

George's home base was supposed to be a Methodist church building in Stillwater that had been without a regular pastor for six months. The previous pastor, James Harrington, had died of dysentery. When George and Caroline arrived, they were unable to find any Methodists to give them lodging. They spent their first night in a flophouse. The next day, George discovered that the few remaining members of the Stillwater Methodist Church had joined the local Presbyterian Church, while others had simply faded away. His difficulties compounded from there.

Hobart had given him a circuit that ran along both the Minnesota and Wisconsin sides of the St. Croix River. George's biggest challenge was finding safe places to ford the river on horseback.

George began his work in the tiny Willow River settlement, where he found twenty Methodists, including a family willing to house him and Caroline. Willow River became his headquarters, and he and Caroline decamped from Stillwater. They found a small house, and Caroline set up housekeeping. It was the first of many homes she organized. Looking back years later, Caroline described in her diary her first home with George as "small, simple, plain but comfortable." And she said this about him: "My kind, loving husband with his books and papers invested our home with a halo."[13]

Three more Minnesota settlements were added to George's circuit in 1852 when a preacher assigned to another circuit failed to show up. Among George's additional responsibilities was Kaposia, a settlement that is now part of the city of St. Paul and was then populated by Indians and territorial government agents. A few whites had married Mdewakaton Dakota Indians, and it was George's first experience with racially mixed families. How he felt about it, he did not record. But he acknowledged he was uncomfortable with the Indians, and they with him. "The Indians did not come inside the church, but lounged outside and made no discord."[14]

George preached three times every Sunday in at least three different locations. His day began early, riding his horse Prince and staying overnight at his last stop before returning to Willow River the next day. His circuit stretched about one hundred miles from one end to the other. With so many missions, he held worship services not just on Sundays but also midweek. George somehow kept his sense of humor, writing of how at one house where he preached, he was surrounded by sliced pumpkin rings drying from the ceiling. "As the ceiling was low, the pumpkins interfered with my head as I stood up to preach."[15]

The lumber settlements along the St. Croix River were populated entirely by men. George would stay at the boardinghouses, eat dinner with the men, and when they learned he was a preacher, they invited him to preach. His most constant companion was his horse, Prince. He got home to Caroline once a week.

In the winter, George traveled by sleigh up the frozen St. Croix River. The most dangerous time of the year was the early spring when the ice began to melt, and George had to head inland on horseback. "The peril of traveling on the ice is beyond the comprehension of one who has not experienced it, and yet familiarity with this danger induces indifference."

On a trip to Taylor Falls on a blustery March day, George followed a road on the west side of the St. Croix River. The road led him to a dead end at a swamp. He tried to cut overland to find the main road, and it began to snow. "I had no sign of a path." Surrounding him was dense forest. "I knew there was an unbroken forest all the way to Lake Superior," he wrote. "I knew I was lost."[16]

Suddenly his horse "took fright and wheeled round." In front of him was an Ojibwa Indian with a gun lashed to his saddle. "I knew I was in his power." George attempted to ask him if he knew the way to a lumber settlement. The Ojibwa man seemed not to understand until George made a motion like he was sawing a log. He then signaled George to follow. He was led along trail through the woods. "He followed a blind trail in which he had been traveling, and I fell into line and followed him for more than an hour. When we struck the main road he motioned me to the North, and he crossed the road and disappeared." George made it to Taylor Falls that night, forever grateful for his Ojibwa guide.

><><

Soon after settling into frontier life, Caroline became pregnant, and in May 1852, the Richardsons' first son was born. He was named George for his father, and his middle name, Owen, was for a friend in Willow Creek. He was known as "Owen" for the rest of his life.[17]

Prince drowned during the spring flooding from the snow melt. George gave no other details about the accident, but he wrote that Prince had become part of the family: "We thought if any horse ever went to heaven it would be Prince." Years later, Owen wrote in his memoir that his father was swept from his horse while trying to ford a frozen stream. Indians pulled George from the water, but the horse drowned. When the Indians found the carcass, Owen wrote, they gave George the horseshoes and ate the horse.[18]

At midyear, George was paid $180 by the Methodist conference for his work, but it was not enough to meet his expenses—or even purchase another horse. George was sick of circuit riding and the dangers of the frontier, and now he had a family to support. He accepted a teaching post in Galena, Illinois—a job arranged by Hobart. George resigned as a traveling Methodist preacher, sold his saddle and books to pay his debts, and he and his young family departed by riverboat for Galena in September 1852. That was not, however, the last George and Caroline would see of Presiding Elder Chauncey Hobart. In the fullness of time, Hobart would reel them back.

In their new home, slavery would land on their doorstep, demanding not just their words but their actions.

<h1>7</h1>

ACROSS THAT BRIDGE

*Lean toward the whispers of your own heart, discover the universal truth,
and follow its dictates. Know that the truth always leads to love and
perpetuation of peace . . . Hold only love, only peace in your heart,
knowing the battle of good to overcome evil is already won.*

JOHN LEWIS | 2012

Like my ancestor, George Richardson, I've been scribbling in notebooks
since I was a teenager. As an adult, I worked as a reporter for three California newspapers for a quarter-century, writing about everything from city
councils to street gangs, murder trials to zoning hearings, toxic waste dumps
to elections. I covered the presidential campaigns of Michael Dukakis, Bill
Clinton, and George H. W. Bush. My last reporting stint was with *The Sacramento Bee,* where I covered state politics and the Legislature for nearly a
decade. I filled a lot of notebooks.

In the mid-1990s, that meant writing about one politician in particu-
lar: Willie Lewis Brown Jr., the flamboyant and exceedingly controversial
Speaker of the California Assembly, and arguably the most powerful African
American politician in the United States until the election of Barack Obama.
Combing public records, and conducting hundreds of interviews, I wrote a
biography of Brown for the University of California Press.

In researching the book, I had to construct the history of racial segregation in East Texas where Brown grew up. I spent a month in Mineola, the
small town where he was born and reared. I found a Black guide who daily
introduced me to people who told me their stories. I learned about the phrase
"whitecapping": the practice of whites doing everything from throwing rocks
at Blacks to randomly shooting up their homes. In the 1930s and '40s, carloads
of whites would patrol the Black neighborhoods of Mineola. Signs on tele-
phone poles read "No niggers after dark." The practice of whitecapping did
not subside until long after Brown left home for San Francisco in the 1950s.

By the mid-1990s, Mineola was refashioning itself as a tourist destination with cute bed-and-breakfasts, and segregation was officially over. But my Black guides took me to the cemetery. A chain link fence separated the white side from the Black side of the graveyard. In death, segregation remained. The fence came down a few years later.

Soon after my book was published in 1997, I did something that stunned my journalistic colleagues and the denizens of the narrow world of California politics: I quit and went to seminary. Many of my friends thought I had lost my mind, which in a way, I had. My own path to the Episcopal priesthood was not a straight line. It never is for anyone.

How did I get from there to here? How did I go from being a driven journalist to the priesthood in the Episcopal Church? Presidents George H. W. Bush and Bill Clinton had something to do with it—as did Willie Brown. Indirectly.

I was coming into my own as journalist. I was exactly where I wanted to be. I worked hard and won a reputation for turning over rocks, digging hard, and asking tough questions. I took great pride when Assemblyman Richard Katz said "Jim Richardson is the one reporter you don't want to see walking toward to you in the hallway. You know the questions won't be good." And Assemblyman Katz was one of those politicians I respected for his honesty and dedication to public service.

But the harder I worked, the more I felt something missing in my life. My spiritual life was nonexistent. I had long since quit going to church and, in more candid moments, I had to admit I was not sure there was a God. The world seemed full of people convinced they knew God's "plan," and that if I would just "accept" Jesus Christ as my "personal Lord and Savior" my life would be fine and, as an added bonus, I'd get a pass into heaven. The journalist in me screamed it was self-serving nonsense. Those who hawked these religious insurance policies always seemed to have a political agenda, usually on the far right. The real world where I lived—a world full of political machinations, warfare, crime, street gangs, racism, and the pollution of the earth—made me say, "If this is God's plan, we need another plan."

I hit my emotional and spiritual bottom in the fall of 1986. I had moved to Sacramento and a new reporting job. I was doing well professionally, but that seemed to make the rest of my life feel vacant. I was in the midst of what the mystics called "the dark night of the soul," although I did not possess the language to call it that. So, I did what I usually did when I felt low.

I went fishing.

I climbed into my old rusty Ford Bronco and headed north four hours to the mountains north of Mount Lassen on the northern edge of California to a place called Hat Creek—my favorite spot on earth, not just for fishing, but for sorting out life. I slept in my truck, and I was up before dawn standing in the cold stream.

I took my first cast and hooked a very large trout. At that moment I had a sense of God's presence that is hard to describe. I could feel this presence telling me I would be fine, that I was loved, that I had always been loved, and that my life would take new turns, but to stop worrying. I let the fish go and sat on the bank for a good long while. I fished the rest of the morning and went home knowing something inside me had shifted.

I won't tell you that my life became immediately wonderful or that all my problems were solved. Life is not a straight line. But I began to notice other moments—small moments—that I would now call holy. I also began to hear yearning in me, long buried, that I needed to serve the poor and marginalized, but not necessarily through a charity. Journalism, though noble, was no longer enough for me. I began to realize I needed to do this somehow through a church. I yet had no idea how, let alone what church.

A couple of years later I met Lori, my future wife, at a *Sacramento Bee* office party. She was an editor, and I was a reporter, so I felt a little mismatched at first. But I could tell she was interested in many topics from the titles on her bookshelf—from Soviet nuclear defense policy and Russian literature to fine art and cooking—and she was an enthusiastic traveler as well. A Texas native and self-described "Air Force brat," Lori was accustomed to moving often and to far-flung places. But, as I learned, she longed for permanence and felt a special affinity for the wideness of the cosmos and the treasures of public libraries that provided a touchstone for her wherever she went. As we got to know each other, and our relationship deepened, we talked about everything—even God things. Before long we were talking about how we wanted to find a faith community together.

One morning we picked up *The Sacramento Bee,* and there was a story about Barbara Harris—a *Black* woman—who was being consecrated as the first female bishop in the Episcopal Church.[1] Not only that, Harris was the first woman bishop in the Anglican Communion, the worldwide federation of churches linked to the Church of England. That hit me like a bolt out of heaven. Could it be that the Episcopal Church—the church that had spurned my questions about the Vietnam War—had changed? We had to find out.

We looked for an Episcopal Church in the *Yellow Pages* and found several. We checked out a few. One Sunday evening we went to a "folk mass" at Trinity Cathedral, a couple of miles from our house in Sacramento. I did not then know why it was called a "cathedral," nor did I care.

The priest who was presiding that evening, Don Brown, was the dean of the Cathedral—the senior pastor. He preached that evening about how he didn't know all the answers, and the Episcopal Church didn't know all the answers, but he would walk with us in asking questions and searching for answers. No question was out of bounds, no answer off limits. He told of how the church where we were sitting was open and involved in the community. He certainly appealed to my journalistic instincts. I was hooked. And I had a lot of questions.

I could not then have fathomed that two decades later, I would be sitting in the dean's chair.

><><

In the mid-1990s, Lori and I became more involved at Trinity Cathedral. I learned a cathedral has nothing to do with architecture. Trinity Cathedral, with its modest brick architecture, has no flying buttresses. It is so designated as a cathedral because it is the headquarters of the local bishop whose official chair—or *cathedra*—gives the building its designation.

I was asked to head our community "outreach" ministries—our programs that serve the poor, hungry, and homeless in the community. A few years later, I was elected to the vestry—the board of directors of the cathedral—and eventually appointed by Dean Brown as senior warden, the chair of the board.

Meanwhile, Lori, after moving from being a night metro news editor into a daytime features editor, also got more involved at Trinity Cathedral, leading adult spiritual education classes and cooking dinners for large gatherings of a hundred or more. After I left the vestry, she served on the vestry and became a junior warden, which is something like vice president. Somehow, we did all this while juggling our stressful and consuming jobs on a large, urban newspaper.

In the midst of all that, my old gnawing feeling returned that I might become a priest. Truthfully, I was resistant to the idea of being a priest, but the nudging would not cease. I looked for ways to say "no" and could scarcely talk about it with anyone—even Lori—for fear of embarrassing myself by voicing an idea that was completely out of the norm for a newsroom.

Yet I also recalled Carl Gracely from my teenage years and how he had quit his business career to become a priest. He had moved to California and so happened to be my parents' priest in the Bay Area. I could not pretend to forget his example. Carl presided at our wedding. Lori, who had been baptized as an infant in the Roman Catholic Church, decided it was a very good thing that Episcopal priests had wives when Carl's wife, Gwynn, backed her decision not to have a male relative walk her down the aisle.

By 1992 I was on *The Sacramento Bee* team covering the presidential election. And then it hit me. I had to say "yes" to this new vocation. I can even tell you the moment: I was covering a speech by President George H. W. Bush at the Fairmont Hotel in San Francisco. I stood in the press area, hearing him give the same speech I had heard over and over. It could well have been Bill Clinton that day giving the same speech. But that particular day I was covering Bush. I could hear a voice inside me telling me that it was time to stop covering the same speech and say "yes" to the priesthood. I began to talk openly about it with friends and family.

At first, Lori thought I was crazy. Gradually she became cautiously enthusiastic about my calling. She had always been independent, so being the sole breadwinner for a few years didn't seem to faze her.

A number of my friends were dumbfounded, seeing my new direction as a radical departure from being a rational journalist. But I never saw it that way. For me, journalism and the priesthood are two sides of the same coin. Both vocations attempt—though imperfectly—to bring light into darkness. There is an old mission statement about journalism that applies equally to the priesthood: "to comfort the afflicted and afflict the comfortable."[2]

When I finally understood how both vocations dovetailed, I could say "yes" to the priesthood. But it took me a few more years to get there. I had one unfinished journalism project to complete: my book about Willie Brown. I was awarded an Alicia Patterson journalism grant in 1993 to work on the book, and I was given a year's leave from *The Sacramento Bee*. The year away from daily journalism was gift on many levels. Not only did I work on the book, I had time for serious spiritual discernment.

After returning to the *Bee,* I began working my way through the complicated ordination process of the Episcopal Church, which entails psychological and medical exams, interviews by committees, working with a spiritual director, and approval by the local bishop. And all that would happen before applying to a seminary.

With the Willie Brown book set for publication in the fall of 1996, and jumping through the many hoops with approval of my bishop, I felt free to enter the Church Divinity School of the Pacific in Berkeley—the Episcopal seminary serving the Pacific Rim—to earn a master of divinity degree.

"That won't work," Lori said flatly. "You can't possibly go back to school after two decades, and at the same time, promote your book. That's just not possible." I soon saw her wisdom. Meanwhile, Gregory Favre, the editor-in-chief of *The Sacramento Bee,* was enormously generous in giving me time to promote the book. The next year turned out to be among my most productive as a reporter. I needed the extra year.

Finally, it came time to bid farewell to my first career. I gave my notice, and I braced myself for the reaction. I was relieved when Editor Favre said: "I would try to make you stay but I never argue with God." But I was also in for a good deal of ribbing. Dan Walters, longtime political columnist, gave me a glow-in-the-dark plastic Virgin Mary statue at a going-away luncheon at Frank Fat's, the legendary hang-out of politicians, lobbyists, and reporters near the California State Capitol. I still have that glow-in-the-dark Virgin Mary.

With the farewells done, our plan was that Lori would keep working as an editor at *The Bee* as I embarked on the adventure of being a middle-aged graduate student.

And that is when my second thoughts nearly overwhelmed me—and when my father gave me George Richardson's "Recollections of My Life-work"—the "journal."

After my weekend reading the journal, I headed off to seminary in Berkeley. My inner struggles came with me, as they do for everyone. I began to think of my future life in ordained ministry as joining the family business. I could not help but feel that somehow George and Caroline Richardson were nudging me along, telling me to stiffen my spine, buck up, and get on with the Lord's work.

I graduated from seminary in 2000 and was ordained an Episcopal priest a few months later. I also returned to Trinity Cathedral in Sacramento where I served as an assistant priest for several years.

And that was only a start.

>~×~<

Ten years and three church assignments later, I was serving as the rector (senior priest) of St. Paul's Memorial Church in Charlottesville, Virginia. One evening, Lori and I were invited to a reception at the annual Virginia Festival of the Book to meet Congressman John Lewis. He was one of the original "Freedom Riders." Over the span of his remarkable life, Lewis had been arrested more than forty times in acts of civil disobedience protesting racial injustice.

He had recently written a short memoir, *Across That Bridge*, recalling the lessons of a lifetime, including his experience as a young man on the Edmund Pettus Bridge in Selma, Alabama. Lewis was savagely beaten by the police that day. Four decades later, when I met him, he still bore the scars on his face.

The room was crowded at the Charlottesville reception, but I managed to make my way over to Lewis to introduce myself. I told him I was a pastor in a local church. He wanted to know more. I told him about my book about Willie Brown. He wanted to know more. Then I told him about my abolitionist ancestors and the journal of George Richardson, and how I wanted to write this book. He pulled me to a corner and wanted to know more.

When I finished telling him the story of my ancestors, John Lewis—one of the bravest, most faithful men I have ever met—shook my hand and said, "Keep testifying."

FREEDOM RIDE

Times chariot wheels roll'd swiftly on
While groaning millions wept and prayed
Minds half enlightened labored on
O when shall tyranny be stayed?

CAROLINE RICHARDSON | "THE PROMISE BEING
MADE MUST BE KEPT," 1863

Before the dominance of railroads, the most important Mississippi River port between St. Paul and St. Louis was Galena, Illinois. Today the town caters to tourists. But in the early nineteenth century, Galena was bigger than Chicago. A history of Galena published by the federal Works Progress Administration in 1930s during the New Deal described the town: "In 1826, while Chicago was still a swamp village, Galena was a bustling outpost swarming with miners, gamblers, traders, rivermen and trappers."[1]

The key to Galena's growth was the nearby lead mines. The ore was dug out of the hills and brought to Galena for loading on barges heading down river. The traders and trappers could purchase hogs, horses, and human beings on Galena's market square. Galena also had its share of bars and brothels, making the town target-rich for Christian missionaries. Methodists showed up in 1828 to clean up the town and push for the abolition of slavery, which was not outlawed in Illinois for another twenty years. The Methodists did well, building a church in Galena in the 1830s, and then tearing it down to build a larger church in 1856. That church building still stands.

Galena became a magnet for the most important Northern political figures of nineteenth-century America. Abraham Lincoln stumped in Galena for the Republicans' first presidential candidate, John C. Frémont in 1856. Frederick Douglass, the ex-slave prophet of freedom, spoke for the cause of abolitionism.[2]

By the mid-1850s, Galena was a microcosm of the national schism over slavery. The Mississippi River gave the town a peculiar Southern flavor, and it was an island of Democrats surrounded by a heavily Republican

Congressional district. In other ways, Galena was a Union town. When war broke out, Galena produced no fewer than nine Union generals, including Ulysses S. Grant, who had worked in his brothers' tannery in Galena. At the end of the Civil War, the town gave Grant a house, though he hardly ever lived there. Grant quipped that his only ambition after the war was to be mayor of Galena so he could get a sidewalk built in front of his house.[3]

The Richardson's oldest son, Owen, two-years-old at the time, claimed in his memoir that their Galena Methodist congregation included Grant's parents.[4] But George Richardson made no such boast in his journal of meeting the general or his parents, and in fact, Grant's parents lived in Ohio when the Richardsons lived in Galena. Postwar memories could be fuzzy.

Nonetheless, George made political connections in Galena that served him well, including Republican Elihu Washburne who represented Galena in Congress. His brother Cadwallader (who spelled his last name without the "e" at the end) also served in Congress, became a Union general in the Civil War and would become George's commanding officer.[5]

Soon after settling in Galena in September 1852, George took a teaching post in the town school while Caroline opened a private school. Caroline's school soon grew to more than one hundred pupils, an early testament to her skill as a teacher. The couple bought a house, the first they owned. Caroline was soon overwhelmed, so they hired a housekeeper, Margaret "Maggie" Harshman.[6]

George found it difficult to discipline his Irish immigrant pupils. A sixteen-year-old boy attacked him with a knife, but George ducked the blow and held the boy with his strong left arm while waiting for the constable. The boy's mother came and hit George with a bat, and he subdued her as well. Both mother and son were arrested and fined the next day by Henry Park, the justice of the peace.[7]

More significantly, George and Judge Park shared a cause—and a secret—that could have landed them in prison: in the spring of 1854, they assisted at least one escaped slave to freedom.

"Just as I was going to bed one evening, I heard a light rap at my front door," George wrote. When he opened the door, it was Judge Park. "Put out the light," the judge told him. "He had a fugitive slave and wished me to shelter her," George wrote in his journal. "I did not hesitate a moment."[8]

In "Recollections of My Lifework," George wrote that her name was

"Kitty," though in his first draft he called her "Katie." The first draft offers another detail: "She was a good sized, well made full black woman, 24 years old."[9] We are left to guess the reasons for the differences in the two drafts.

When Judge Parker brought Kitty—or Katie—into their house, George and Caroline Richardson became "station masters" on the Underground Railroad (those who led escaped slaves on their journeys, like Harriet Tubman, were "conductors"). Caroline, although pregnant, prepared a bed for Kitty in the attic garret. "She was beyond the reach of her pursuers," George wrote. "We asked no questions that night. We only knew she was a human being panting for freedom."

By taking in Kitty on that 1854 night, the Richardsons put themselves at risk of arrest and imprisonment. Although slavery had been abolished in Illinois, the federal Fugitive Slave Act made it illegal to harbor escaped slaves in "free" states. Southern slaveholders had won passage of a law that virtually invalidated state's rights to abolish slavery by forcing the return of slaves to their owners. The Fugitive Slave Act verged on legalizing slavery everywhere, thus enraging Northern abolitionists. The law would be upheld three years later by the United States Supreme Court in its notorious Dred Scott decision. The high court's ruling would permit slave owners to maintain their "property rights" over other human beings when visiting states that had banned slavery. They might not be able to purchase a slave in "free" states, but they could bring the enslaved with them from another state.[10]

Safe inside the Richardsons' home, Kitty told her story: her master, a Texan named McCracken, brought her to Illinois as a wet nurse for his baby daughter while his family was visiting friends in Galena, the McDowell family. McCracken had promised Kitty her freedom if she came with them to Illinois, but he reneged. No manumission papers were forthcoming. Instead, her owner prepared to return to Texas and take Kitty with him. She feared being sold as a field hand once she was no longer needed to nurse the McCrackens' baby.

A kitchen maid in the McDowell household helped Kitty plot her escape. When the appointed evening came, the maid instructed Kitty to simply walk out the door and cross the street. She was quickly retrieved by Judge Park, who was legally responsible for enforcing the Fugitive Slave Act but instead took her to the Richardsons' house a few blocks away. Though George gives no hint in his journal about how Judge Park was certain the Richardsons would take her in, he and Caroline were fully prepared for Kitty's arrival. The transfer from Judge Park's carriage took only seconds. Their home was the perfect place to hide her.

All involved in the plot were right to be nervous about getting caught. Sympathies in Galena were with the slaveholders. The next day, the police searched the town for the escaped slave. "Nobody had suspected me of being an abolitionist," George wrote, "and nobody crept around under our windows to eavesdrop, and the police never came to search our house. Many houses were searched. The whole police force were on the lookout for our guest."[11]

George and Caroline—who was pregnant with their second child—knew exactly how to evade detection and where to take her when the search died down. The Richardsons either learned on the fly—which does not seem likely—or they were well briefed. They might even have been more experienced in smuggling escaped slaves to freedom than George let on decades later in his journal.

George never revealed in "Recollections of My Lifework" the names of his co-conspirators, other than Judge Park, nor did George use the phrase "Underground Railroad" in his book. Many years later, in the midst of the Civil War, George wrote a letter home describing a sermon he delivered to a "colored" congregation in Memphis telling his listeners how he had "kept a depot on the underground rail road." He left the hint that he was involved helping in the escape of other slaves besides Kitty.

George did not record how long Kitty stayed hidden in their attic, but it was certainly several days and perhaps weeks. He wrote years later that arrangements were made "for spiriting her away." When the time came for her transfer to the next stop, Caroline dressed Kitty in men's clothing and hid her in plain sight. Kitty and George walked together two miles through Galena's streets to meet her "conductor." George and Kitty started their stroll at 7:30 p.m. under the streetlamps. "Businessmen were just passing up the street on their way home, and the police were on duty." Somewhere on the road outside of Galena they met a horse-and-wagon that took Kitty to the next stop along the Underground Railroad on her way to Canada and freedom.

George never recorded their route out of town or the exact rendezvous point, but it's clear that he knew exactly what to do, who to contact, and where to go. "Those who knew who helped Kitty get away, were true to the secret entrusted to them," he wrote. They never revealed those secrets even after emancipation. The story in the journal is tantalizing by what's left out.

Years later, George wrote an account of Kitty's escape for a friend who wanted to publish it in a book. "McCracken never knew what became of his 'property.' If he is anxious to know he can find out by addressing Rev GW Richardson, Austin, Texas."[12]

The escape of Kitty was a major turning point for George and Caroline. From that moment on their commitment to abolishing slavery shifted from the abstract to the real. The cause of emancipation increasingly became their consuming passion and would take them places they scarcely could have imagined as a young couple from western New York who had settled in the Midwestern frontier.

✥

When Lori and I began retracing George Richardson's steps, our first stop was Galena, Illinois. By the twenty-first century, Galena had become a thriving tourist destination with bed-and-breakfasts and fine restaurants. Galena is well preserved from its pre-Civil War days. The town's commercial district still has a low skyline of antebellum red brick buildings, and many of the modest houses of that era still stand. Ulysses S. Grant's home has been maintained as a tourist attraction. The nearby Grant Museum displays a hologram of President Grant and his wife greeting visitors. The Grant family pew in the Methodist church is marked.

Steve Repp, the public library archivist, helped us find George Richardson in a city directory from the 1850s. He pointed out on a map where the Richardson house still stands. The directory gave no address, listing it as a house on Dodge Street near Hill Street, only a short walk from the center of town. He also told us that the account in George Richardson's journal is one of the few confirmations that the Underground Railroad was active in Galena.

We found three plain brick houses on the hill. We could not tell which house belonged to the Richardsons. One of the adjacent houses belonged to John A. Rawlins, Galena's city attorney at the time the Richardsons were neighbors. Rawlins was Grant's closest aide and confidante and is counted as one of the generals Galena sent to the Civil War. Rawlins later served as secretary of war when Grant became president.[13] The Richardsons made no mention of Rawlins in their journals and diaries, but I wonder if he was in on the secret of Kitty and the Underground Railroad? If Rawlins was part of the plot, it would have lent an added layer of protection for all involved.

We asked Repp if he could figure out the route George took to get Kitty out of town. He mulled over the map and then traced a likely route. All possible routes would have led through town to the main highway. We walked the route, and, indeed, it would have been hard to get Kitty away unseen except at night and in disguise.

〉━〈

In July 1854—not long after Kitty escaped—the Richardsons' second child was born, David Fay Richardson, who would become my great-grandfather and the first in the line of those who conveyed the journal eventually reaching me. George was now thirty and Caroline twenty-nine.[14]

A month after David Fay's birth, George helped organize a large religious revival near the town of Elizabeth, about fifteen miles northeast of Galena in the heart of the lead-mining region. Elizabeth was initially established as Apple River Fort in the 1830s during the Black Hawk War. Abraham Lincoln was a veteran of that short and vicious war. So was Chauncey Hobart.[15]

What set this revival apart is how it focused on evangelizing African Americans laboring in the mines. "During this meeting the Spirit of Labor came on me as never before," George wrote. "God gave me words and faith and access to hearts, so I found it easy to lead sinners to Christ, and Christians to a higher life."[16]

Hobart helped organize the revival and recorded in his memoir that roughly one thousand people attended—fully one-third of them Black.

"During this revival the people fell by scores as if dead, even upon the children there was an awful consciousness of God's presence," Hobart wrote. "Galena was redeemed from its character of lawlessness and has since been the home of many earnest, noble Christians and strong churches."[17]

And Hobart still had an eye out for the Richardsons.

〉━〈

Lori and I ended the first leg of what would be many trips spanning many years with a visit to the site of the religious revival at the Apple River Fort east of Galena. It is still off the beaten track. There weren't many visitors on the day we visited. The rustic wooden fort has been reconstructed and used for reenactments of the Black Hawk War and its connection to Lincoln. But no mention was made at the fort of the religious revival that drew so many African Americans led by abolitionists including George Richardson and Chauncey Hobart. We walked the grounds and headed back on the road.

⤜ 9 ⤛

DAGGER STROKES

Walk with me, Lord! Walk with me!
Walk with me, Lord! Walk with me!
While I'm on, Lord, this tedious journey,
I need Jesus, to walk with me.

"WALK WITH ME LORD!"
RECORDED BY MAHALIA JACKSON IN 1949

With two young children in tow, Caroline gave up teaching and with it her income. The couple could no longer afford their housekeeper, Margaret Harshman. Nor could they keep up the payments on their Galena house for much longer.[1]

George yearned to reenter the Methodist ministry, and he certainly talked to Hobart during the revival at Elizabeth. "My heart had learned some lessons of love and obedience during the two years I had been in Galena," he wrote in his journal.

The Richardsons returned to Wisconsin—and he to the life of Methodist circuit riding. Hobart brought George back as a senior preacher, putting him in charge of other preachers. On horseback once again, George was relicensed as a Methodist preacher in August 1854. His second stint as a traveling preacher was about to prove far more trying than the first, both personally and professionally.[2]

His new charge was near Platteville in southwestern Wisconsin, not far from Galena. Platteville survived on the lead and zinc mines. George was assigned four preachers under his supervision, and he visited each of his churches once a month. He had about three hundred Methodists in his circuit; combined, they composed his largest congregation to date. Although his new responsibilities came with a parsonage, he and Caroline found it uninhabitable for the harsh winter. They took rooms at a large farmhouse in nearby Lafayette County, Wisconsin. The couple had two-year-old Owen and infant David.

Within a year, Chauncey Hobart moved George back to the Minnesota territory where he had begun his ministry. But, before George could move, he was stricken with typhoid fever.[3] He was laid up for four weeks, and "some of the time my life was despaired of" he remembered. George did not make it to his new congregation in Prescott, Minnesota, until October 1855. "My people had waited patiently for my recovery and prayer had been made for me without ceasing."

Caroline was pregnant with their third child, so she moved back with her parents in Wisconsin while George settled in Prescott. He was away for the birth of their daughter, Caroline Lucretia, or "Carrie" as they called her. The birth was hard, and Caroline had a difficult recovery. She stayed with her parents until the ice melted in the spring of 1856. A week after rejoining George in Prescott, her mother suddenly died. "My wife, as long as she lived, was thankful she was with her mother through the winter."

Nor had George recovered fully from typhoid fever. He had regular chills and attacks. Keeping up with his circuit proved impossible. Hobart moved George yet again, this time to Hastings, Minnesota, on the west side of the Mississippi River. It proved even worse. "The membership was small, and a very different class of people from what I had at Prescott," George wrote, describing his new flock. His new flock did not respond well to his first sermon. "I soon found myself floundering." So George kept talking and talking. "I failed so I could not stop [his underline]."[4]

The next day, George talked to the congregation's leader, "Brother" Twitchell, about making the parsonage habitable. Twitchell replied: "The conference has sent us a preacher, and we must take care of him whether he is good for anything or not." George said it felt like a "cruel dagger stroke."[5]

An even crueler dagger stroke followed: Their baby daughter, Carrie, died on September 3, 1856—barely nine months old. "Strangers were kind and sympathizing, but there was a terrible vacancy in our hearts and home."[6] George was bereft and could not conduct a funeral himself. No Methodist preachers were available for the burial, so a Presbyterian pastor volunteered.

"We laid away the little form, that had been the home of the undeveloped soul, in the Hastings cemetery, about two miles west of town." Although nothing more was written in "Recollections of My Lifework" about Carrie's death, the loss of their child never left George and Caroline. Decades later, long after the Civil War, when they moved to a new farm, the Richardsons reinterred their baby's remains in a new cemetery.

No words survive in Caroline's diary about her infant daughter's death. Three pages were torn out in a section written in 1856, the same year Carrie died. The jagged stubs the pages stick out from the binding. Perhaps those pages spoke of the delight at her daughter's birth and then the worries about her sickness. The one page from 1856 not torn out is a poem she wrote lamenting the death of her brother, Myron, who had died many years earlier as a teenager. Perhaps Caroline wrote the poem not just as for her long-deceased brother but to pour out her raw grief about her baby daughter:

> It was long we watched thy bed-side
> With alternate hope and fear
> And prayed to see life's spring-tide
> Till death approached thee near
>
> I' was hard to see thee fading
> With each succeeding day
> And to note how uncomplaining
> Thy chastened heart did stay
>
> But we know thou hast escaped
> Earth's trifles, joys and fears
> That might have downed thy spirit
> In the lapse of coming years.[7]

Thirty-year-old Caroline did not write another word in her diary for another five years—not until 1861, in the horror of the Civil War.

><><

Soon after Carrie's death, George collapsed from exhaustion and grief. He felt he could do nothing right with his church in Hastings. During a Sunday service, he embarrassed himself when he began singing a hymn before the choir could find the page in the hymnal. The choir felt insulted, and the congregation soon divided along those who sided with the choir and those who sided with their pastor—a dividing line that certainly must have spoken of deeper conflicts in the congregation than just music. The church elders forced George to step down. "I had so far damaged my ability to do good, that it would be useless for me to remain."[8]

He looked again for a teaching job. In January 1857, the trustees of Hamline University, the newly established Methodist school in Red Wing, Minnesota, elected George as the chair of mathematics.[9] How he came to their attention, he did not say, but no doubt Chauncey Hobart had something to do with it. Yet George turned it down. George wrote that he wanted to take the position but did not want to give in to his detractors in Hastings by resigning from the ministry. If he ever regretted that decision, he never recorded it.

Seven months later George was assigned to a new circuit at Kenyon, Minnesota. He purchased 160 acres hoping to supplement his income by farming. The house on the property was in disrepair, and there was no parsonage with his new preaching assignment. As winter approached, George felt increasingly anxious about building a secure house and barn, "and a hundred other things to be done so we could live when the snow became deep."

And Caroline was pregnant again.

In November, George set out with a team of borrowed oxen for Hastings to buy lumber. It took him four days to get there, and the snow was already falling. When he returned with the lumber, Caroline had given birth to their third son, Francis Asbury, who they would always call Frank. "The mother and babe were in the open house, and the snow was drifting through the cracks, and lay in small drifts on her bed."[10]

Neighbors came to the rescue, and within a week of Frank's birth, they had built the Richardsons a new house with the lumber hauled through the snow from Hastings.

In the spring of 1857, George planted crops, hoping to support the family while he preached. But farming went poorly and was made worse by the economic "Panic of 1857," as it came to be known.[11] The crash and resulting depression was the first worldwide financial crisis of the Industrial Age. With declining demand for American products in Europe, the value of land declined in the West, and with it, farm prices. Farmers like the Richardsons went broke as their crops rotted in the fields.

George sold his horse in the spring of 1858 and abandoned the farm at Kenyon.[12] He considered his experiment of "half farming and half preaching" a fiasco. The financial crisis was far beyond his control, but he felt keenly responsible for the failure. "I have never been able to understand that I accomplished any good for myself or anybody else during the short conference year I was at Kenyon," he wrote. "But God does not count mistakes as unpardonable sins."

Caroline summed up her feelings by writing a poem in a letter to her husband:

> "And tho' we've sometimes trod the sand
> With sore and bleeding feet
> I've ever found thy firm strong hand
> Stretched forth to guide and keep."[13]

George was assigned yet another preaching post, this time in Spring Valley, Minnesota, about seventy-five miles from Kenyon. Railroads did not reach this outpost, and the roads were muddy and rutted. The people of Spring Valley brought horse-and-wagon teams to fetch George and his family. He was emotionally spent and so was his new community. When hailstorms wrecked the crops on many of the farms, George hit the emotional bottom.

And then his new charges lifted him up.

George arrived on his first Sunday for worship in Spring Valley, held in a schoolhouse. The building was packed, and the people were delighted to greet him.[14]

"There came over me such an overwhelming sense of responsibility of caring for these scattered flocks, that I could scarcely go on with the services." He stood to preach. "The reaction was great." His congregation kept coming back week after week to hear him preach. "There seemed to be no flagging in the sermons."

The people of Spring Valley were as much a gift to the Richardsons as they were to them. On Thanksgiving Day—and his birthday—Caroline made a rice pudding and cake with sugar and raisins she had been saving for a special occasion. They invited six of their nearest neighbors to join them. "A rice pudding and a cake were a strange sight on that circuit that year," George wrote.[15]

In the spring of 1859, Caroline was pregnant with their fifth child, Earl Mercein, born that fall. He was called "E.M." and outlived all of his siblings, dying in 1947, a mere six years before I was born. He was known to my father and his sister as "Uncle Earl."

George had finally found his footing and considered 1859–1860 the most productive and fulfilling period of his life up until then. He conducted revivals, visited the sick, baptized babies and adults, won converts, and ministered to young and old alike. His people showed him their appreciation in ways big and small. He began to love the preaching life more deeply than ever before. To read his journal for the year of 1859 is to hear a man who, after enduring bitter disappointments, financial ruin, physical calamity, and the tragedy of losing a child, was now thriving in his vocation and his family life.

But the world far away was about to explode, and with it, life on the prairie.

PART II

THE SLAUGHTER PEN

Negroes, like other people, act upon motives. Why should they do anything
for us, if we will do nothing for them? If they stake their lives for us, they
must be prompted by the strongest motive—even the promise of freedom.
And the promise being made, must be kept.

ABRAHAM LINCOLN | LETTER TO JAMES C. CONKLING, AUGUST 26, 1863

Minnesota had been a state for barely three years when South Carolina, one
of the original thirteen, decided it no longer wanted to be in the same country
with Minnesota or any other northern state. It so happened that Alexander
Ramsey, Minnesota's governor, was in Washington, DC, at the outbreak of
war in April 1861 and earned the distinction of volunteering his state as the
first to commit troops to fight the "Southern Rebellion."[1]

Minnesota paid a fearsome price for the honor.

By the end of the Civil War, Minnesota had sent nearly half its young
adult men—more than twenty-six thousand soldiers—to the front. More
than twenty-five hundred did not return.[2] Minnesota regiments served in
nearly every major battle and in every theater. George Richardson, Chauncey
Hobart and many other pastors and priests, representing nearly every Christian denomination, served among them.

Led by Hobart, Minnesota's Methodist preachers had little doubt about
the righteousness of the Union cause. Crushing the rebellion and abolishing
slavery were one-and-the-same holy cause. They fervently believed that only
a Union victory would bring the downfall of slavery and the liberation of
African Americans. Their biggest frustration was that Lincoln did not free
the slaves immediately.

After the Civil War, apologists for the Southern "Lost Cause" claimed that
the Confederacy fought for "state's rights," which was postwar propaganda.
The Confederacy had no respect for states claiming their rights to abolish
slavery. Prewar Southern leaders made abundantly clear their cause was the
preservation of slavery based on race. Alexander Stephens, the vice president
of the Confederacy, asserted in 1861 that the foundation of the new nation

would rest "upon the great truth that the negro is not equal to the white man; that slavery subordination to the superior race is his natural and normal condition. This, our new government, is the first, in the history of the world, based upon this great physical, philosophical, and moral truth."[3]

But for the brothers John and Charles Wesley, the English founders of Methodism, slavery was a heinous sin. The Wesleys had supported the British political movement to end the slave trade. Their stance was embraced especially by Northern Methodists including Hobart and George Richardson.[4]

The growth of Methodism in the United States brought with it the same tensions and conflicts already seething throughout the country, particularly around slavery. Many Southern Methodist pastors, and at least one bishop, owned slaves.

Northern and Southern Methodist factions clashed at their 1844 national conference. The flash point: one of the church's five bishops, James O. Andrew of Georgia, owned slaves—and proudly so. He became the living symbol of hypocrisy for the Northern Methodists. The conference voted to suspend Bishop Andrew until he divested himself of his slaves, which he would not do.[5]

In response, the Southerners voted to secede from their national church and organize their own Methodist Church. Northern and Southern Methodists would not to be reunited for another generation, and then only after splitting along racial lines.

In the opinion of Abel Stevens, a contemporaneous Methodist historian, the Methodist split was nothing less than the opening salvo of the war: "This stupendous rupture, it cannot be doubted," he wrote, "was the effective beginning of the great national rupture which soon after startled the world with the greatest civil war of modern history."[6] Stevens noted that the split left the Southern Methodists as the "chief religious denomination of the Southern states," while the Northern Methodist Church, "became the most energetic antislavery body in the nation."

Hobart, as the presiding elder in Minnesota, put himself into the thick of the national conflict. "We, as a conference, were known to be among the radicals on the question of slavery," he wrote in his memoir.[7] As they prepared for the next Methodist national convention, "there was a good deal of figuring among the brethren so as to send an ultra anti-slavery delegation to represent the [Minnesota-Wisconsin] conference."

Hobart was one of the three delegates elected from Minnesota sent to the Methodist convention in Indianapolis in 1856. Hobart and his allies pushed a resolution to excommunicate any Methodist who owned slaves. Despite the efforts of the abolitionist Midwesterners, the abolitionist Methodists failed to win the required two-thirds majority and their proposal failed.

At the next national convention in 1860 in Buffalo, New York—only a few months before the outbreak of war—Hobart and the Minnesota delegation pushed their proposal again, and failed again. By then it didn't much matter. The Southern Methodists had already bolted the church. Cannons—not canons—and soldiers—not pastors—would settle the issue. "All through the following summer, political agitation and threats of national disunion hung like a dark cloud over the land," Hobart recalled. "War was inevitable."[8]

✂━✂

In the summer of 1860, Hobart assigned George Richardson to Northfield, Minnesota—and it was a plum assignment.[9] Northfield still had a frontier flavor, but it was developing as a prosperous regional center of commerce with two colleges, Carleton and St. Olaf, that would grow in educational stature and national prominence. The Richardsons' second son, David (my great-grandfather), years later would graduate from Carleton and settle in Northfield. My grandfather, Russell, would attend Carlton, though never graduate. Three generations of Richardsons considered Northfield the family home, although their patriarch, George, never did.

George did not have much time to enjoy Northfield or his budding family. He rode a circuit with five congregations and was seldom home except on the Sundays when he preached in Northfield. The rest of his time he rotated among the other four missions. The missions were two hours apart by horseback, "hardly giving me time to eat or breathe between sermons."[10]

His message struck the common themes for a Methodist preacher in his day: sin, redemption, living a moral and temperate life. He recorded the outlines to his sermons in a small brown notebook, along with many other details about his ministry. He also recorded where and when he gave his sermons to avoid repeating himself in the same place. It is hard to tell from the outlines whether he preached about slavery, but a number of his sermons hit on the theme of the equality of all humanity as members of "God's family."[11] He asked his listeners, "What are the obligations growing out of those relations?" and he would answer his own question: "to defend and encourage, love and cherish the brotherhood." He implored his congregations to live pure lives that they might "associate with angels." It does not take much of a leap to connect the dots in his outlines to the abolition of slavery.

In the tumultuous election of 1860, George voted for Abraham Lincoln. Decades later, his son, Owen, wrote in his own memoir how his father voted in a saloon and had to cajole the bartender into giving him a ballot.[12] His father's vote for Lincoln was among Owen's earliest childhood memories:

> On election day father took me to the polls when he went to vote for Lincoln. The voting place was in the hotel barroom. The clerk challenged father's right to vote on the ground that he had not been a citizen of the precinct long enough. I remember father's defense, 'This is a federal election. I am a citizen of the United States. I am entitled to vote for a presidential candidate. I do not wish to vote for any state or county candidate.' Father held his ballot in his hand while the Judge looked up the law and found that father was entitled to vote for Lincoln. I saw father deposit his ballot. I was very angry to see father so treated.

With the outbreak of war in 1861, the men from George's congregations began enlisting. The first to go was a man named Miller. "He was eating his dinner when a neighbor came in and told him Fort Sumter had been fired on. He left his dinner unfinished, and ran all the way to Faribault—12 miles—to the recruiting office and enrolled his name and was sworn in."[13]

Miller joined the First Regiment Minnesota Volunteer Infantry and fought in the first major battle of the war, known by Northerners as "First Bull Run" in Manassas, Virginia.[14] The engagement was a debacle for the Union, and the Minnesota regiment took heavy casualties. Word came back to Northfield that Miller was among the dead.

Chauncey Hobart was also among the first Minnesota volunteers. The Methodist elder joined the Army as a chaplain and followed a Minnesota regiment to Kentucky.[15] The Minnesota Methodist conference met that fall without Hobart, but still felt his dominating presence. The conference approved resolutions endorsing Lincoln's prosecution of the war and urging the President to free the slaves. The Minnesota Methodists also endorsed Gen.

John Frémont's order emancipating the enslaved in Missouri (Lincoln later rescinded that order on the grounds that the general exceeded his authority). George wrote in "Recollections of My Lifework" that the Methodists' resolutions recognized "the fact that slavery must die before the rebellion could be put down."[16]

At the conference, George got yet another preaching assignment, in Hudson, Wisconsin. "Everybody seemed glad I had come." But as George was moving his household goods, he jumped from a wagon and caught a foot in the spokes of a wheel.[17] His ankle broke in two places, the bone piercing the skin. He was taken to his new parsonage, where a surgeon was summoned. He was bedridden for more than a month, and by his own description, he endured more pain than when he had lost his right forearm as a young man. At least he did not lose his foot.

George gave his first sermon in his new church while sitting on a chair on December 1, 1861. He soon asked to be transferred back to Minnesota. The Methodist elders assigned the Richardsons to Lake City, Minnesota, and a new circuit including several places he had served years earlier. "This was a year of hard work, but everything was harmonious."[18]

Caroline was soon pregnant for the sixth and final time. Their last child, Mary Emma, was born April 27, 1863, in Lake City. She was known ever after as "Emma."[19]

As a child, Emma was described as "delicate," and she suffered from various maladies throughout her life. She was thin and small. Of all of the children of Caroline and George Richardson, Emma resembled her father the most—and they drew closer over the decades. Photographs in Richardson family albums show that the sons had round faces resembling their mother. But Emma had the long face and high cheekbones of her father, and his red hair as a child.[20] And, unlike her older brothers, Emma had her father's scholarly bent.

⟩⟫⟨⟪

In the fall of 1863, as the Civil War raged on battlefields with names like Gettysburg and Chickamauga, the Minnesota Methodists went on about their business evangelizing the frontier—but the pall of the battlefields hung over the Methodist annual conference. "A good many of the ministers and laymen are away in the Army," George wrote, "and we have all we can do to keep from going backwards [in organizing new congregations]."[21]

The conference passed more resolutions supporting the war effort and George Richardson felt increasingly sidelined and irrelevant. He felt that the routine of church business and the pettiness of church disputes were insignificant compared to the battlefields far from Minnesota. "Such patriotic speeches and resolutions kindled my patriotism to a white heat," George wrote.[22]

Outwardly, his ministry was doing well. He was now a respected pastor, a troubleshooter, and a sought-after preacher. He was appointed to Red Wing, Minnesota, a prestigious posting because it was in the locale of the Methodist school, Hamline University. His congregation included professors and students, and he found their company stimulating. His family thrived in Red Wing, where his children could get a good education.

But George Richardson was restless to do his part to save the Union and end slavery. "I knew of none of my relations that bore the family name that were in the war. I was ashamed to have my children feel that none of their relatives helped to save the Union."[23]

His first step was through the United States Christian Commission, established soon after the calamitous Battle of Bull Run and the reports of suffering and neglect of Union soldiers. Under the auspices of the Young Men's Christian Association (YMCA), the Christian Commission organized Protestant pastors, seminarians, and laypeople to bring medical supplies, books, and religious materials to Union soldiers in camps, hospitals, and prisons. The federal government paid for transportation and rations; the churches provided the volunteers.

Chauncey Hobart returned to Minnesota in late 1863 from his stint as a Union chaplain, and then he and George together joined the Christian Commission.[24] In January 1864, the pair of Methodist preachers got their first assignment: ferrying medical supplies to the battlefields near Nashville. "The account of the suffering among the soldiers reached us from every quarter," George wrote. "Many a box of sanitary goods from Northern homes was hurrying to the front."[25]

The carnage on the Tennessee countryside was immense: the Battle of Shiloh, with twenty-three thousand casualties, achieved the distinction of being the bloodiest single battle up to that point in the Civil War. Hobart had served as a chaplain in that battle.

Then came the Battle of Stones River, about thirty miles south of Nashville near the town of Murfreesboro. The spot was strategically unimportant but was where the two armies collided. When the fighting was over there were more than twenty-four thousand dead and wounded. The Union suffered almost one-third wounded or killed—achieving the distinction of the highest percentage of casualties of any major battle in the war.[26]

And that is where George Richardson and Chauncey Hobart were sent.

Bones and bodies were still being buried a year later from the Stones River Battlefield when the pair of pastors arrived on January 13, 1864. "I was on this battle ground 13 months after the fight, but there was still evidence of great slaughter on both sides," George wrote.[27]

The ferocious fighting was confined in a small, flat plain, with low lying bogs and a few rises that were just high enough to defend but not see over. This was not a battlefield sweeping for miles like at Gettysburg. Soldiers here would have been hard pressed to see more than a few yards ahead, and it would have been impossible to see into the surrounding thick woods.

A year after the fighting, George and Hobart walked into these woods to see for themselves the place the soldiers dubbed the "Slaughter Pen." Their guide was a chaplain from Michigan by the name of Patterson.[28]

The Union Army retreated into these woods, and the Confederate Army gave chase. But it was a trap. The federals hid in rock outcroppings stretching across the forest floor. The rocks made natural trenches. Once the rebels were deep into the woods, they were mowed down—and the ambush turned the tide of the battle—and so it became known forevermore as the "Slaughter Pen."

After the slaughter, federal troops buried their own dead but left the rebel corpses to rot. As George described in his journal, "I saw one place where the bodies had been piled up and rails had been piled on them. We noticed as we passed that the hogs had rooted away the rails, and were scattering the bones in every direction."

A year later, the trees were still filled with bullet holes higher than a soldier's head. George learned soldiers shoot too high.

"Some of our party wanted to stop the ambulance and pick up a skull or some other bones as a relic of the war," George wrote. "Bro Hobart said, 'No, let the bones of these men remain in oblivion. So perish all the enemies of our Government. Drive on.'"

><><

The first time I read the journal, I knew I had to walk this same ground as my ancestor, and so it was that a century after he had recorded his experience, Lori and I walked into the Slaughter Pen. The day was overcast and drizzly, and the air was cold and heavy. We walked across a meadow and found a trail into the woods.

The trees were dense, and we could not see far into the forest. In the rock outcroppings, the National Park Service had set up steel cutouts in the shape of soldiers pointing guns. The eerie silhouettes appeared as rusty ghosts. We crouched next to them. A ghostly chill surrounded us. The soil of the trail soaked with blood so long ago still seemed to ooze with death. We did not linger.

><><

Hobart and George reported to a hospital camp in Murfreesboro and found soldiers still convalescing from their wounds a year after the battle.[29] More soldiers with fresh wounds arrived daily from distant battles. Hobart was assigned to the Zollikoffer Barracks, an old hotel housing about two-thousand soldiers. George was assigned to a hospital camp about two miles away. The two also worked at a refugee camp at an abandoned medical school. The refugees were Southerners loyal to the Union who had fled their Confederate neighbors.

"There were very many Union men and women, and they had suffered everything it was possible for them to suffer, from their rebel neighbors and rebel soldiers," George wrote. "Here were hundreds of people—poor-sick-emaciated, driven from their homes because they were Union people. Under such circumstances their loyalty was intense."[30]

George gave them Bibles and religious tracts but discovered that only one in ten could read. In his view, slavery had degraded not just enslaved

Blacks, but poor rural Southern whites as well. "Here was a sample of the degrading effects of slavery."

George visited makeshift hospital camps in Murfreesboro and Nashville, and was appalled at the conditions. He was especially outraged that officers were stealing the medical supplies meant for wounded soldiers. "I found also that there was much more suffering than necessary, if officers, the surgeons and hospital nurses had all done their duty."[31]

He ventured into the smallpox camps. "I found this neglect took its worst form in small-pox hospitals." He willingly exposed himself to the disease that could maim or kill so easily. One night, asleep, he felt violently feverish and, groping in the dark, could feel sores on his forehead. When he awoke in the morning, the symptoms were gone. It had been a frightening nightmare. But despite his sleeping terrors, he returned to the camps again and again.[32]

A year after the slaughter, the Stones River Battlefield had become a garrison for Black Union soldiers. Escaped slaves were arriving daily near Nashville and enlisting in the Union Army.

George visited schools in Nashville that had been set up for the formerly enslaved, and he was deeply moved. "I noticed the eagerness with which these children of oppression snatched the first chance for an education."[33] He saw three generations—grandparents, parents, and children—sitting in the same room learning to read and write. "It was the building up of a new hope and a new life."

His experiences with Black soldiers would shape the rest of his life. "Among the first things to be considered by the philanthropic people of the North, after providing the ex-slave with food, was to provide for his education and this seemed to be God's order, if the slave was to be changed to a citizen, he must have education to meet the responsibilities of citizenship."[34]

Other than his encounter several years earlier with Kitty (and maybe other escaped slaves unmentioned in the journal), this was the first time he had mingled with African Americans for any length of time. At first, he found his stereotypes confirmed. "I was very little acquainted with the Negro characteristics and peculiarities, and there were many things that seemed funny to me, that a person acquainted with them would not notice."[35]

A few days later, George encountered his first "colored" Union regiment. Although George did not mention it in his journal, he probably saw Black soldiers building a national cemetery at Murfreesboro for the Union dead. He brought the Black soldiers spelling books. "The eagerness to learn to read, and to hear the gospel which did not have for its text—'Servants obey your masters'—attracted my attention," he wrote.

Earlier in the war, the Fugitive Slave Act was still in place and many Union Army regiments routinely—and tragically—returned escaped slaves to their former owners. But that did not staunch the flow of thousands of slaves escaping, crossing the battle lines, and attempting to enlist in the federal Army.

Maj. Gen. Benjamin Butler of Massachusetts, an antislavery former Congressman, came up with an ingenious legal theory to avoid returning escaped slaves to their former masters. The ex-slaves were considered "contraband" of war because they had been the "property" of Southerners. He reasoned that if the ex-slaves were "contraband," then they could be confiscated by the Army as the spoils of war and could enlist as Union soldiers. The Black soldiers became known as "Contrabands."

George relished Butler's reasoning: "It chose to make a man of the Contraband, and then it chose to put a gun in his hand, and allow him to help save the Union," George wrote. "The order to return the slaves to their masters after they had come into our lines, was countermanded, and now they were free. The master was not allowed to hunt slaves after they came to us for protection," George wrote.[36]

The first Black regiments were given exotic, foreign legion-sounding names, like the "17th Corps de Afrique Infantry," which eventually morphed into the Eighty-Eighth us Colored Infantry. By the end of the war, more than 178,000 Blacks had served in the Union Army. Casualties among Black soldiers were enormous, and a full one-third of them died.[37]

George Richardson had not yet witnessed a battle. But his experience at Stones River moved him deeply. His racial stereotypes began to shift. He was impressed not only by the plight of ex-slaves but also by their determination to enlist in the Army to fight their ex-masters. If he ever had any previous doubts, he knew then that the cause of Black Americans was his cause. He yearned to join them, and not just on brief missions of mercy for the Sanitary Commission, but in the Army at the front.

"I decided then and there to take a place as Chaplain of a Negro Regiment if such an opportunity offered," he wrote in "Recollections of My Lifework."[38]

But he had to pull strings to get into such a regiment.

The War Department required that Black regiments must have white officers (a few Blacks became officers by the end of the war, but they were the exception).[39] Officer positions in the "colored" units became among the most sought after by white officers. For some, these posts were a quick way to promotion. But for many others, including George Richardson, joining the "colored" Army units was fulfilling the mission of their lives.

"There was no lack of white soldiers who volunteered to be detached from their Regiments and given places in colored Regiments," George wrote.[40]

A few white officers became famous, such as Col. Robert Gould Shaw of the Fifty-Fourth Massachusetts Colored Infantry, celebrated in the twentieth-century movie *Glory*. But most white officers in Black regiments served without fame or fanfare, especially in the western battlefields of Tennessee and Mississippi, far from the nation's capital and battlefields of Virginia.

Historian Joseph T. Glatthaar in his book about white officers in Black regiments noted that religion motivated the most determined white volunteers: "Just as evangelical religion had been a driving force with abolitionists, because it branded slavery a sin and demanded that its converts work actively to terminate the evil wherever it existed, so it was with whites who elected to command Black soldiers."[41]

The bulk of the white officers in the Black regiments, he wrote, came from the hotbeds of the evangelical tent revivals in the Second Great Awakening—the same revivals that fired up George's youthful faith and propelled him into the ministry. "Spearheading this religious influence in the ranks of the white officers was the clergy itself," Glatthaar wrote.

The War Department was flooded with applications from whites requesting commissions in Black regiments. The bar was high, and acceptance became selective.

George had a few connections who could help him. Before leaving Nashville, he wrote his request to Brig. Gen. Augustus Chetlain, who was organizing Black troops in Tennessee and Kentucky. Chetlain, as it happened, was from Galena, Illinois.[42]

Chetlain made it clear to all applicants that he wanted only white officers with the highest of motives, and none were welcome if they believed it a "sacrifice" to serve with Black soldiers. He looked askance at those desiring only "appointment simply for higher rank."[43]

Many years later, George's oldest son Owen wrote in his own memoir that his father used his connection with another general from Galena, Cadwallader Washburn, who was then commanding Union occupation forces in Memphis.[44] Washburn's brother, Elihu, represented Galena in Congress, and his nod was all it took to win for an applicant a coveted Army commission.

What Owen apparently didn't know was Chetlain and Washburn were close friends and political allies—and his father probably knew both. Owen also noted that Galena's most prominent general was Ulysses S. Grant and claimed that Grant had parents living in Galena whom his father knew. In fact, Grant's parents lived in Ohio. But Grant's chief of staff, John Rawlins, had been the Richardsons' next-door neighbor in Galena.

By whatever means he used, George Richardson had enough connections to get into the Army despite his age—nearly forty—and with only one arm.

With his work done for the Christian Commission in Tennessee, George returned to Minnesota. He was barely home when orders arrived for him to return to Tennessee and report to the Army in Memphis.

On May 14, 1864, George boarded the Mississippi River steamboat *Canada,* bound for war. As the steamboat made its way downriver, he wrote the first of many letters home to Caroline.[45]

"The stream of water and of time are constantly bearing me farther from you," he wrote. "I have a calmness in my own feelings corresponding with all things around me. I feel a satisfaction in believing I am in the path of duty. I have no knowledge of what the future may be, but I believe it will all be right." In the margin of his letter, he added, "Keep up good courage and trust in God."

Most of his letters began with "Dear Wife," but sometimes he wrote "Dear Home."[46] George Richardson had left behind his wife and five children. The oldest, Owen, was twelve, and the youngest, Emma, was barely a year old. He would see very little of them in the years ahead. Aboard the steamboat *Canada,* he had set his course not just for the duration a war but for the rest of his life. His course would carry him and his family to places he could not then imagine—and at great risk to not just his own life, but to theirs.

His orders were to report as chaplain to the Seventh US Colored Heavy Artillery Regiment posted at Fort Pickering, Memphis, Tennessee. Union Army chaplain George Richardson would soon find himself in a muddy, mosquito-infested fortress, under constant threat from raiding Confederates, and joining the most martyred African American regiment of the Civil War.

In my training to be an Episcopal priest, I worked for a summer as a chaplain at a big urban hospital, Sutter General in Sacramento. Working as a chaplain was a rite of passage known as clinical pastoral education, or "CPE," as it is called seminary shorthand. As CPE chaplains, we spent half of our time with patients in the hospital rooms and the other half interacting with each other in group therapy. Given what we were going through in the hospital rooms, we were much in need of the group therapy, though I would imagine it would have been a foreign concept to my Civil War chaplain ancestor.

I was assigned to the Intensive Care Unit at Sutter General. That meant I was around death and dying every day, all day, and all summer long. Mostly I offered my silent presence just sitting with family members, holding hands, listening. I soon memorized the Twenty-Third Psalm. These encounters inevitably brought forth my own distant memories of pain and disability.

One of the patients who touched me most deeply was a ninety-two-year-old man named Ben Brown. His physical health was gradually failing with age, but he taught me much from his experience about spiritual health. In time, I would preside at his funeral—my first as a priest.

I found Ben's name on the daily hospital roster of patients. He had listed himself as "Episcopalian," and I always went looking for the Episcopalians regardless of what unit they were in. After I introduced myself, I checked to be sure that he was an Episcopalian.

"Yeah, I guess I am," he replied. "I was born that way, baptized that way, and I was defrocked as a priest."[47]

I was quite taken aback.

The next day, we talked for more than an hour. I learned Ben had been an Episcopal priest as a young man. He had served as the Navy chaplain at the Battle of Guadalcanal in World War II. The battle for the Pacific island raged for six months, and thousands of Americans and Japanese died of their wounds and malaria. Food and medical supplies were in short supply. At one point Ben figured that the ratio of chaplains to men made him chaplain to fifty thousand marines.

As the first casualties turned into a torrent, the marines set up a hospital under a large tent. Then it began to rain without ceasing. He said the water flowed unabated across the muddy floor of the tent. They laid boards on the ground next to the beds so that the doctors, nurses, and chaplains would not sink into the mud. He told me how he did what he could with young men—many of them teens—with limbs blown off and their eyes blinded. He received little "care packages" from stateside with socks and small personal items. "Was I supposed to give these to young guys whose feet had been blown off? The folks at home didn't really get it."

Ben considered Guadalcanal the most important event of his life. But it nearly broke him.

When the war was over, Ben asked his bishop to release him from being priest—"defrocked." He felt done.

That summer I saw Ben nearly every day until he was discharged home. I continued to see him after my chaplaincy was officially completed at the hospital. I returned in the fall to seminary in Berkeley, but when I was home for the weekend, I would go see Ben. I learned how he was always questioning whether he was fulfilling God's purpose in the world. The question of himself went beyond institutions. He said he could not believe in any church that tried to contain God and exclude most of humanity. He inspired me to keep asking that same question of myself.

Ben gave me something else—something tangible to remember him by: the Bible he carried at Guadalcanal. He died quietly in his sleep a few hours after I last saw him.

A year after Ben died, Bishop Jerry Lamb ordained me a priest at Trinity Cathedral, Sacramento. We used Ben's Bible at my ordination ceremony. And I thought of my ancestor, a chaplain in a war long ago.

II

THE FORT PILLOW BOYS

If men have been murdered after capture,
retaliation must be resorted to promptly.

ULYSSES S. GRANT | APRIL 12, 1864

The steamboat *Canada* churned downriver in May 1864 carrying newly minted Army Chaplain George Richardson and a contingent of Union soldiers bound for the battlefields of Tennessee and Mississippi. As the paddle wheeler ventured farther south into what had been Confederate territory, it passed Fort Pillow, a remote outpost that lay in ruins overlooking the Mississippi River in Tennessee. George knew well the significance of Fort Pillow to the men with whom he would soon serve—and he would describe it years later in his journal. "I went past Fort Pillow," he wrote, noting that the Confederates had "cruelly butchered the prisoners."[1]

The executed prisoners were Black Union soldiers.

Fort Pillow had been built by the Confederates early in the war but was easily captured by the Union Army.[2] As Grant's Army continued south, he left behind Black troops to hold the fort. On April 12, 1864—barely a month before George Richardson saw it from the deck of his steamboat on his way to Memphis—a brigade of rebel raiders captured Fort Pillow, led by Confederate Lt. Gen. Nathan Bedford Forrest, who had been a slave catcher before the war.[3] After the war, Forrest went on to become the Ku Klux Klan's first "Grand Wizard," perpetrating more atrocities.

The Union defenders at Fort Pillow were overwhelmed by Forrest's raiders and surrendered. What happened next is considered the worst war crime of the Civil War. The rebels proceeded to butcher their Black Union Army prisoners. Those trying to escape were chased down, shot, or hacked to death. When they finished, Forrest's raiders disappeared back into the Tennessee countryside, taking more than one hundred prisoners with them. A few Union soldiers still managed to get away to tell their story, and the massacre soon made headlines in Northern newspapers.[4]

Forrest and the Confederates had no intention of holding the fort. They had come to kill and capture Black Union soldiers. Forrest filed a dispatch after boasting: "The river was dyed with the blood of the slaughtered for two hundred yards. . . . It is hoped that these facts will demonstrate to the Northern people that negro soldiers cannot cope with Southerners."

Grant noted in his memoir that Forrest later sanitized his reports and "left out the part which shocks humanity to read."[5]

The reaction in the North was not as Forrest expected. Black Union soldiers sought revenge, and Grant suspended prisoner exchanges for the remainder of the war.[6]

The Fort Pillow massacre has remained subject to sharp arguments into our own time. Soon after the massacre, accusations of corruption and incompetence haunted the white Union officers who had left Fort Pillow without enough men or arms to defend it. Apologists for the Confederacy later claimed—with scant evidence—that the atrocity was the fault of a few renegade soldiers whose officers had lost control.

But that conclusion is preposterous.

"It has been asserted again and again that Forrest did not order a massacre. He did not need to," historian Dudley Taylor Cornish concluded in his seminal book on Black Union soldiers written in the 1950s. "Most damaging of all," Cornish continued, "is his own report written three days after the capture of the fort. There is no suggestion that his men were 'out of control.' There is, on the contrary, a kind of gory exultation."[7]

Beyond dispute is that the rebels conducted an orgy of killing. There were 593 federal soldiers on the roster at Fort Pillow on the day it was attacked by Forrest and his men. The Union soldiers were outnumbered two-to-one by the Confederate raiders. More than two hundred Black soldiers were executed after they had surrendered. The Confederates lost between fifteen and twenty men. Forrest did nothing to stop it and bragged about it afterwards.[8]

Fort Pillow had no strategic value to either side. At first glance, the fort's height above the river made it virtually invulnerable to attack from riverboats. The threat was not from the river, but from the land. A year before the massacre, Grant's forces went around it, capturing Memphis to the south without bothering with Fort Pillow. The fort was left cut off, and the Confederates retreated from it. The Union Army began using Fort Pillow not to defend the river, but as a base for suppressing Confederate guerrillas in the western Tennessee countryside.

With the fall of Vicksburg on July 4, 1863, the Union succeeded in splitting the Confederacy and cutting it off from the Mississippi River as a rebel highway for troops and commerce. But Fort Pillow held by the Union was just as vulnerable to attack from the land as it had been when the Confederates held it. Gen. William T. Sherman believed Fort Pillow an unnecessary drain on Union resources needed for his drive into the Deep South. But Fort Pillow remained garrisoned by Black soldiers borrowed from occupation troops in Memphis.

By April 1864, Sherman ordered Fort Pillow closed, but the order never arrived.[9] The commanding general in Memphis, Gen. Stephen Hurlbut, ignored Sherman's order. The reason Hurlbut did so remains unclear; some have speculated that the Union general was profiting from Fort Pillow as a black-market trading post. Or, just as plausibly, he did not care about the "colored" soldiers garrisoning it. By the time orders were finally issued to abandon Fort Pillow, it was too late. The fort had become a tempting target for Forrest's guerrillas—and doubly so because it was occupied by Black troops; the rebels dubbed it a "mongrel garrison."[10]

The shock of the massacre was quickly felt in the North, and Congress launched an investigation. Gen. Hurlbut was sacked. The *New York Spectator* ran a story under the headline: "The Rebel Butcheries Confirmed—Heart Sickening Details—The Sick, Wounded and Unarmed Murdered in Cold Blood."[11] The newspaper reported that the "barbarity" of Forrest's army "must convince even the most skeptical that it is the intention of the rebel authorities not to recognize the officers and men of our colored regiments as entitled to the treatment accorded by all civilized nations to prisoners of war."

Two days after the massacre, an incensed Maj. Gen. Augustus Chetlain, the commander of all the US colored regiments, wrote to his Galena friend and political ally, Congressman Elihu Washburne. "This is the most infernal outrage that has been committed since the war began," Chetlain wrote. "If this is to be the game of the enemy they will soon learn that it is one at which two can play. . . . I feel the blood of these heroes must be avenged."[12]

Black soldiers throughout the Union Army began wearing headbands emblazoned with "Remember Fort Pillow!" The motto traveled to the Eastern theater and the Virginia battlefields. There were reports that when Black soldiers caught Confederate soldiers, they dispatched them with cries of "Remember Fort Pillow."[13]

The aftershocks from the Fort Pillow massacre reverberated far beyond its significance as a brutal raid in a backwater fort. The so-called "Radical Republicans" in Congress were convinced that the Confederacy's official policy was to execute all Black Union soldiers. President Lincoln's cabinet heatedly discussed the massacre, with Secretary of the Interior John Usher recommending that any captured soldiers from Forrest's units should be executed. Others cautioned that retaliation would spin out of control.

The number of whites volunteering as officers in Black regiments declined with the realization that the Confederates would not spare them if captured.[14] Gen. Chetlain blamed the drop in white officer volunteers on the failure of the Union to immediately retaliate against the Confederates for the Fort Pillow massacre. The decline in white volunteers may have helped one-armed George Richardson win swift acceptance into the Army. If he ever hesitated to join the Army because of the Fort Pillow massacre, he never recorded it.

The Sixth US Colored Heavy Artillery Regiment was so decimated at Fort Pillow that it was reorganized and renamed the Seventh US Colored Heavy Artillery Regiment and pulled back to the relative safety of Fort Pickering, Memphis, where George was to join them as their chaplain. He stayed with the regiment for the remainder of the war and another year after that until he was mustered out of the Army. The newly reconstituted regiment dubbed themselves the "Fort Pillow Boys."[15]

The Fort Pillow Boys made it their holy cause to capture and kill Forrest.

The Fort Pillow massacre had one other tragic consequence: Grant suspended prisoner exchanges in the Western theater under his command until Black soldiers were treated as prisoners of war. The Confederates would make no such concession. The Confederates continued to execute captured Black Union soldiers or return them to slavery. Secretary of War Edwin Stanton soon followed Grant's lead and suspended all prisoner exchanges in all theaters for the remainder of the war.[16]

The end of prisoner exchanges made almost inevitable the horrific conditions at Andersonville, Georgia, where 45,000 federal soldiers were jammed into a camp designed to hold a quarter as many men. By the end of the war, 13,000 Union soldiers died in captivity. Among those imprisoned at Andersonville were the 139 captured white survivors of Fort Pillow. Most perished.

><><

Ten days after the massacre, Lizzie Wayt Booth went to the site of the massacre to look for the body of her husband, Maj. Lionel Booth, the slain commander of Fort Pillow. His body was never found, likely dumped in the river by Forrest's raiders.[17]

One of the Black survivors of the massacre gave Lizzie Booth a flag smeared with blood because it had been used as a bandage. She brought the bloody flag to Fort Pickering in Memphis where the new "colored" regiment was organizing.

"Soldiers, this flag I give you," she told the Black soldiers, "knowing that you will ever remember the last words of my noble husband: 'Never surrender the flag to traitors.'"

As she presented the flag, the soldiers at Fort Pickering knelt in front of her, and then they took an oath to avenge the victims of Fort Pillow.

The Fort Pillow flag hung over the Memphis fort for the remainder of the war. For the Black soldiers at Fort Pickering, the bloody flag represented their holy cause. They would scour the countryside looking for Forrest and his men, though they would never catch them. George Richardson, now almost forty, would be among them.

⟋⟍ *12* ⟋⟍

FORT PICKERING

Princes, this clay must be your bed,
In spite of all your towers,
The tall, the wise, the *rebel head*
Must lie as low as ours!

HYMN SUNG BY BLACK SOLDIERS | 1864

George Richardson arrived in Memphis on Sunday May 22, 1864—a month after the Fort Pillow massacre. He wore no insignias of rank. Union and Confederate chaplains wore the same uniform, always black, fitting with their grim task of ministering to the wounded and dying for both sides. Even their buttons were black, not shiny like other officers. By midafternoon George was already caring for soldiers at a Memphis convalescent hospital.[1]

The next morning, he reported for duty at Gen. Chetlain's headquarters and found the commanding general "cordial and glad to see me."[2] He brought with him a signed endorsement from Chauncey Hobart and was commissioned as Chaplain to the Seventh US Colored Heavy Artillery Regiment.[3] The regiment was filled with the men of the Sixth US Colored who had evaded death at Fort Pillow.

A month after the massacre, decomposing corpses were still washing ashore in Memphis. In one of his first letters home, George reported: "Yesterday the body of one of the Fort Pillow men came floating down and was taken ashore and buried by some of our Reg."[4]

He soon met one of the Fort Pillow survivors, a Black soldier who had narrowly missed being killed and managed to make his way to Memphis.[5] "I saw one black man that the rebels missed at Ft. Pillow," George wrote Caroline. "He said the way he escaped murder was to drop down on his face and appear dead. The rebs shot another man wounding him badly and he fell right across him. When the reb came up with his pistol he shot the wounded man through the head killing him instantly. This fellow lay still under the dead man till he saw the reb had no more cartridges—then he raised up and told him he would follow him, and as the reb had nothing to kill him with he took him along. He went with them about 50 miles and escaped and came back to camp."

Years later, George remembered how the massacre haunted his soldiers.[6] He filled page after page of his journal with their stories. George recorded the story of Capt. Charles Epeneter and his lieutenant, who escaped after he "was shot through the ear after the rebels had got into the fort." After being captured, they escaped, and in disguise made their way back to Union lines. George recorded how Forrest's raiders repeatedly entered the field hospital shooting wounded Union soldiers or smashing them with the butts of their guns. Black soldiers were forced to stand up and were shot dead. Epeneter's immediate superior, Maj. William Bradford, was captured, taken to the woods and executed.[7]

"My heart grows sick at their tales of horror," George wrote to Caroline.[8]

As a new chaplain, George Richardson found Fort Pickering oddly bucolic. "The lawn in front of my door is covered with a beautiful carpet of red-top and white clover in full bloom—on which the officers are stretching and lolling under the shade of some fine cedar."[9]

Fort Pickering, laid out like a long cigar, sprawled above the Mississippi riverbank on the southern edge of Memphis. The fort had been built atop Chickasaw burial mounds a half-century before the Civil War. The burial mounds made perfect ramparts. The Army built barracks, hospitals and storage bunkers inside the fort, and placed cannons facing the river within easy range of hostile riverboats.

His first night at Fort Pickering, George slept on the floor inside a wooden building reserved for white officers. The Quartermaster gave him two blankets and he wrapped his overcoat around his boots for a pillow. That was the only night he would sleep in a whites-only building.

George found conditions inside the fort a "disappointment."[10] He was struck by the inequality between the Black enlisted men and the white officers; the Black soldiers lived in tents pitched on the lawn or in the mud while the white officers lived in comfortable houses. George decided to pitch his own tent near the men in front of the infirmary. He had lived in a tent as an itinerant preacher, and it was good enough now. He slept in his tent near his men for the remainder of the war. By mid-summer, he wrote in a letter to his wife, "I prefer my tent."[11]

He wrote home that that he "began to harden myself to the soldiers fare."[12]

His only complaints in the months ahead were about not having enough dry socks—and the lack of a prosthetic right arm that he had ordered but had not arrived.[13]

Although still spring, the muggy Memphis weather felt to George like Minnesota in the summer. "The dust in the streets and in the Fort where the men drill is very bad."[14] There was only one cistern for drinking water so he and others drank river water. His tent was hot from "the burning rays upon the canvas."

George made the rounds at hospitals, getting acquainted with the officers and soldiers. While there were reports of mediocre white officers in Black regiments elsewhere, George found the officers of his regiment worthy of their ranks. "They were mostly good men, and took as good care of the soldiers under them as they could."

In another letter home, George recounted how he had introduced himself as an "abolitionist" to his Black soldiers.[15] He told them that *his* Methodist denomination opposed slavery and his own involvement in the cause: "I had received colored children into one of the public schools in Wisconsin—had preached for the Colored Church in Galena, and had kept a depot on the underground rail road." The letter is the only known written admission that he was, indeed, a conspirator on the Underground Railroad and not just a hastily drafted recruit on the night that he spirited Kitty to freedom.

Within a week, George preached his first funeral for a Black soldier, held inside a ramshackle brick building converted for prayer meetings. "As I came up they were singing then followed a prayer very simple—somewhat earnest and in the old sacred Baptist tone," he wrote in a letter home. "I really thought we were going to preach a funeral sermon, but it was a revival sermon."[16]

George scheduled Sunday worship services and devised a plan for schooling the soldiers.[17] "The regular plan of my work was to visit the hospital every day—to look after the sick and dying, and give the dead a soldiers burial—to be present at dress parade every Sunday morning and to offer prayer—to preach at 2 pm in the improvised chapel, and sometimes preach Sunday night—to hold meetings for prayer and exhortation at least three times between Sundays."

During the rest of the week, he taught the formerly enslaved soldiers reading and writing. "I find the men are nearly all anxious to learn but what can I do among 800 men? I think I shall take a school of the colored noncommissioned officers and put them through the best I can. The white officers are so busy with their other duties I can expect but little help from them."[18]

He soon got reinforcements from two white women, Mary Redman and Ellen Fuller, who taught in George's makeshift school.[19] The regiment's colonel, who supported educating the Black soldiers, let the women board with his family. The demand for schooling by the Black soldiers was great, and George needed more teachers. He wrote his wife inquiring whether Ella Fay, one of her nieces, would be willing to come to Memphis to teach the soldiers.[20] Caroline's reply is lost, but Ella did not come.

George was assigned a Black orderly, Sam Slocum, to care for the regimental chapel, school room and George's horse.[21] He soon learned Slocum had a gift for preaching. "He was the best preacher I had in the Reg't," George recalled in his journal years later. "He could not read a word but he knew a good deal of the Bible by hearing white ministers read it, and he remembered a great many texts."

George asked Slocum to preach to the soldiers on Sundays. Their work together represented George's first of many partnerships with Black preachers. George quoted at length in the journal one of Slocum's sermons, and it is a rare snapshot of a Black preacher in the midst of the Civil War.[22]

"As a race" Slocum preached, "they had been trodden down and oppressed—they did not own their wives nor their children, nor their own bodies or souls—often whipped for going to a prayer meeting—often obliged to have the overseer in the meeting should talk about being free."

As soldiers, Slocum continued, "we are only half free." But "by and by, when we have served our time out in the Army, we shall muster out, and be as free as white men . . . be counted as citizens and not cattle." He exhorted the men that God wanted them to fight for their wives and children who were still enslaved. "It is God who has moved the friends of liberty to give us this chance. We must do the rest for ourselves."

"Now God is lifting us up above all our enemies round about. Bless his name!"

George was keenly aware that his soldiers came from many Christian traditions, or none at all, and so he set about to organize a non-denominational "Soldiers Christian Association."[23] Any soldier—Black or white—professing to be a Christian and leading a moral life could join. The men wrote their own "confession of faith" or creed. "I intend to have all the religious persons among the soldiers and officers, and officers wives if they will, join the same Church," he wrote in a letter home.[24] "I have no idea of having one organization for the whites and another for the blacks."

George enjoyed preaching to the Black troops. "I never enjoyed myself any better preaching anywhere than I do here," he wrote. "I have an inward satisfaction that I am just where I ought to be."[25]

Yet, most of the time at Fort Pickering, life was dull, dirty, and monotonous, with sobering reminders that there was a war raging a few miles away. "The gunboats are passing up and down the river almost every day ready to pay their respects to the guerrillas if they should chance to discover them. At 10 o'clock this morning we heard heavy cannonading a few miles below."[26]

That spring, he tended to the wounded survivors who had made it to the fort from Brice's Crossroads, Mississippi, where Forrest had once again routed Union troops. "They are all cut to pieces," George wrote in a letter home.[27]

By summer, George was short on socks and shirts, and he still needed a new prosthetic right arm. He paid ninety dollars for a new arm before leaving Minnesota, but it had not shown up. George wrote Caroline requesting that she ask Chauncey Hobart to make inquiries about his prosthetic arm and send it south with another chaplain bound for the front; George made several such pleas before a new arm arrived.

George readily acknowledged that his deprivations were nothing as compared to those of the Black troops. Then as now, summer in Memphis was hot and sticky. The soldiers suffered from fevers, bed bugs, fleas, and diarrhea from drinking polluted river water. "Quite a number of the men are sick, two or three have died since I came here," George wrote.[28]

Death was an ever present companion. Another white officer, Humphrey Hood, a surgeon from Litchfield, Illinois, assigned to the Third US Colored Heavy Artillery Regiment at Fort Pickering, wrote home: "The sick list continues large," Hood wrote. "Several have died." Judging by his letters, he detested every minute at Fort Pickering.

Hood's letters are in the archive at the Abraham Lincoln Presidential Library and Museum in Springfield, Illinois.[29] Hood is also featured in one of the display cases in the museum. Unmentioned in the display are the surgeon's attitudes about the Black soldiers he served. Calling them "darkies" in his letters, he disparaged their oath to avenge Fort Pillow as a "ridiculous farce." His characterization of the soldiers he served are in sharp contrast to George Richardson's letters.

The surgeon complained frequently about bad food, and packages that rarely arrived from home containing good food. Hood's morale steadily sank. In one of Hood's letters, he thanked his wife for two bottles of snuff that had safely arrived. "I'm feeling much better tonight—almost quite well."

Hood loathed the chaplain assigned to his regiment, Chauncey P. Taylor.[30] Hood wrote that Chaplain Taylor was "a disgrace to his profession," because he never visited the sick in the hospital, and "does nothing and makes no effort to do anything." George Richardson made no mention of Chaplain Taylor, or Hood, in his letters or journal. Nor did Hood mention George Richardson. There is no evidence they knew each other.

There were a few diversions. The white officers—including George—went into town to the Oak Gallery photography studio to have their portraits taken. The photos were small, about the size of a baseball card, with "J. W. Taft, Artist" on the back. Civil War soldiers gave the cartes de visite, sometimes called "cabinet cards," to each other as souvenirs.[31]

The cards had another more sobering purpose: Soldiers mailed them home so that their loved ones could remember them if they did not return. Eight such Civil War era cards of soldiers have survived among George's mementos. George also collected mass-produced portrait cards of Abraham Lincoln, Mary Todd Lincoln and Gen. Grant. There are no photographs of Black soldiers in George's collection—the Black soldiers would not have been welcome in the white photography studio in Memphis. But he had one card in his photo collection of an unnamed Black pastor from the 1870s, likely Charles Madison during his work in Austin, Texas.[32]

George's own Civil War photo card shows him in his black chaplain's frock coat with the top button clasped in the fashion of Civil War officers. In the photograph, he is leaning his right arm atop a chair, with a prosthetic hand on his missing right forearm. Three copies of the black-and-white portrait cards survive, plus a larger colorized version. One of his grandchildren later wrote that it was the only photograph showing him with an artificial hand. The photography studio probably supplied the hand as a prop for the many amputee soldiers posing for pictures. George never mentions in "Recollections of My Lifework" owning a fake hand—he might have considered it vain. His prosthetic arm was utilitarian with a clip on the end for hooks and eating utensils.[33]

When George first set foot at Fort Pickering in 1864, he brought with him typical white stereotypes of Blacks as lazy. His believed that Black soldiers did not have much "vital energy," and that they would flee rather than fight. "I am disappointed in the colored troops," he wrote a month after his arrival. "It is a greater change for field hands to become soldiers than for white men generally."[34]

That summer, his attitude about the fighting mettle of Black soldiers would take a dramatic turn. In August, both the Third and Seventh US Colored Artillery Regiments left Fort Pickering for battles in Mississippi.

George Richardson would go with them.

13

SNAKES

Hold up my goings in thy paths, *that* my footsteps slip not.
PSALM 17: 5 | KING JAMES VERSION

On a sticky summer afternoon, Union Army chaplain George Richardson stood at the gate of Fort Pickering watching his soldiers march out under a flag emblazoned in gold letters: "Fort Pillow Apr 12 1864."

There was no mistaking the soldiers' mission: search for Nathan Bedford Forrest and avenge the massacre at Fort Pillow. "They cheered lustily," George wrote home. "There is no flinching, no playing sick." The Mississippi River mosquitos were especially vicious that August, and the soldiers were delighted to escape the confines of the fort.[1]

"Everything is all alive in camp today to give Forrest and his men a taste of what they gave them at Fort Pillow," he continued in his letter. "It makes me feel sober to see these men and officers fitting up for a fight in earnest."

He knew he would never see many of them again.

An officer gave him his gold watch for safekeeping and his wife's address if he did not return.

"I have not had any thing come so hard since I left home," he wrote. "The men in the ranks on the side next to me all tried to get hold of my hand and bid me good bye, but I could not shake hands with many of them as they were passing, so I stepped back from the line and said to them 'Good bye boys, I shake hands with you all in my heart.'"

He knew if the Black soldiers passing through the gates were captured, the Confederates would execute them or return them to slavery. He had heard the rumors white officers also would be executed if captured. At best, "some of them, in all probability, [would] be left on the bloody field and some may pine in rebel prisons," he wrote. Despite that, he wanted to join his soldiers on the field of battle. "Even the Chaplain feels an itching restlessness to be where there is danger."

George had been ordered to stay behind as a nonessential noncombatant.

Finally, he could stand it no further, so he jumped on a wagon and accompanied his soldiers for several miles before walking back to the fort.

The "colored" artillery regiment traveled as infantry. George referred to it as a "raid," but his regiment's mission was part of a larger federal invasion of northern Mississippi led by Gen. Andrew Jackson Smith.[2] The Union Army moved in force south into Mississippi toward the town of Oxford where the commanding generals believed—erroneously—that that they would find Forrest.

Within three days of his regiment's departure, George was angling to join them. He soon got permission. "I intend to stay with them until they move," George wrote Caroline, telling her not to expect more letters from him for a time. He talked his way onto a railroad car reserved for Brig. Gen. Benjamin Grierson's staff, bound for Mississippi. "After a long wait we were informed that the cars were ready for our party—the colored boys to be put on top of the cars, and the rest of us were to take best chance we could inside the freight cars," he wrote in a letter home. "The country along the line of the R. R. over which we must travel was infested with guerrillas and traveling was dangerous."[3]

As the train rumbled south "the desolations of war were everywhere visible along the road. About half the fields were uncultivated," he wrote in a letter home. The towns along the way were in ruins, mostly "chimneys and a few brick walls to tell us they were villages."[4]

George began shuttling roughly eighty miles between Fort Pickering in Memphis and the regiment's headquarters in Oxford, Mississippi. He brought messages south to Gen. Andrew Jackson Smith, and then on his return trip he cared for the wounded on the train back to Memphis.

The raiders did not find Forrest in Oxford, nor would they find him for the remainder of the war. The Union Army burned the town square before continuing the search for the Confederate general and his guerrillas in the Mississippi countryside.

On the night before one of these raids, George camped with his soldiers somewhere in Mississippi. Where exactly he was, he did not say. Years later, he recalled that the soldiers showed him extra respect because of his missing right forearm. They believed he had lost it in battle. He did not dissuade them of that belief.[5]

The night was hot and rainy, and the soldiers ate their rations and slept in the open. George slept nearby under a tarp, held up with sticks and open at both ends. Many years later, he described the scene in "Recollections of My Life-work": "When the men were preparing to lie down for the night, I heard the hum of voices from hundreds of men at the same time. I got up and walked out to where our men were, and found they were saying their evening prayers."[6]

The moment was seared forever into his memory.

"The voice of prayer from so many at the same time, made the place seem wonderfully sacred. I said, 'Surely God is in this place.'"[7]

⬥

The killing fields of Mississippi mentioned by my ancestor are about a three-hour drive south of Memphis. I went searching for where he and the Black soldiers he served slept on that night before the raid.[7]

I had a hunch where to look.

As it happens, the Duncan Grey Episcopal Retreat Center was built on the ground where Black Union regiments camped the night before a raid on a Confederate bridge. One of these units could have been George Richardson's.

The peaceful retreat center displays Union Army artifacts unearthed from the surrounding fields and woods, including canteens and bullets. But I came not looking for artifacts but wondering if I could still hear the echo of these men at prayer on what was, for many, the last night of their lives on earth. I wondered if I would find this place as sacred as my ancestor found it.

A dirt road leads about a mile from the retreat center to a nearby meadow where the Union soldiers slept. I was there in late spring, and it was already hot and muggy, and the air was packed with bugs. It rained every afternoon. The meadow was thick with wet grass and thistles, the ground spongy and soggy. I was thankful for having an air-conditioned room at the retreat center for the night.

I left the road, wading through the wet grass into the meadow. My shoes were soon soaked and muddy. I found a rotting log to sit on, and I stayed a long while, alone with my thoughts.

I pictured the soldiers emerging from the woods on foot and horseback to set up camp. Their target, the Confederate bridge, was still a few miles away.

I wondered if the gunfire from the raid could be heard from this meadow. I wondered how many died. The Union raiders that day wrecked the bridge, disrupting the Confederate supply lines before departing.

When I walked back to the retreat center, I found a piece of rusting iron, half-buried in the road. Maybe it was from an old farm wagon, or maybe it fell off a wagon carrying supplies for the soldiers. I held the iron plate and then dropped it back onto the road. It belonged there. I was not there for artifacts.

The next day, I hiked with a friend a couple of miles to an old Black Baptist church graveyard. Most of the tombstones were from the twentieth century. But nearly hidden in the woods, half covered with prickly vines, were the graves of people born in the 1850s and '60s—people born into slavery.

Perhaps, as enslaved children, they had heard the gunfire from the raid on the Confederate bridge. I wondered what they thought as they saw Union soldiers—*Black* Union soldiers—charging out of the woods. Were they startled? Amazed? What stories did they tell their children about this remarkable day?

As we walked through the cemetery, an elderly Black man got out of his pickup truck to put flowers on his mother's grave. It was Mother's Day. He used a golf club to brush the grass ahead of him as he walked. I asked him why.

"Sweeping for snakes."

I asked how many types of snakes in Mississippi might be poisonous.

"All of them."

14

REBS AND REFUGEES

Come on boys, if you want a heap of fun and to kill some Yankees.

NATHAN BEDFORD FORREST | JULY 1862

After the raid into Mississippi, George returned to Fort Pickering where he "found everything quiet." A letter was waiting for him from Caroline, asking if he was safe. But before he could pen his reply, Memphis was under attack by Forrest and his guerrilla raiders.

While the Union troops were in Mississippi looking for him, Forrest and his men had circled behind them back to Memphis. Forrest's spies in Memphis were "thick as flies," as an admiring biographer wrote.[1] His spies slipped out of the city to report not only the positions of federal troops but also the whereabouts of their generals.

At 3 a.m. on August 21, 1864, Forrest's Confederate cavalry charged through the Union picket lines and rode straight into the center of Memphis. They aimed to capture Gen. Cadwallader Washburn, the commanding general of Union forces in Memphis, who had replaced Hurlbut after the debacle at Fort Pillow. He would have been a rich prize. Washburn was the brother of Congressman Elihu Washburne, who represented Galena in the US House of Representatives and had assisted George Richardson in getting into the Union Army.

Gen. Cadwallader Washburn (who spelled his last name without an "e") was considered a "political general," but he quickly acquired military experience in the western theater and earned the confidence of Gen. Grant particularly for his administrative skill.[2] Both were from Galena.

In Memphis, Washburn remained a close confidante of Grant, and regularly corresponded with his brother Elihu in Washington. Elihu, in turn, protected Grant's political interests with President Lincoln. Gen. Washburn would have been a major catch, indeed, for Nathan Bedford Forrest.[3]

With the rebel troops bearing down on him, Gen. Washburn escaped from his quarters in the center of Memphis wearing only his nightshirt.

Confederate raiders shot at him as he ran through an alley. Washburn found refuge in Fort Pickering about a mile from his headquarters.

Fort Pickering was, as George described, "nearly stripped of all the soldiers fit for duty." Years later, George wrote in his journal that Forrest could have captured Fort Pickering and Washburn if had he pressed the attack, "for we were not expecting an attack when Gen. Smith was chasing the very fellow that attacked us."[4]

Forrest's pluck became the stuff of Confederate lore—as did Washburn's embarrassment at fleeing in his nightclothes. Confederate apologists called it the "Second Battle of Memphis," but it was really a raid, not a battle. Forrest had no chance of recapturing the city. His aim was to free Confederate prisoners and embarrass the Union commanders—and Forrest succeeded at that. But he did not capture Washburn and paid a fearsome price for his pluck; Forrest lost a quarter of his men and horses in the raid.

George was asleep when the raid began. "I slept quietly perfectly unconscious of any danger near."[5] Black refugees, many of them the wives and children of the soldiers camping outside the fort, streamed inside. "The Fort was alive with men and women from the town" who thought Forrest was out to capture and re-enslave them. George hid three refugees inside his tent until the danger passed.

By 6 a.m., three hours into their raid, Forrest and his men fled Memphis, leaving their wounded and dead behind for the Union to pick up. The wounded from both sides were brought into Fort Pickering all during the night and into the next morning. "A large portion were fatally wounded," George wrote his wife. "Three have died since they were brought into the fort."[6]

Surgeon Hood and Chaplain Richardson went to work. "I was among the wounded of both armies," George wrote, "for we made no difference whether they were friends or foes. I received messages from the dying which they sent to their friends in the South and in the North."

The wounds were ghastly. "It is astonishing with what fortitude our wounded bear their suffering," George wrote. "I stooped over one man about 40 years old. 'My dear sir, where did they hurt you?' 'Here,' said he as he moved down the clothes and showed where the ball entered his bowels and came out at his side."

George came upon a fatally wounded federal soldier from Illinois who told him: "Tell my folks I died in peace and with my last breath prayed that God would protect them."

George ministered to a severely injured Confederate soldier from Forrest's brigade. "A wounded rebel gave me his name and the address of his friends in middle Tennessee, and wished me to write them if he should not get well," George wrote his wife. "When I thought how he and his comrades treated our Reg. at Fort Pillow I felt that he ought to die. His left leg was shot all to pieces just above the knee. He will fight no more."

George did not say whether he wrote the requested letter or if the wounded rebel survived.

The raid on Memphis left the Union soldiers and their leaders jittery. "We thank the Lord we are safe," George wrote. "Maybe somebody will be awake next time."

Two days after Forrest's raid, Fort Pickering was shaken by rumors that Forrest was again raiding Memphis. The fort's big guns sounded three warning shots. "The officers armed the convalescents and brought them into line of battle. There was a most frightful stampede for the fort. Six-mule teams, hacks, drags and buggys [*sic*] charging at the top of their speed were jamming against each other to see which should get to the fort first. The citizens, black and white, poured along the sidewalks in hot haste to find a place of safety."[7]

The gunboats prepared to push off from the docks. "Where's the rebs? Where's the rebs?" George remembered everyone shouting. But by noon, there was no Confederate invasion. As it turned out, the scare had been the result of pickets firing and cleaning their guns, and other pickets interpreted their shots as an alarm.

Forrest's raid on Memphis humiliated Washburn, and his humiliation was well noted by his Union Army rivals, particularly Gen. Stephen Hurlbut, who had been sacked after the Fort Pillow massacre. "Well, they removed me from command because I couldn't keep Forrest out of West Tennessee," Hurlbut huffed, "but apparently Washburn can't keep him out of his bedroom."[8]

Hurlbut, who was in Memphis awaiting reassignment the night of the raid, apparently was unaware that he, too, had been a target of Forrest's raiders. The only reason Hurlbut was not captured was he had slept elsewhere that night. Where he slept became the topic of ribald innuendo.

In September 1864, George accompanied his regiment on another raid into northern Mississippi with the aim of capturing or killing Forrest. George's mission was escorting the wife of a colonel who was sick in the regiment's field camp. Gen. Washburn gave George a pass to take the colonel's wife aboard a troop train to Mississippi so that she could care for her husband. Washburn warned them that the route was infested with guerrillas and "traveling was dangerous."[9]

Their train stopped in Holly Springs, Mississippi, about fifty miles southeast of Memphis. Exploring the town, George found an abandoned school building. "I looked the ground over carefully and decided that this was a central point to establish a Freedmen's School." He later wrote to the Bureau of Refugees, Freedmen, and Abandoned Lands—commonly called "the Freedmen's Bureau"—urging it to purchase the building and establish a school for freed slaves. After the war, the Methodists took his advice, and it became the site of Rust University. It was the first of George Richardson's contributions to the higher education of African Americans.

George found the Union soldiers encamped near the Tallahatchie River north of Oxford. He was invited by the Third US Colored—Surgeon Hood's unit—to join them for supper. "They had Boston Crackers beef that they had confiscated & coffee with sugar and condensed milk. I have not had so good a supper in for two months," he wrote Caroline.[10]

Bedding down for the night, he could hear the Black soldiers "singing their religious songs until some time after I lay down, and when the singing ceased I heard the low subdued voice of prayer from every part of the camp."

The next day, George talked with a few whites in the vicinity and found them terrified of his regiment. "I find that that our Reg[iment] is regarded with a feeling of dread and horror, both by the citizens and soldiers. They are regarded as the ghost of the Reg[iment] murdered at Fort Pillow, and the horrid specter haunts their waking as well as sleeping dreams."

There was "heavy skirmishing" in the area, he later recalled. He was given two hours to retrieve the sick Union colonel and depart. With the colonel's wife, the three made it back by train to Fort Pickering.

Caroline expressed her worry about his safety, writing him a letter about a terrifying dream she had of him dying in the war. Her letter is lost, but George replied. "If I should be injured or killed I know it would be a dreadful blow on you," he wrote Caroline. "Your dream was only what may yet take place. I expected when I took a Chaplaincy to be where there is danger. But if I am in the path of duty, as I feel that I am, I have this confidence, that God can preserve me here as well as at home if it will be most for his glory. I shall be as careful as I can to keep out of danger, but when duty calls me into danger, it would be wrong to shirk."[11]

Shirking was definitely not in George Richardson's constitution.

><><

After returning to Memphis from Mississippi, George Richardson found himself at the confluence not only of war and peace, but also the politics of Protestant sexual mores, marriage rights, and white racial attitudes. The boiling point in his small corner of the war was part of a larger political inferno in the nation's capital involving death benefits for widows of Black soldiers. It is a story ignored in most histories of the Civil War.

Many of the Black soldiers escaping slavery brought with them their wives and children, and they camped outside Fort Pickering. Plantation owners typically had a minister give a perfunctory wedding rite for the enslaved, but the marriages were not considered legal, nor was it recorded in court or church registers. The "mock" marriage could not keep masters from separating couples and selling their children. The threat became an effective weapon used by owners to control the enslaved. Even if a slave owner kept the families together, they were usually broken up when owners died.[12]

"It was the habit among the slaves," George noted in his journal, "when they were sold away from their plantation, to take a new wife. The masters encouraged this. The relation of husband and wife was not recognized by law."[13]

Yet, as George observed, "in many instances the marriage relation was sacredly maintained."

Nor were slave marriages considered legal in the North.

In the midst of war, slave marriages erupted as an issue for the Army and for Congress. By midsummer 1864, the refugee camp outside Fort Pickering was bulging with women and children. The Army found itself with hundreds of mouths to feed. By winter, Gen. Washburn determined that the refugee camp was "not favorable to military discipline." In his view, the women in the camp had no legal right to stay near the soldiers because they were not legally married. The general decided to designate the women as "refugees" and remove them from the vicinity of Fort Pickering. Orders were issued to confine the women to a new refugee camp on President's Island in the middle of the Mississippi River about five miles downriver from Fort Pickering.

"The Contraband Camp is getting so thronged here that there is an effort to move some of the colored folks," George wrote Caroline.[14]

President's Island is now a large sandbar in the middle of the river. A century later, it is easy to see why the Black soldiers were so alarmed at the prospect of their families being exiled to the marshy, mosquito-infested sandbar. Modern Memphis consigns necessary-but-toxic industries to President's Island, with gravel quarries and large fuel tanks.

The soldiers pleaded for help with their chaplain. "Our boys became very much alarmed at the prospect of losing their wives."[15]

George invented an ingenious plan: if the legality of marriages was the issue, he would perform mass "legal" weddings and exploit Washburn's penchant for procedures. "Women that have certificates that they are married and their husbands in the Army are allowed to remain. So the men come to me for certification," George wrote Caroline. "I tell them I cannot give certificates that they are married unless I do it myself. So they come in to be married according to law."[16]

George convinced sympathetic white officers to delay enforcing Washburn's order for a week. He obtained passes for the soldiers to bring their wives into the fort so that they could be lawfully married. "The tide began to roll," he wrote in his journal, "and for a week I had plenty to do."[17]

George registered each of the marriages in his notebook and gave each couple a certificate attesting to the legality of their marriage.[18] The first of the marriage ceremonies was held on January 21, 1865, for a Randolph Biggers and Maria Bowers. George did another later that day for a Solomon Higgins and Sarah Jackson.

"They came in squads, and finally I was obliged to marry them in squads," he wrote. "I would stand several couples on the floor at once and have the groom take the right hand of the bride in his own, and then I would use a ceremony that married each couple at the same time."[19]

George presided at sixteen marriages on January 26 and twenty-three more the next day. He recorded the names of Absalom and Agnes Fields; Washington and Elizabeth Autrie. The sympathetic white officers served as witnesses, including a Lt. Smith and a Capt. Washburn from Iowa (whether the latter was related to the commanding general is not known). There were so many marriages that George was assigned a clerk to help with the paperwork.

The marriages at Fort Pickering continued steadily through 1865. He continued performing weddings for Black soldiers after the war ended. George glued an extra page in his notebook near the end of 1865 to record more marriages, labeling it page "61a." The top of the page is stamped with an eagle clutching the flag in its talons, and below is the motto, in all capital letters:

NO MORE DISUNION—NO MORE SECESSION—NO MORE SLAVERY

"When I married a couple, I made a record of it in my own book, then made out a certificate, giving age, color, height, etc., and returned it to the Freedmens [*sic*] Bureau for permanent record, then made another certificate for the bride, showing that she was the lawful wife of a soldier. This gave her exemption from the Order to remove refugees to President's Island."

After George was finished with each ceremony, the soldiers and their wives were legally married in the eyes of the Union Army. Gen. Washburn backed down and granted a reprieve to the newly married women, sparing them from being rounded up and imprisoned in a camp.

A one-armed Methodist chaplain had defeated a general, the Army bureaucracy, and a racist legal double standard.

How Washburn reacted is not known. He left no memoir. He had come from a Galena antislavery family, and perhaps George had softened him up by reminding him of his roots. After the war, Washburn founded General Mills, the food giant, served in Congress, and became governor of Wisconsin. He probably forgot the clever one-armed preacher.

There was another political subtext to the issue of slave marriages, though whether George Richardson was aware of it is not known. The widows of Black soldiers killed in the war were ineligible for survivor pensions because the federal government had ruled that the ex-slaves were not legally married.

Lizzie Booth, the widow of Fort Pillow's commander, Lionel Booth, made the plight of Black soldiers' widows her passionate political cause.[20] She traveled to Washington, DC, pleading with President Lincoln to provide for the widows of Black soldiers. Lincoln sent her to Congress, which a few months later approved death benefits—though smaller than for white soldier's widows—if the Black widows could produce a marriage certificate. George Richardson's mass weddings at Fort Pickering produced the needed paperwork for at least a few.

✿ *15* ✿

LICKED

Our history has been but a track of blood.

FREDERICK DOUGLASS | SEPTEMBER 29, 1865

As the Civil War drew to a close, the Seventh US Colored Heavy Artillery Regiment was redesignated as the Fifty-Fifth US Colored Infantry and deployed to picket lines outside their fort in Memphis. The big guns of Fort Pickering were no longer necessary. George Richardson continued sleeping in his tent inside the fort but spent most of his days outside with the soldiers.[1]

In his off hours, he gravitated to Collins Chapel, "a church for the Colored people," he called it. He was deeply impressed by the preaching and teaching of the Black pastor, Reverend Bryant (first name unknown), and his daughter, Ida. The Bryants were well educated; Ida had a degree from Oberlin College in Ohio that George had hoped to attend as a young man.

In the century following the Civil War, Collins Chapel would become known as the oldest Colored Methodist Episcopal Church in continuous use, and a landmark in one of the major Black Protestant denominations in the United States (later renamed Christian Methodist Episcopal Church). George delighted assisting at Collins Chapel as a pastor, and his letters home had a playful tone as the end of the war drew near. "Tell that little red headed baby [Emma] how de do for papa."[2]

George and another Union chaplain led revival meetings in Memphis, and more than a thousand people came. On weekdays the Collins church building was used as a school to teach reading, writing and arithmetic to the formerly enslaved. His work at Collins Chapel became the model George would follow years later in Texas.

He wrote Caroline that being a Methodist gave him credibility with ex-slaves because his denomination had opposed slavery before the war, and he had helped slaves to freedom. "I told them," he wrote, "I belonged to a church that had one of her Bishops mobbed and one of her preachers hung and many more shamefully treated" because they "did not believe in the Divine right of slavery."[3]

George believed that Blacks could have organized into Methodist congregations had there been interest by the hierarchy of the Northern, white-dominated church. But there was no interest. The opportunity was lost with far-reaching consequences. Methodism remained sharply segregated along racial lines well into the twentieth century. One feeble attempt was made to organize a racially integrated Methodist Church in Tennessee, but the experiment soon foundered. George wrote that a brave Methodist bishop—the name is illegible in the journal—favored building racially integrated churches but the idea "was a thousand years ahead of the times."[4]

Surrendering to that reality, George wrote a letter to Methodist bishop Edward Ames, who was then in charge of organizing Methodist Churches in the war-torn South. George recommended that the only way to make headway planting new Methodist churches was to organize congregations and districts along racial lines and then give them equal status for resources and voting at annual Methodist conventions. "The whites had not reached a state of grace in which they would willingly belong to the same congregation with the Negroes," George wrote.[5]

His idea went nowhere.

George Richardson was at his post in Fort Pickering when he heard the news of the surrender of Confederate general Robert E. Lee at Appomattox Court House in April 1865. George's excitement still bursts off the page of a letter he wrote home to Caroline:[6]

"The great events which came tumbling upon us so rapidly were too much for my ardent nature," he wrote. "The closing of the war—the disbanding our Army—the return of the long absent ones—the enthusiastic public greetings—but better still—the long and silent embrace of wives, mothers and sisters—which is more eloquent than words—and then the hearts that will bleed anew over those that will never be received on earth—All—all these thoughts were too much to bear at once."

Decades later, he described in "Recollections of My Lifework" the jubilation at the end of the war:

The city [of Memphis] was illuminated and guns were fired and there was wild joy among all the Union men. It meant that the hardships of the field were about at an end. It meant that the soldiers, after an honorable discharge, could return to their families, and to their peaceful occupations. It meant that the thousands of prisoners who had languished in military prisons or in prison pens would at once be liberated, and breathe the air of freedom once more. It meant that the principles for which our nation had contended for four years had at last triumphed, and that America would henceforth be 'the land of the free and the home of the brave.' It meant that the four and a half million of men, women and children of African dissent [*sic*] would have a chance to become intelligent American citizens; and this class were very demonstrative in their joy.[7]

But the rejoicing was short-lived when word reached Memphis that President Lincoln had been assassinated. "We were stunned and stupefied this morning," George wrote Caroline. "Truly the depths of hellish malice has not yet been fathomed."[8]

George blamed slave owners for Lincoln's murder. "I think we were too magnanimous. This will rouse our nation to strike the last blows with a severity that was due the crimes of our enemies—and our motto must now be 'Death to traitors.'"[9]

George also predicted, wrongly, that the new president, Andrew Johnson, would handle the Confederates with "rough hands" and that all vestiges of slavery would be crushed once and for all. "But one thing will be the result: the more speedy overthrow, and humiliation of the South, and the immediate and thorough emancipation of slavery."

George wondered whether Nathan Bedford Forrest would be arrested or allowed to surrender. The Confederate architect of the Fort Pillow massacre still represented a raw wound for George and his regiment. "Forrest will shortly come," George correctly predicted.[10]

In fact, Forrest surrendered and then continued his war upon Northern occupiers and the freed slaves. Vigilante violence erupted in the Tennessee countryside for months, and then years. The stain of Forrest's legacy would be stamped on the nation as he became the first "Grand Wizard" of the Ku Klux Klan.

Sitting in his study nearly four decades later, writing his journal, George Richardson was still pondering the meaning of Lincoln's murder: "It is very difficult now, at a distance of 37 years from that awful tragedy, to form any adequate idea of the crushing blow it was to every loyal Union man, woman and child in the Nation."[11]

As the news of President Lincoln's death filtered through the ranks at Fort Pickering, a delegation of Black soldiers asked George to speak at Collins Chapel. "It was a pitiful sight to see the consternation it produced among the ex-slaves," he recorded in his journal. "They said 'now that Lincoln is dead, we shall be sent back to the plantations to be slaves forever.'"[12]

When he arrived at Collins Chapel, the church was packed with Black soldiers. "At the church I found a large congregation that had been moved by one impulse to go to the house of God in this the greatest calamity of their lives. They had just begun to taste the sweets of freedom, and now it was dashed from their lips forever."

He began to preach.

George told them that their freedom could not be taken away. God had "surely seen their affliction." He compared Lincoln to Moses, saying neither prophet made it to the Promised Land but that both had guaranteed the freedom of their people. "I saw their faces brighten as I talked with them in this strain about forty minutes."

Of this he was sure: "The Nation's victory in arms over which we have just been rejoicing, is a pledge that the principles of liberty will triumph, and slavery cannot longer exist on American soil. God can brush aside those who oppose him in this contest against American slavery."[13]

He would soon see slavery re-emerging by other means on American soil.

A few days after his sermon, he wrote to Caroline about his experience. "The Congregation at Collins Chapel seems to have adopted me," he wrote. "The Speech I made them the Monday after the assassination of the president and the sermon I preached for them a week ago last Sunday, seems to have canonized me in their estimation."[14]

George gingerly raised the possibility of moving his family to Tennessee so that he could continue working among African Americans. "I don't know but my work will henceforth be for the benefit of the colored people. I know this that I desire to use the fragment of life, where I can do the most good."

Caroline's reply is lost, but judging from George's next letters, her concern was not the cause, it was the location. In his next letter, he pleaded with her to wait until he'd returned to Minnesota before making up her mind. "I cannot decide definitely on the future till after I have had a talk with you for I cannot comprehend your letters."

The immediate aftermath of the war was chaotic in Tennessee. Union officers who had been captured at Fort Pillow and imprisoned made their way back to Fort Pickering, bringing news of who had died. They also gave chilling first-hand accounts of the slaughter at Fort Pillow. The survivors told him that many Black soldiers, rather than being shot, had been sold into slavery. "My heart grows sick at their tales of horror," George wrote to Caroline.[15]

The death toll of Union soldiers continued to escalate after the close of the war. George witnessed the worst tragedy in the war's immediate aftermath.[16] On April 26, 1865, the steamboat *Sultana* made its way up the Mississippi River, overloaded with newly released Union prisoners of war. Many of them were very sick including those imprisoned in the notorious camp at Andersonville, Georgia.

A few miles north of Memphis, at about 2 a.m., a boiler blew up, and the steamboat quickly sank. More than seventeen hundred perished in the Mississippi River. "At daylight the dead bodies could be seen drifting past the fort like flood wood," George wrote in his journal.[17] A lieutenant was dispatched with a small boat and squad to gather up floating bodies. As bodies were recovered, an unidentified woman in town prepared the remains. "I gave them a Christian burial."

The *Sultana* disaster was the worst peacetime maritime accident in US history, eclipsing even the loss of life at the sinking of the *Titanic* a half-century later. "I have seen some wounded men, and hundreds of sick in the Hospitals but this occurrence made my heart sick," he wrote Caroline two days later. "Surely these are the days of unprecedented calamity."

The *Sultana* was scarcely mentioned by the newspapers. The country was numbed by so much death and the assassination of President Lincoln that the sinking of the *Sultana* quickly faded from national memory. But for George Richardson, the *Sultana* was a microcosm of the war. Decades later, he reflected in his journal:

The rejoicing of our regiment over the return of our officers who had been held prisoners for a year and this immediately followed by the awful tragedy of the Sultana in sight of our Fort, was a miniature picture of the mingled joy and sorrow all over the North. Joy for those who had survived and returned, and sorrow for the hundreds of thousands who never would return.[18]

Several units of the Union Army remained at Fort Pickering, deemed necessary for occupation of the South and the new, but ill-fated, federal program of Reconstruction. George stayed in the Army for almost another year after the close of the war. "Soldiering in the time of peace is dull business, and yet we were not wholly without sensations. There were small detachments of men in the South who were unwilling to return to civil life, and it was necessary to have a strong force on the picket lines around Memphis."[19]

The countryside remained dangerous. A contingent from the Third US Colored, including a surgeon (not Hood) and a lieutenant, had gone beyond the picket lines to gather wood and were killed in an ambush. The guerrillas were captured and sentenced to death by hanging. George was assigned as the "spiritual adviser" for one of the condemned prisoners. "I remembered the way he received his sentence with bitter cursing." George was relieved when the prisoner asked for a Catholic priest. "I did not feel the least twinge of sorrow or regret when the drop fell."[20]

In June 1865, George was given leave to go to Minnesota to see his family. It was the first time he had been home in fourteen months. It took three days of travel to get there. His daughter, Emma, had been a year old when he had left. "The hard part of my visit was that she did not know me, I was a stranger to her all the time I was at home."[21]

His leave was brief. He returned to Fort Pickering two weeks later. "The government had given us no clue as to the length of time we should be retained in the service. Leaving home this time was harder than the first."

Soldiers and officers in the garrison were restless to get out of the Army. Humphrey Hood, the fort surgeon, wrote letters home boiling with frustration, at other times, with humor. "Our time will come I guess," Hood wrote his wife, "unless we are to have a war with France there is certainly no use for so many men."[22]

In autumn 1865, George Richardson and another Army chaplain named Brown (his first name is lost) of the Eighty-Eighth US Colored Infantry, left Memphis by horseback, heading into western Tennessee and Arkansas "to learn what we could of the condition of the freedmen."[23]

The two Union chaplains believed that as pastors they would be safe in their travels, but they soon discovered their sense of safety was illusory. The threat of violence seemingly seethed at every turn. George's journal paints a picture of the war's physical ruin—"the marks of war" as he put it. Where houses once stood, there were only chimneys. The fields lay unplanted. His journal also describes white fear of Black retribution and white hatred of the Union Army—and its chaplains.

The chaplains encountered whites "wild" with fury about the outcome of the war and the continuing occupation of the Union Army. "The everlasting wail about the 'nigger' was sung with some variations from time we arrived to the time we left—the nigger is ungrateful—the nigger will lie—the nigger will steal—the nigger won't work—the nigger is getting so saucy that he is unendurable."[24]

In Arkansas, the pair encountered farmers whose homes and lands had been stripped bare by both armies. But the white farmers only blamed "the niggers" and the Freedmen's Bureau, which had been redistributing land and attempting to prevent whites from punishing their ex-slaves.

The traveling chaplains met an Arkansas ex-Confederate soldier willing to guide them.[25] The threesome became a foursome when another former Confederate soldier, who was wounded and sick, asked to travel with them on his way home. The Union chaplains got into a roaring argument with their guide about slavery, the causes of the war, and who had the better Army. "I went to fight to keep the niggers from being my equals," George quoted him. Fed up with the argument, George replied: "The niggers licked you."[26]

The wounded Confederate soldier tipped off the chaplains that their Arkansas guide was leading them into an ambush. They were grateful for their tipster: "His gentleness had won our hearts." George and his companion managed to slip away and found safety at the encampment of the Third US Colored Infantry Regiment near Mound City in the swamps across the river from Memphis. Mound City had been a field hospital and was where the wounded from Fort Pillow had been taken in the days following the massacre. They spent the night at the field hospital before moving on.[27]

Next the Army chaplains stayed with "Free Joe"—Joseph Harris, a slave who had been emancipated before the war by his owner.[28] He had purchased his wife's and children's freedom. Harris appeared to have the only farm that was thriving in the region. Harris's son Harry was engaged to be married to Ida Bryant, the daughter of the pastor of Collins Chapel in Memphis. Harris was doing so well he leased acreage to other Blacks. George was much impressed by "Free Joe" Harris and his connection to Collins Chapel. He referred to him as a "gentleman."[29]

A few nights later, their host could not have been more different—a white Methodist pastor, the William McFerrin, who explained how he had been ruined because the "Yankees had robbed him" of his slaves. George found his self-serving screed beyond his endurance. "With my abolition sentiments, which were bred in the bone, and had grown with my growth, it was hard to reconcile this statement of Parson McFerrin with my idea of Christianity, and especially with the calling of a minister of the gospel."[30]

McFerrin's sons, who had been in the Confederate Army, especially perturbed George. He called one a "liar" and the other "a simpering fop." The evening had been "a tempest," he wrote. The Union chaplains departed the next morning, shaking the dust from their feet.[31]

That night the pair of Army chaplains met with "colored folks" at a Methodist church. Whites lurked, listening warily to what the chaplains had to say. George talked that night about the importance of education and "just compensation" for sharecroppers. "As the colored people had no land," he told them, "it was necessary for them to work and earn a living."[32] He urged them not to move away. In hindsight, George Richardson was overly optimistic that Southern white landowners would give Blacks a fair break, but his eyes were gradually opening about how sharecropping was little removed from slavery.

Making his way back Memphis with his traveling companion, George learned he would be discharged in early 1866. While waiting, he continued leading worship services at Collins Chapel, visiting the sick, and "giving the men who died a soldier's burial."[33]

The Black soldiers in his regiment approached him about remaining in Memphis to build a racially integrated church. He was tempted. "The pressure that was brought to bear almost made me feel that it was my duty to do it. But the unsettled condition of the country made me unwilling to take my family to the South, and I would not undertake this kind of work without my family with me."[34]

His letters home reflected how his heart was set on staying in Memphis. He wrote Caroline that she should investigate "what shape the title is in" on their land in Minnesota so they could sell it. He suggested she and their children could move Memphis to "build a first class school that will make us a good living and educate our family and furnish us a home."[35]

A day later, he wrote her another letter about moving to Memphis: "I do not know certainly yet what we can do, but if there should be no opening to go teaching I think I shall go into itinerant work, unless you interpose some serious objection."[36]

Caroline's reply cannot be found, but the idea of moving his family to Memphis soon disappeared from his letters. George steeled himself to take up the life once again of a traveling preacher in Minnesota. He was discharged from the US Army on January 22, 1866.[37]

His soldiers—the "Fort Pillow Boys" as he still called them—gave one more try at convincing him to stay in Memphis. Two of them met him at the dock as he was departing with a message that "they were sure would change my purpose to go North." They had mustered out a week earlier and decided to stay in Memphis rather than return to the Deep South. The men proposed building a combined Methodist-Baptist church with George Richardson as their pastor.[38]

"They gathered as many as they could of the scattered regiment," George wrote in his journal. "They wanted to band together so that these institutions should be under the control of the boys of the Fort Pillow regiment." They had even formed a committee and pledged $1,000 for the project from their final Army pay—a monumental sum at the time.

"This committee met me at the landing just as I was ready to go aboard the steamer. They urged me to stay and be their preacher. They knew me and knew I would be true to them. They knew I would be of great service to them in their new relation to the Southern people. It was hard to disappoint these men who had clung to me so confidingly. But I had to tell the committee I have been away from my family most of two years, and I will not under any circumstances be separated from them any longer."[39]

Years later, he confided to his journal his other reason for turning down their offer: he did not think it safe for his wife and children to live in Memphis. Caroline's concerns were well-founded. His enthusiasm of a few months earlier about staying had dampened with the reality of what he encountered in the countryside where he had been nearly ambushed. There were regular reports of marauding bands of Southern whites killing Northerners and ex-slaves. "The city was full of a lawless element, the refuse of both armies, and there was robbery and murder going on every night."

Yet George immediately regretted his decision to leave Memphis, and his regret only deepened in the years ahead. His dream of building a school for the freed slaves would not leave him. "After all these reasons I could muster for not continuing to work for the colored people, I felt that I was neglecting a great opportunity to do good. I promised myself to resume the work in some shape as soon as the boys were a little older, and the country was settled."[40]

As he boarded the riverboat for Minnesota, he was joined by one of the Black mustered-out soldiers, Abraham Davenport—George's last orderly. Davenport, who had been enslaved before the war, told George he was not going back to Mississippi and the plantations, fearing that the old order was still much alive. Davenport asked to go north to Minnesota, and George promised to take him and find him work.[41]

George kept his promise to Davenport, who not long after found work at a riverboat port in Winona, Minnesota. But many more years would pass before George Richardson kept the other promise he had made to himself on his last day in Memphis—that he would work with the formerly enslaved. Minnesota winters and failing health would nearly kill him before he could discover how.

FIGURE 1. Daguerreotype of the Richardson family in Galena, Illinois, circa 1855. Seated, left to right, Owen (child); Caroline; George; and David (child). Standing, Margaret Harshmann, housekeeper. The Richardsons helped at least one enslaved woman reach freedom on the Underground Railroad in Galena. This daguerreotype is the earliest known depiction of the Richardsons. It is two inches wide, three inches long, and placed under glass inside a small, hinged case. Author's Collection.

FIGURE 2. Caroline, age forty, seated with Emma Richardson in 1865. Caroline mailed the photo to George at Fort Pickering, Memphis, near the end of the Civil War. Author's Collection.

FIGURE 3. George Richardson posed for this portrait at a studio in Memphis in 1864 when he was serving as chaplain to the Seventh US Colored Heavy Artillery Regiment posted at Fort Pickering. Civil War soldiers had photos like this made into small cartes de viste, or "cabinet cards," which they mailed home and gave each other. In this portrait, George Richardson is wearing his Army chaplain black coat, the same uniform worn by chaplains on both sides. He posed with a fake right hand resting on the back of the chair, covering his missing forearm. The studio also enlarged and colorized the portrait. The colorized version has hand-drawn outlines of his coat, the chair, his prosthetic right hand, and his hair red. Author's Collection.

FIGURE 4. "Cabinet card" portrait of Chauncey Hobart taken in Red Wing, Minnesota, probably in the 1860s. Hobart served as a Union Army chaplain at the Battle of Shiloh and was the Methodist presiding elder of Minnesota and Wisconsin. He was mentor to George and Caroline Richardson for thirty-six years. Caroline is buried in Hobart's family plot in Red Wing, Minnesota. Author's Collection.

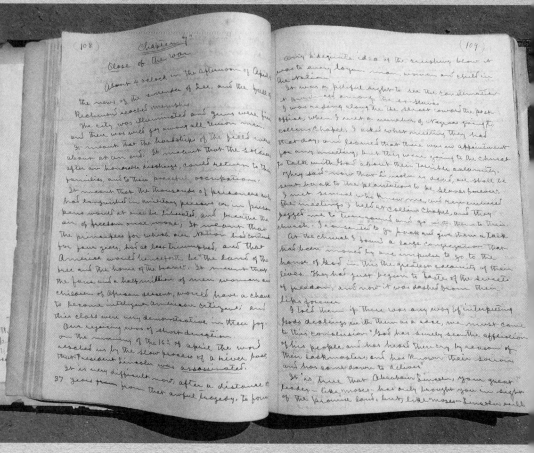

FIGURE 5. Pages from George Richardson's journal, "Recollections of My Lifework," describing the end of the Civil War as he experienced it in Memphis. "It meant that the four and a half million of men, women and children of African dissent [*sic*] would have a chance to become intelligent American citizens; and this class were very demonstrative in their joy." Author's Collection.

FIGURE 6. Owen Richardson, when he was about twenty, circa 1870s. The oldest son of George and Caroline Richardson, Owen hatched the plan to take his father to Dallas, Texas, to recuperate in 1875. Ten years later, he became the first president of Samuel Huston College in Austin. Author's Collection.

FIGURE 7. Portrait of George Richardson taken in Austin in 1876. He had noticeably aged in the decade after the Civil War; his hair and beard were graying and his face gaunt. This was probably taken soon after the school he founded with Black pastor Jeremiah Webster moved from Dallas to Austin. Author's Collection.

FIGURE 8. Rare "cabinet card" portrait of a Black pastor, name and date unknown but likely Charles Madison. The photo was found in an envelope containing George Richardson's photographs and cabinet cards and is the only photograph of a Black person in his collection. The portrait is likely one of three Black pastors with whom he was close: Jeremiah Webster, Mack Henson, or Madison. The photograph was taken at the R. Poole studio in Nashville, which was established in the 1870s, after the Civil War. Madison is the only one of the three from Tennessee. Madison was the pastor at Wesley Church in Austin used as the first building in what became Samuel Huston College. Author's Collection.

FIGURE 9. Caroline Fay Richardson, circa mid-1880s, likely when she was acting president of Samuel Huston College in Austin, Texas. Her oldest son, Owen, had resigned as president and her husband, George, was traveling in the Hill Country bringing books and tending to his flock in Black settlements. She was more effective than both of them running the school. Author's Collection.

FIGURE 10. Portrait of Emma Richardson, age twenty-five, upon her graduation in 1888 from Hamline University in Minnesota. She had already worked as a teacher at the Richardson family school in Dallas and again in Austin. After graduation from Hamline, she returned to Texas as a teacher in Fort Worth. Author's Collection.

FIGURE 11. Rachel Elizabeth "Lily" Silver, circa 1880s, who had been the family teacher of the Richardson children when they lived on a farm in Minnesota in the 1860s and '70s. When the children were grown, she returned home to Nova Scotia. In 1889, Owen arranged to bring her to Texas to marry his father following Caroline's death. Lily died in 1907 and is buried with George and Emma in Denver. Author's Collection.

FIGURE 12. Last formal portrait of George Richardson, 1909, on what would be his final visit to Minnesota, baptizing two of great-grandsons, Harold and Paul, and delivering a farewell sermon. He got a haircut before having his picture taken. Author's Collection.

FIGURE 13. One of the last known snapshots of George Richardson, taken a few weeks before his death in August 1911. He is seated in the middle in front of his Denver house. On the left is daughter, Emma, and kneeling on the right is Russell Richardson, the author's grandfather at age sixteen. Standing, from left to right, are Jennie Milne Richardson; her husband, Earl Mercein Richardson (fourth son of George and Caroline); and their daughter, Jessie Emma. George kept his missing right forearm hidden from view. Author's Collection.

FIGURE 14. Portrait of Emma Richardson, circa 1930s, when she was a teacher in Denver. She lived with and cared for her father until his death and finished his journal. Her remains are buried under the same tombstone in Denver as her father and stepmother, Lily. Author's Collection.

FIGURE 15. David Fay Richardson, circa 1900, owned a furniture store in Northfield, Minnesota. He was the second son of Caroline and George Richardson and the author's great grandfather. David Fay Richardson likely received the journal after his father's death in 1911. He, in turn, gave it to his son, Russell. Author's Collection.

FIGURE 16. Russell David Richardson, grandfather of the author, was an oil company executive. This photo was taken in 1949 on a business trip to Kobe, Japan. The journal of his grandfather, George Richardson, came to him, and he gave it his son, David. Author's collection.

FIGURE 17. David C. Richardson, the author's father, in December 1963. He gave George Richardson's journal to the author (whose middle name is David) in 1997 at a pivotal moment in his life. Author's Collection.

FIGURE 18. The author's wife, Lori Korleski Richardson, left, with Madge Richardson Walsh, right, the author's aunt, taken in October 2010 in Redding, California. Madge was the family archivist and genealogist and preserved many of the photographs and documents used in this book. She died in 2015. Photo by James Richardson. Author's Collection.

FIGURE 19. Larry Earvin, left, president of Huston-Tillotson University from 2000 to 2015, gave the author a tour of the campus in 2004. Earvin was succeeded by Colette Pierce Burnette. The author spoke at her installation. Photo by Lori Korleski Richardson. Author's Collection.

FIGURE 20. Our journey at an end, we reached the Fairmount Cemetery in Denver and the tombstone of George Richardson; Elizabeth "Lily" Silver Richardson, his second wife; and his daughter Mary Emma Richardson. Her name is inscribed on the side of the tombstone. Photo by Robert D. Tonsing. Used by permission.

WAR CRIMINAL PARK

Our American Christians are too busy saving the souls of white
Christians from burning in hellfire to save the lives of black ones
from present[ly] burning in fires kindled by white Christians.

IDA B. WELLS | 1894

Two centuries of American racial injustice intersect in Memphis.

Soon after the war, white Memphis citizens, wanting no reminders that
Black Union soldiers had once occupied their city, had ripped down the Fort
Pickering's ramparts. A century later, a few mounds and rusting iron fixtures
in the ground are all that remain. The highest mound has a square-shaped
depression where a cannon was likely placed, pointing toward the river.

Black soldiers, mustering out of the Army, settled nearby. Their neighbor-
hood was for a time known as "Fort Pickering." But whites had it renamed
"French Fort." And where the fort once stood, the sign said "Chicasaw
Heritage Park."

In May 1866—barely a year after the close of the war—whites rampaged
through the Black neighborhood reestablishing the old order. In three days
of white terror, forty-two Black men, women, and children were murdered;
there were at least five rapes; ninety-one homes, four churches, and twelve
schools were burned. The *Memphis Argus* preposterously claimed, "the whole
blame of this tragic and bloody riot lies as usual with the poor, ignorant,
and deluded blacks."[1]

A Congressional investigation under the leadership of Galena congressman Elihu Washburne—the brother of George's commanding general in
Memphis—concluded otherwise: "The outbreak of the disturbance resulting
from collision between some policemen and discharged colored soldiers was
seized upon as a pretext for an organized and bloody massacre of the colored
people of Memphis, regardless of age, sex, or condition." The investigators
further concluded that the violence was not just perpetrated by a few renegade vigilantes but was sanctioned by Memphis officials.

"The mob, finding itself under the protection and guidance of official authority, and sustained by a powerful public sentiment behind, actuated by feelings of the most deadly hatred to the colored race, and particularly those who wore the uniform of the republic, proceeded with deliberation to the commission of crimes and the perpetration of horrors which can scarcely find a parallel in the history of civilized or barbarous nations."[2]

Further, the report concluded that whites targeted Blacks who had been Union soldiers—the men George Richardson had served with only a few months earlier. Had he stayed, he might have been among the casualties.

With Lincoln dead, succeeded by a white supremacist, Andrew Johnson, nothing was done by the federal government to curb the violence against Blacks in Memphis—or anywhere else.

Even worse was to come.

In 1878, a yellow fever epidemic decimated Memphis. Much like the Covid-19 pandemic in the twenty-first century, the yellow fever epidemic brought into sharp relief the difference between white privilege and the lack of it among Blacks. Whites fled Memphis—twenty-five thousand, half the population—evacuating on trains and horses. Blacks and poor whites, with no means to get out, could not escape. Five thousand—probably more—died from yellow fever. The estimates are probably low, especially for Blacks. One tally put the death toll of infected whites at 70 percent. White officials in Memphis would assert, with no firm evidence, that the death toll among Blacks was lower. Chances are, however, that given their poor living conditions and sanitation, it was far higher.[3]

A brave handful of Catholic, Episcopalian, and Anglican nuns cared for the sick—white and Black. One by one, all of the nuns succumbed to yellow fever. Collectively known as the "Martyrs of Memphis," the nuns are commemorated as saints by the Episcopal Church yearly on September 9. St. Mary's Episcopal Cathedral in Memphis is dedicated to their memory with stained glass windows depicting the nuns caring for the yellow fever victims. We visited the cathedral on one of our visits. We then walked to Collins Chapel, a block away, now listed on the National Register of Historic places. The wooden church of George Richardson's era was replaced with a brick building after the massacre of 1866.[4]

Black survivors of the yellow fever epidemic included Ida B. Wells, who lost both parents and her infant brother to the yellow fever epidemic in Holly Springs, a few miles south of Memphis. After they died, she moved to

Memphis and became a crusading journalist, documenting lynching against Blacks as the co-owner of the *Memphis Free Speech and Headlight* newspaper.[5]

In 1892, Wells found herself in the crosshairs of the white power structure when she wrote: "Nobody in this section of the country believes the old thread-bare lie that Negro men rape white women. If Southern white men are not careful, they will overreach themselves and public sentiment will have a reaction; a conclusion will then be reached which will be very damaging to the moral reputation of their women."[6]

A white mob came looking for her, but she was away making speeches in New York. Had they found her she certainly would have been lynched. The mob settled for destroying her newspaper office and putting her out of business.

Her friends pleaded with her to not return to Memphis. Wells relocated to Chicago where she continued publishing pamphlets against lynching and became one of the founders of the National Association for the Advancement of Colored People. Ida Wells was the most prominent and outspoken Black woman civil rights leader of the late nineteenth century.

Memphis continued into the next century as a locus of violent white reaction against Black civil rights. Martin Luther King Jr. came to Memphis to support Black sanitation workers demanding safe working conditions after three garbage collectors were crushed to death by a malfunctioning truck.[7] King was murdered within walking distance of the ruins of Fort Pickering. The Lorraine Motel, where King was shot on a balcony, is now the site of the National Civil Rights Museum.

><><

On my first trip to Memphis, I walked the route of Gen. Cadwallader the night of his narrow escape from capture by the Confederates.[8] Halfway between Washburn's headquarters and Fort Pickering is the where the Lorraine Motel would be built a century later. The general would have run near that spot to reach the safety of the fort.

The house where Washburn's headquarters once stood is now a minor league baseball park for the Memphis Redbirds, the farm team of the St. Louis Cardinals. On my walk, I found a marker near an entrance to the ballpark gleefully described Washburn's flight from Nathan Bedford Forrest's raiders.

The marker mentioned Forrest's brother, Jesse, who led the charge into Washburn's headquarters: "He escaped capture by decamping through the back door in his night clothes. His uniform and sword seized by raiders under Lt. Col. Jesse Forrest, were returned next day under flag of truce."

When I returned a few years later, the marker was gone. But there is still a street near the stadium called "General Washburn's Escape Alley."

I looked for what I could find of Fort Pickering where my ancestor had slept in a tent during the Civil War. It was not on modern maps. There were no historical markers designating the fort's location. The Memphis Public Library used a nineteenth-century map of Memphis to point me to the spot (the reference librarian had never heard of Fort Pickering).

Even with the Memphis Public Library's help, I was not sure if I had found it. As it turned out, my first day's effort was off by about a mile. The next day, I went to another location that seemed more probable, but it took a second visit a few years later to confirm I had the correct place. By then, a small brass plate marking the spot had been placed near the remnants of an Indian burial mound that had been converted into a cannon rampart in the war.

Twentieth century Memphis was dotted with numerous historical markers and monuments to the Confederate Army. Nathan Bedford Forrest and his wife were buried under a grandiose statue in a park named for him. On my first visit, a friend winced as we drove by, and called it "War Criminal Park."

By the time of my second visit in 2013, a debate had erupted about renaming Forrest Park. By then, Memphis was two-thirds Black, and it seemed unconscionable that a park dedicated to a hero of white supremacy and terrorism still existed. Yet Confederate commemorative groups argued vociferously that the renaming of parks dishonored the Confederate dead. After several raucous meetings, the Memphis City Council voted in February 2013 to remove Forrest's name from the park, along with the names of Jefferson Davis Park and Confederate Park. For the first time since the close of the Civil War, the defenders of "the Lost Cause" did not prevail. Forrest's remains were disinterred and transferred two hundred miles away to the National Confederate Museum in Columbia, Tennessee. After his statue was removed, protesters in 2020 spray painted "Black Lives Matter" along the sidewalk but did not deface the pedestal.[9]

More Confederate statues have been removed in Memphis and parks renamed with more innocuous sounding titles: Nathan Bedford Forrest Park was renamed Health Sciences Park and Jefferson Davis Park was renamed River Garden Park.[10] Yet there are no monuments in Memphis to the Black soldiers who served in the Civil War and died for their country and freedom. There are no monuments in Memphis for those who were butchered at the hands of Forrest and his rebels at Fort Pillow a few miles north. There are no monuments commemorating how whites butchered Blacks in their homes and businesses in 1866.

The small marker at Fort Pickering mentions only that Union soldiers had occupied the fort and that it was "an artillery redoubt and magazine." There is no mention of that the soldiers in the "artillery redoubt" were a "colored" regiment. The marker itself is tucked under the trees and off to the side of a footpath.

There is one monument in Memphis where I lingered.

About a half-mile north of the ruins of Fort Pickering is a modernistic metal-and-concrete sculpture dedicated to the victims of the yellow fever epidemic. Erected in 1971, almost a century after the plague that killed so many, the sculpture depicts gaunt victims floating in midair. The monument was built atop a mass grave for more than fifteen hundred people who died in the epidemic. A nearby historical marker calls them "Memphis Martyrs."

It wasn't easy to find the monument, hidden down a hill on "Channel 3 Drive" behind a television station overlooking the Mississippi River.

At least it is there.

PART III

～ 17 ～

OWEN

Hear the right, O Lord, attend unto my cry,
give ear unto my prayer, *that goeth* not out of feigned lips.
PSALM 17: 1 | KING JAMES VERSION

Mustered out of the Army one year after the official close of the Civil War, George Richardson boarded a riverboat in Memphis bound north to Minnesota. He arrived home in Red Wing on a Sunday morning in January 1866 just as his family was dressing for church. As George recalled in his journal, the housekeeper, a Miss Parker, did not recognize him, and she went to the kitchen to tell Caroline that "there was a gentleman in the parlor."[1]

When Caroline came to the door, "she was taken somewhat by surprise to find her husband," he wrote. "Of course there was a sensation among the children when they learned who the caller was."

Army chaplain George Richardson had been away for two years, and with only one leave home. "Home again! I breathed freer," he recalled in the journal. "I did not need to think of anything but being home for a month." But he was a stranger to his daughter Emma, almost three. "She would have it for a long time that I was a visitor, and that I had a home somewhere else."

His four sons immediately recognized him and "we very soon fell into our old fashioned frolicsome ways." His oldest son, Owen, was only fourteen but already enrolled at Hamline University taking classes with men six or seven years older than he was.

David Fay Richardson—who would become my great-grandfather—was eleven, small for his age, and enrolled in the Red Wing Public School.[2] He was doing well with declamation, a popular nineteenth-century academic discipline of memorizing and presenting famous speeches. George was soon coaching him on his recitals. George made no mention in the journal of his other two sons, Frank and Mercein, during this period. Indeed, he rarely mentioned them at all in "Recollections of My Lifework."

George had no job, and there were no openings on the Methodist circuit. Idleness did not suit him. Eventually, a position opened in Winona, sixty-five miles down the Mississippi River. George took the post and roomed with his cousin, Levi Richardson. He was away from home once again. George visited his family once a month. His situation was less than ideal, but he quickly immersed himself again in the minutia of church work.

In September 1866, he was assigned to a circuit in Red Wing and rejoined his family. The circuit had seven preaching "posts," and so he was away most of the week. He found a smaller house more centrally located in his preaching circuit, and so the Richardsons gave up their house in Red Wing and moved into the country.

George went house-to-house in his new circuit to win converts. He proselytized the town drunk in one settlement and brought him to an altar call to accept Jesus. He threw himself back into his old life, perhaps trying to forget the horrors he had seen in the war. Indeed, he was no closer emotionally to his family than when he had been posted in Memphis. If anything, he was more distant. To read the pages of his journal recounting this period is to hear a man who was escaping depression by working himself into total exhaustion.

In March 1867 George reached the end of his tether after buying an eighty-acre farm at "County Line," a rural, windswept community in Goodhue County near Red Wing on the Mississippi River. Years later, he justified the purchase as necessary to show his boys the value of hard work. Owen was nearly fifteen years old and two of his brothers were "old enough to do some work." George took out a mortgage to pay for the land. "I mention this purchase because it had very much to do with my after life, and my ministerial work."[3]

His sons worked on the farm, and the family made payments on the mortgage, but George noted: "We were all beginners at the farming business, and not always working to the best advantage."

His former Army orderly, Abraham Davenport, rejoined George and his family at County Line to work on the farm. The boys were soon released from farm work to continue their education with Elizabeth "Lily" Silver, a single woman from Nova Scotia, who was the family's teacher. Caroline hired another woman to help her with household chores. All seemed to go well for a time.

But George's life began to unravel beginning with a property conflict between an elderly couple and their son-in-law who were members in one his congregations. After witnessing war and its aftermath, the dispute must have felt trivial to George. He tried to mediate the conflict, but his effort backfired. The dispute split the congregation, and the entire Methodist circuit imploded. "I would be glad to skip this year in writing up my life work, but it had so much to do with the remainder of my life that I cannot leave it out."[4]

His congregants left and joined the Congregationalists down the road. "My three years' work at that point seemed to be lost. My intense anxiety to head off this strife, and save God's heritage from damage affected my health."[5]

By 1870, George had been reassigned twice more to other congregations. The last one, in Mazeppa and Bear Valley about thirty miles south of Red Wing, did not go well. "I was completely broken down, and should have given up the charge. But I was determined to fill out the year if possible. Every sermon I preached during the balance of the year caused severe pain in my right lung."[6]

He described in his journal migraine-like symptoms: "I had suffered for two or three years with a burning heat at the nerve center on the top of my head, and that portion of my head was sore to the touch. This nervousness had greatly interfered with my sleeping." Owen later recalled in his memoir that his father took to his bed for weeks at a time. "I was frightened thinking [about] my father who had been confined to his bed for several weeks."[7]

In September 1871, George asked church authorities to be relieved of pastoral duties and retire. "This was a sad experience. I was still in the prime of life, so far as years were concerned," he wrote in his journal. "It was very hard to get grace enough to submit gracefully to the inevitable."[8]

His request was granted. George Richardson was forty-seven years old.

His mother, Margaret, who had moved in with his family at County Line, died in 1872. He buried her in a plot on the southeast corner of his farm at County Line. The remains of his baby daughter, Carrie, were reinterred with those of his mother. "Now my Mother and babe rest in the same grave. A small granite headstone marks the spot."[9] The graves and tombstones were still there more than a century later.

In September 1875, George Richardson sat on his front porch at his Minnesota farm feeling glum. He was fifty-one years old and believed his best years were behind him. All he could see ahead of him was the grave, and he could barely provide for his family. "My prospects for usefulness to my family or the church was not very flattering," he wrote in his journal. "I felt sure I should die with consumption within a year."[10]

But George also remembered the day as a "bright and sunny afternoon." It was at this moment that his oldest son, Owen, sat down with him on the front porch.[11]

"Pa," Owen began. "If I will give up my school and go to Texas with you this fall, will you go? It is possible the climate will help you."

"Yes," George replied. "I will go anywhere if there is chance to get well."

Owen told him the rest of the family would stay behind. "I found that my wife and boys had talked that matter over before Owen spoke to me about it. I had wished to have the way open for something like this, and the bare possibility that it could be realized cured me of the blues at once."

Many decades later, Owen wrote his version of the move to Texas.[12] The effort to get George out of Minnesota included the town physician, Dr. Hughes, who cornered Owen on the street, warning him: "I am afraid one more year in Minnesota will be his last." The doctor suggested that Owen drop out of school and take his father to Texas. The doctor told Owen he was educated enough to get a teaching job in Texas and could resume his own schooling later.

Owen corresponded with the Fort Worth school board about possible teaching jobs but got no assurance of a post. He went ahead anyway to Texas. When he got there, he discovered that the school board he had corresponded with had no actual school. With no prospect for a teaching position, Owen contacted Pastor L. H. Carhart, who had worked with George in Minnesota years earlier.[13] Carhart was building a new Methodist church in Dallas. Carhart offered Owen a job to digging ditches for the foundation. That was good enough; Owen sent for his father.

George had no funds to get to Dallas, so he borrowed fifty dollars from a generous Methodist, a Mr. Boothroyd. "I left home the last of November [1875] with conflicting hopes and fears as to the result of my experiment."[14]

George Richardson would never live in Minnesota again.

Most of my Richardson relatives still live in Minnesota, not far from where our ancestors lived. When I was growing up, we regularly drove to Minnesota to visit cousins. The adults shared many meals and many cocktails but avoided controversial topics like religion, politics, and race. The life and work of our George and Caroline Richardson did not come up in conversations that I ever heard.

But that would change.

After Lori and I finished exploring the battlefields and forts of Tennessee in 2015, we headed northward to Stillwater, one of the many Minnesota frontier outposts where my ancestors lived.[15] We stayed with Jeanette Richardson Nelson, whose Uncle Russell was my grandfather. Her father's first name, Fay, was the maiden name of Caroline Richardson, George's wife.

Jeanette was an enthusiastic supporter of this book project. She was the last of my parents' generation, and sadly, she died before its completion.

Jeanette looked like a Richardson—like me—with a long face and sunken cheekbones. She was born in Northfield and grew up a few miles north on a farm. She lived much of her life in Stillwater where George Richardson had been the pastor of the Methodist Church in the 1850s. Jeanette and her husband, Dwayne, were long active in that church.

We arrived after a long day on the road but sat up for hours talking about George and Caroline and their progeny. Jeanette filled in many gaps for me about who was related to whom, and she wanted to know everything I knew about our ancestors. I outlined what I had learned from reading George's journal.

I asked whether her parents ever talked about George and Caroline Richardson. "No, they never told any stories about them," she said. "The only time they were mentioned was in connection to Methodist churches."

The next day we set forth, with Jeanette behind the wheel, looking for places that we never could have found on our own. We drove along the St. Croix River with its heavily wooded bluffs. George would have navigated the dirt roads along the river by horseback or horse and wagon. I remembered his story of getting lost in the winter. Just driving along these roads I could see how.

We were slowed along the way by rain and hail squalls, and farm tractors lumbering up and down the road. Jeanette took us to the farm at County Line where George struggled in the years after the Civil War. We found the tiny graveyard where George had buried his mother and infant daughter. As we walked past tombstones, a cold wind snapped across the fields through bent trees into the graveyard. The wind made it hard for us to hear each other talk.

Another cousin, Scott Harris, met us there. For many years, Scott has looked after the graveyard. He showed us the family graves and a new headstone for George's mother, Margaret, inscribed with the dates 1793–1872. The headstone had begun to sink, and Scott reset it. "That replacement was put in there without anyone from the family being there to see it done right," Scott mentioned.

We emerged from the graveyard and walked up a slope toward the farm. Corn stubble from the previous season gave the ground a brown-yellow tinge; the soil was still too soggy for planting. The fields were laid out on uneven terrain. It was easy to imagine the difficulty plowing this land before the advent of tractors. No wonder George's health was broken, and Owen was ready to call it quits and move to Texas.

Onward we traveled to Northfield and Red Wing, making more stops at farms, houses, schools, and graveyards where generations of Richardsons lived, worked, and were buried. Along the highway, we passed large windmills generating electricity. The wind never seems to stop along the St. Croix River.

On Sunday we attended worship with Jeanette and her husband at the First United Methodist Church in Stillwater. The building where George served as pastor in the 1850s was torn down long ago. The congregation moved to a new location, but the church still mentions him in their history. Jeanette had seen to that.

It was Mother's Day, and candles were lit for each mom. The church had a woman pastor, which would have been a startling development in the time of George Richardson. The worship style was informal and the lively guitar music definitely not from his era. After the service, the pastor and several of her congregants asked me to tell the story of George and Caroline Richardson. I was happy to comply.

Back at Jeanette's house, we poured through old photo albums and talked more about George and Caroline Richardson and their legacy. Our visit to Stillwater had broken open a conversation that lay dormant in our family for generations.

George Richardson's journal was the catalyst.

~ 18 ~

TEXAS BURNING

None but niggers & alligators can exist there at all.

TEXAS STATE LEGISLATOR JAMES W. TRUITT | 1875

In the decades before the Civil War, Southern white farmers began migrating to East Texas looking for cheap land. They brought with them slaves, and within a few years the eastern one-third of Texas became known as the "Black Belt." Seen on a map, the Black Belt extended from Corpus Christi at the southern tip of Texas, north to Austin, Waco, Dallas, Dennison, and east to the Sabine River.[1]

Most of the Black Belt was humid, woody, swampy, and prone to flooding. The land was poor for cattle grazing but better suited for growing cotton, sugar cane, and corn. The geography, economics, and politics of East Texas had more in common with the Dixie states to the east than with the dry open Texas Range to the west. Planters, not cowboys, dominated East Texas.

The Black Belt was also where Texas's biggest cities grew. Dallas began as a trading post in the 1830s at the intersection of the Caddo trail and a ford in the wide Trinity River. Thirty years later, at the outbreak of the Civil War, Dallas had grown into a town with seven hundred people, including ninety-seven enslaved Blacks. East Texas would send thousands of its white sons to fight and die for the Confederacy.[2]

In the upheaval after the Civil War, freed slaves left their former masters looking for a better life. The exodus of slaves from the plantations represented one of the largest migrations in American history. Many Blacks flocked to Dallas, settling in ramshackle "Freedmen towns" springing up throughout the city. Most of the formerly enslaved were hoping to find land of their own, but like many Blacks throughout the South, ended up submitting to a system of tenant "sharecropper" farming that was barely removed from slavery. To enforce the system, white Confederate Army veterans established a chapter of the Ku Klux Klan in Dallas three years after the end of the war.

Yet there were glimmers of hope for Blacks of East Texas. A year after the founding of the Klan, the Texas Legislature provided funds for public education throughout the state, and theoretically at least, including money for Black schools.

Major railroad lines intersected in Dallas and the city became the commercial hub of Texas. Grains and cotton were shipped east from Dallas, and Dallas was the last supply stop for settlers heading west. Industries sprouted including cottonseed oil mills. The population of Dallas more than doubled in the year the rail lines were completed in 1873. New towns blossomed throughout the Black Belt of East Texas, with Dallas as the economic and political center.

But racial segregation was codified and rigidly enforced everywhere that whites built new towns. Whippings, warning shots, arson, and lynching were in the arsenal to keep intact the old order of white supremacy with Blacks at the very bottom.

It was into this old order that George and Owen Richardson descended in 1876.

>≻⤙⤚⤛⤜≺

When George Richardson stepped off the train in Dallas, he had no prospects for employment—not in a church, not in a school, not in any occupation.[3] He was sick, weary, depressed. He did not know where to find a room or his next meal. He relied entirely on faith—his faith in God, faith in his life mission, and faith in the resourcefulness his oldest son, Owen, who had gone ahead to Texas.

Owen and Pastor Carhart met George at the Dallas train station. George that night bunked in the cabin that Owen called his one-room "shanty." Owen had finished his job digging ditches for Carhart's church, and he was now scraping by as a farmhand on a plantation.[4] They did not stay long at the plantation. Father and son were kicked out. George explained in "Recollections of My Lifework" that the shack was needed for another farmhand. But that was not the entire story.

Owen recorded in his memoir that he was fired because he had unwittingly crossed the rigid Southern caste system.[5] One Sunday, Owen had put on his finest clothes for church. On the way home, his employer saw him and tipped his hat, not realizing he was tipping his hat to one of his field hands. "When we were about mid-way, we met the Colonel and his niece in a fine carriage," Owen wrote. "Of course, as they passed I lifted my hat in salutation."

The plantation owner summoned Owen to his office. To remind Owen of his place, he sent a Black field hand to retrieve him. "You are the first man to work on my plantation who could afford better clothes that I ever wore," the planter told Owen. He fired Owen and ordered him to vacate the shack and leave the plantation.

"But Colonel, I have just spent all you paid me for furniture and all the money I brought with me to refit the cabin."

His plea went nowhere.

"I insist you vacate immediately," the planter replied.

Owen was paid twenty dollars, and with that, he and his father were evicted.

George and Owen moved into town, and Pastor Carhart gave them a room in his parsonage until they could find a room to rent. George continued recuperating from his ailments while Owen found odd jobs hauling firewood, working at a lunch counter, and clerking at a cotton market. "Father was alone most of the day light," Owen wrote. "Never-the-less he gained strength rapidly."[6]

The Texas climate agreed with George, he later wrote in his journal. "In the course of two months I began to feel the benefit of the change of climate. My intense nervousness began to subside."[7] His migraine symptoms disappeared. "I could sleep like a child."

In January 1876, George felt well enough to attend the annual meeting of the West Texas Methodist Conference, the district including much of Texas in the western hills and plateaus. He met the bishop, Edward Gayer Andrews, who was based in Des Moines, Iowa, and was responsible for a vast swatch of territory in the center of the country including Texas.[8]

Methodist bishops were not confined to strictly defined geographic dioceses like their counterparts in the Catholic and Episcopal churches. The Methodist bishops were wide-roaming super-itinerants, presiding at annual regional conferences and overseeing the local presiding elders. Andrews's hagiographer, Francis McConnell, noted, "During that time Bishop Andrews went abroad once and presided over Conferences in almost every State in the Union."[9]

A year younger than George Richardson, Andrews was from New York and was a Union man. He was known to upbraid Northern supporters of the Confederacy. Yet Andrews's commitment to emancipation was lukewarm at best, as was his attitude toward whites who worked with Blacks. "It is no secret," McConnell wrote, "that he cherished very few illusions concerning the work of the Negroes, though he wrought as faithfully as any to help them upward. His rather doubtful attitude toward white work of our Church in the South is also well known."[10]

Despite his reservations, Andrews's name would soon be affixed to a Negro school in Texas.

When George Richardson arrived in Texas, the Methodist conference was racially integrated. Black and white church representatives sat side by side at annual gatherings. George was thrilled at what he saw—and the spark within him kindled with new possibilities.

"Hope that my work was not done began to revive," George wrote. "I cannot describe the joy I felt at the prospect that my days and usefulness might be prolonged and that God might add to my life as many years as he did Hezekiah."[11]

George volunteered for any available preaching post. "When I reported to the conference at Austin I was willing to take work among the white people or colored people wherever I was needed most."

But his initial meeting with Bishop Andrews did not go well. The bishop told him he was not healthy enough to return to the saddle as a traveling itinerant preacher. "Bishop Andrews noticed that the blood had not come back into my cheeks and my voice was not very strong. He knew that the work in any field that he could give me would be rough and trying."

George was impressed by three Black preachers at the conference who would have an enormous impact on him and the Black Methodist Church in Texas in the years ahead: Charles Madison, Mack Henson, and Jeremiah Webster. The three were among the few Black preachers in the conference who could read and write. They articulated to George that the crucial task of their communities was to become literate.[12]

Whether they realized it or not, the three pastors gave George Richardson back his calling, reminding him of the promise he had made to himself a decade earlier on a Mississippi River dock. "My convictions that I had when I left Memphis in 1866 all came back to me. Here among these colored preachers and people is my field of labor."[13]

Like others who had worked to abolish slavery, George understood that the work of emancipation was not over at end of the Civil War. It had only begun. Education, he understood, was critical if the formerly enslaved and their children were to break the bonds of servitude. And they stood little chance of getting an education without a few brave souls like Pastors Madison, Henson and Webster impressing upon whites the importance of education for Blacks. The partnership George Richardson forged with these three African American pastors would have an impact far beyond their lifetimes.

But first, George needed an education from his Black partners. He was to learn from them how the racial caste system remained unbroken, economically benefiting whites. The sharecropping system required Black farmers to give most of what they grew to white landowners. Blacks stood little chance of owning their own land and were in constant danger of being kicked off the land they tilled.

The caste system was increasingly systematized and institutionalized as racial segregation laws were enacted throughout the old Confederacy including Texas. Literacy alone could not overcome poll taxes, segregated schools, poor health care, sharecropping, or Ku Klux Klan terrorism. But literacy represented a start.

George was also taken with the preaching he heard in Black churches, particularly by Larkin Carper, who could not read or write his own name. But Carper was among "the most eloquent men I ever heard," George wrote.[14] Carper repeated scriptural passages and sang hymns entirely from memory. He was among the most successful and innovative Black pastors of the time. He founded St. Paul Methodist church in 1866 in the homes of San Antonio's Black families, and they built a wooden structure in 1872. By the 1880s, the congregation replaced it with a stone church, and replaced it again in 1922. The church is still in use, and a square in San Antonio is named for St. Paul Church. Carper also obtained funds to establish the Lincoln School for Blacks in San Antonio.

"He made a deeper impression on me than any other man in that conference," George wrote in his journal. He wondered what more Carper could do if he could read directly from the Bible. "This discovery gave me a little daylight with regard to the need of our colored preachers. I found that a large majority of the colored men of that conf. had no books except a testament and hymn book, and several lacked a hymn book."

As a former Galena schoolmaster, George Richardson knew something about education. Near the conclusion of the annual Methodist conference, George had another long conversation with Bishop Andrews.[15] "I told him the greatest need these preachers have is help to read and study—that in very many cases the preacher was not ahead of his people, and in some parts of the conference the preachers were not much ahead of where they were at the time of emancipation."

George asked the bishop for permission to organize a school. "I was willing to take hold of this most necessary work by establishing a school for the colored people." He had no idea where or how to organize such a school, or where to find the money. But George Richardson was not without political savvy. He knew the imprimatur of the Methodist bishop would give legitimacy to such a school, and so named it "Andrews Normal College."

The bishop gave his blessing to the enterprise and pledged an unspecified amount of financial support. On the thin reed of that promise a future Black university was built.

❧

George returned to Dallas from the annual Methodist conference and surveyed the quality of education among African Americans.[16] Under Texas law, enacted under pressure from the federal government during the Reconstruction era, white and Black schools were supposed to be treated equally, if separately. The reality was that separate was far from equal. "Texas had provided a pretty fair school fund," he wrote in the journal, "and nominally the white and colored population were on the same footing with regard to it, but practically the Negroes were getting but little benefit from the fund."

George visited two Black schools supported by the Texas public school fund. "At one of these I found a man who had been a Confederate soldier. He was a drunkard," George recorded. "I watched his methods till I saw the children had better be at home." The teacher showed up drunk to school, become "cross and cruel" and then fall asleep in his chair by mid-afternoon. "Then the children would dance around him."[17]

George sought out Pastor Jeremiah Webster, one of the Black preachers he met at the annual Methodist conference.[18] Webster had enlisted as a soldier in a "colored" Union regiment that was deployed to New Orleans. He rose to the rank of sergeant, which was about as high as Blacks could go in the Army. After mustering out, Webster made his way home to Texas. In January 1876, Webster was appointed as the pastor of three-year-old St. Paul Methodist Church in Dallas, founded by formerly enslaved people from Mississippi, Louisiana, and Texas. Some of those in the congregation may have been the soldiers Pastor Webster—or even George Richardson—served with in the Civil War. The church got started with one small wooden building in the heart of a Black neighborhood on the edge of Dallas.

Webster's courage deeply impressed George. Webster told him he was "anxious" to get a school started. In the days ahead, the two crossed the rigid racial boundaries to get the school launched at physical risk to both.

Webster invited George to use his unfinished church building for the school. About all that commended it was a solid roof. "The walls were simply clapboarded and there was a rough floor—it was a very cold place when the Northers swept over Texas," George recalled in his journal.[19]

George, joined by Owen, opened their "colored" school on February 22, 1876, with six pupils, or "scholars" as George called them. Three decades later, George would remember proudly that date. "This school has grown into Samuel Huston College," he wrote in his journal. "It has a history of struggle for existence these 26 years that will never be written up."[20]

When the school opened, instruction was conducted from nine in the morning to four in the afternoon, five days a week. The school charged one dollar a month for tuition. "They were all poor and depended on their daily labor for their existence," George wrote. "If there were two or three in one family that attended school it meant quite a sacrifice to pay 25 cts a week for each."

Somehow the scholars came up with the money. Two months after opening, the school had sixty pupils.

The school gained notice in Dallas, and not all who noticed approved. On Saturday morning, April 22, 1876, Webster and the Richardsons awoke to find the building in flames.[21]

"We were startled by the cry of fire, and on running to the door we discovered that our Church School House was all in a blaze. My son partly dressed and ran barefooted and bareheaded, and found that the rear of the building had been kerosened as high as a person could throw the fluid, and that the flame on the outside was reaching to the roof."

The perpetrators were obvious: "KuKlucks had torched the church," George wrote.

If there were fire brigades in that part of Dallas, none came. George and Owen rescued the school furniture before the building was completely engulfed. "In 30 minutes the dry shell of a house was a heap of smoldering ruin."

By then Webster and the entire neighborhood had arrived.

"It was a pitiful sight to see the despair written on the face of that faithful colored pastor and the members of his flock—men, women and children—as they stood around the smoking brands," George wrote. "They had worked hard, and sacrificed much to build their church and bring it so near completion."

Tears streamed down their faces.

"Our scholars stood about us crying because they could not go to school anymore. We assured them that we would not leave them."

Despair turned into defiance. The Klan, George recalled, could not be allowed to succeed. "The fight would not stop there. If the KuKlucks could not succeed in driving away their teachers by burning the building they would attack the teachers, and their lives would be in jeopardy."

At daylight, George and all the Black pastors in the neighborhood resolved to rebuild the school—and quickly. The pastor of Tabernacle Church signed on immediately (his name is lost). "He was a very impulsive man and said with a great deal of vehemence, 'I'll stand by you and we will not be driven.'"

George went to a lumberyard to purchase materials while the Black pastors rallied enough labor to put up a new building. The neighborhood pitched in to purchase the lumber.

Within hours, they were ready to rebuild. They wanted to make a point with the Ku Klux Klan by rebuilding fast.

"We pressed into service every colored man that could use a saw or drive a nail. That was a busy afternoon. The sound of hammers did not cease till 9 o'clock, then we carried the seats we had saved from the fire, and our building was ready for dedication."

When the new building was finished, they held a ceremony and sang a familiar hymn of praise to the Almighty. "We sang the Doxology in which the great crowd of men and women joined with a will. The notes of praise rang out all over Freedman Town, and the weeping of the morning was turned into joy in the evening."

A short item in *The Dallas Daily Herald* mentioned the fire, noting: "Two men, one white and one black, were seen near the church, going from it, crying fire, at the time the fire was discovered." Almost certainly the two men must have been Jeremiah Webster and George Richardson.[22]

Another local newspaper, the *Dallas Commercial,* reported the school fire and the determination of the Black community to rebuild. "For about six weeks they labored under discouragements that cannot be told," the newspaper reported, recounting the short history of the school before the fire. "People began to comprehend the fact that their school would be a success, and the scholars began to pour in rapidly. About three o'clock last Saturday morning their building was reduced to ashes."

In his journal, George described a photograph in the newspaper depicting that the Richardsons and their scholars standing in front of the rebuilt school. He described Pastor Webster in the photo holding open a Bible. George wrote he would illustrate his journal with the photo, but I have never located it.

The Dallas newspaper article was reprinted in the *St. Paul Pioneer Press,* with an editorial addition commending George and Owen Richardson for their "Minnesota pluck."[23] George wrote that the newspaper article in a Northern newspaper "was of great service to us in our effort to raise money."

The newspaper article may have helped raise money in Minnesota, but it did not help George with his wife. He had not seen Caroline in five months. He wrote to her about the fire—the letter is now lost—but the newspaper article thoroughly alarmed her.

Buried in a box of family mementoes is a letter Caroline wrote to George seven days after the school burning. "I have been trying to get means to get you home," she wrote her husband.[24] She told him she had been away from home when news of the fire arrived. When she walked through the front door, Emma had handed her the newspaper article and his letter. "I was weary and had been very anxious about you."

Caroline wrote that she was nearly overwhelmed with anxiety about George and her oldest son. "Well my own weariness, and the knowledge that probably not only your school but yourselves have hidden human foes who would not hesitate to do anything that darkness would cover to hinder your work nearly overcame me."

She was supporting the family with their farm at County Line, and she still had three sons at home and her young daughter, Emma. To raise money to get George home, she had called the local sheriff to collect a debt for the sale of a team of horses.

At the close of her letter, Caroline softened slightly. "I do not expect you would start for home until your proposed [school] house is built. Well I am thankful that you have thus far outgeneraled the incendiary. . . . But you can never feel any security. Lawless villains will always be ready to do all they can dare, and be able to evade the law."

She was also realistic about something else: she did not trust that the Texas legal authorities would protect the school or her husband. "It may not be an impossible thing that the officers would shield instead of catching them."

At the close of her letter, Caroline again implored George to come home: "If you cannot come home at the time we had expected you to, I shall be more disappointed than I can easily tell." She pointedly informed him that Emma, who had just turned thirteen, would not be sending him any further letters because she expected him home soon. "I asked Emma if she was not going to write you. She is sure that you will be home so soon that it is not worthwhile."

A month after receiving his wife's letter, George was on his way back to Minnesota. But any hopes Caroline had that he was staying would soon be dashed.

19

JEREMIAH WEBSTER

*Of all the forms of negro hate in this world, save me from the one
which clothes itself with the name of the loving Jesus.*

FREDERICK DOUGLASS | 1885

The school in Dallas was nearly broke when George Richardson returned
home to Minnesota. The dollar-a-month tuitions were not enough to support
both George and Owen, let alone purchase school supplies, maintain buildings, and employ teachers. While George went north to raise money—and
mend fences with his wife—Pastor Webster also took to the road, raising
what he could from congregations outside of Dallas.[1]

George wrote in his journal that Webster "traveled through the Southern
part of the state [of Texas] and visited the wealthier congregations in Austin, San Antonio, Houston and Galveston to raise collections for the same
purpose. He was only partially successful, for all our colored congregations
in the city or county were poor."[2]

Caroline raised—or borrowed—enough funds to buy her husband a train
ticket and riverboat passage to Minnesota. He arrived back on the County
Line farm in June 1876 but did not stay long, determined to raise enough
money for the school and return to Texas.[3]

"After taking a short rest at home and helping the boys a little about their
strawberry harvest I started out and visited a number of churches which I
had previously served. My collections were not large."

George traveled for two months by train through Minnesota and Wisconsin, and then by horse and wagon to remote congregations. Whatever
words passed between husband and wife are not known, but they reached
an understanding. "While at home my wife and I arranged that she would
come to me a year later from the following fall and assist in the school work.
She could not tell whether she would be willing to make her home in the
South till she had tried it."

The family was about to split up in a year's time anyway. David would
go to Carleton College in Northfield, while Emma would accompany her

mother to Texas. Their two youngest sons, Frank and Mercein (nineteen and seventeen years old, respectively), would stay behind to manage the Minnesota farm.

George headed back to Texas in August 1876.

Meeting up in Dallas, George and Webster pooled their collections to begin constructing a larger school building. They applied for funds from the Methodist Freedmen's Bureau but got nowhere. The two pastors kicked in their own money to finish the new building at a total cost of $300. They also hired a new teacher, a Miss L.L. Webb, whom George said was "well qualified to take any of the classes."[4]

By mid-November, the school was thriving. The school roster listed 154 pupils, with names including Jefferson Armstrong, Charity Burris, and Minerva Cravens. There were two Middletons, three Scogins, four Parkers, four Wellingtons, and five Claypools. Next to each pupil's name was their age—all were between eight and thirteen—and the name of a parent or guardian. The Richardsons recorded every detail in a long ledger book.[5]

The school continued to grow, and a second building was constructed. Not only were children getting an education, but so were the adults. "We had quite a number in both schools that were past school age."

On December 2, 1876, the school was sanctioned by the city of Dallas and adopted as a Methodist school officially named the Andrews Normal College.[6] The nameplate would change several times in the years to come, but for now, the Methodist bishop had his name on the door.

><><><

At the annual Texas Methodist convention in 1876, a resolution drafted by the Committee on Education commended the efforts of George and Owen Richardson, Pastor Webster, and others involved in launching the school. Owen Richardson was mentioned as its first president.

George quoted the resolution verbatim in his journal: "Your committee would report their conviction that the hand of God is in the enterprise, and that the Messrs Richardson, who have in the face of so much difficulty inaugurated the enterprise, deserve our gratitude and cordial support." The resolution concluded: "The design of the school is to educate preachers and teachers for the Freedmen."[7]

The establishment of Andrews Normal School, however, was among the few bright moments at the annual Texas Methodist Conference. A proposal to split the Texas Methodist church along racial lines tore the conference apart.[8] Even white supporters of the Andrews Normal School favored splitting the conference along racial lines. It was a repeat of the argument George witnessed in Memphis a decade earlier.

"The preachers connected with the white work felt that they could succeed better among the white population if they had a conference of their own," George wrote. "While they were willing to do all they could for the colored brethren they felt they could help them more if they built up strong work among the whites."

Making matters worse, by 1880, Bishop Andrews had moved home to New York, and with him the commitment for a racially integrated church in Texas.[9] The new bishop, whose name cannot be located, had no such commitment. The bishop, George wrote, reminded everyone "the Methodist Episcopal Church considers all souls alike, and that Christian privileges belong to one as well as to another." But the new bishop maintained that the Methodist Church had not "undertaken to control the question of social life," and the church's only interest was "the salvation of souls." It was not the church's concern, he maintained, whether those souls mingled on earth.

George drew back from taking sides publicly. He felt caught in the middle between the white hierarchy represented by his bishop—from whom he desperately needed support for the school—and his Black pastor partners. At the conference, Jeremiah Webster and Mack Henson delivered impassioned speeches against separation, imploring the Methodists to stick together across color lines.[10]

Henson pleaded, "We need our white brethren in conference relation. We need their advice and assistance." But the bishop tipped the scales, responding that the church would "never consent to the degradation of any of her ministers to a second rank," but that individual ministers should "labor among their own people."

When the conference gathered the next day, the bishop called for a vote along color lines. He declared that a majority of each race needed to approve the resolution to separate. The resolution to separate was introduced by one of the Black pastors, Daniel Gregory, who maintained the Black churches should be allowed to grow without white interference.

Pastor Webster stood once more to oppose it and "made an earnest plea that the conference remain as it was." One of the white pastors responded, "the colored ministers would be freer and grown faster."

The final vote was seven white pastors in favor of racial separation, none against; and eighteen Black pastors in favor, and thirteen against. George was still officially a member of the Minnesota Methodist Conference and could not vote.[11]

The resolution allowed the Black Methodists to retain the original name of the conference—West Texas Conference—while the new white Methodist conference was called the Austin Conference.

The white separatist's promise to help the Black churches proved hollow. Once the white Texas Methodists went their own way, they abandoned their efforts to help the Black conference and educate the freed slaves and their descendants.

George offered no opinion in his journal about which way he would have voted on the Methodist racial separation vote. But he had nothing good to say about the Black pastor, Gregory, who had introduced the resolution to split the church along racial lines. George wrote that Gregory was subservient to a white pastor during the celebration of the Lord's Supper, and had "cringed to him because he was a white man, and had once been in authority" thus showing "the utter inability to appreciate the sacredness of sacred things."[12]

To be sure, George Richardson was not fully an integrationist. His guiding principle was that of a missionary: Blacks needed an education so that they could propagate the gospel and become productive citizens. For him, the cause was not about social equality, or even legal equality. His cause was building a better society—and a stronger Methodist Church—by educating Black pastors and their congregations. To do that, whites had an obligation to educate Blacks, and they could not do that from a distance.

But George had not yet connected how justice and equality required more than teaching reading and writing or building churches. That idea would come to him—but that awaited the arrival his wife.

George wrote that Webster was right on one major point: the only way the Black churches and schools could succeed was if the whites helped financially—and they weren't. The whites and their money evaporated. "The West Texas conference started out after the session to do its work without the aid of their white brethren."[13]

George wrote in his journal that if the Black conference was to have any chance of survival, it needed white pastors raising money in the North. And that was one thing he could do. George Richardson chose to join the Black conference and would become the presiding elder—a status he had never attained in Minnesota or anywhere else.

On another level, for George to stick with the Black conference was career suicide in the white Methodist Church. He would find it tough dealing with narrow-minded senior Methodist leaders, even those—including Hobart—with whom he had been close. The coldness he would encounter from other white pastors was not unusual. A contemporary Methodist pastor, John Dixon Long, wrote a book, *Pictures of Slavery*, about being shunned because of his ministry with enslaved Blacks.

"I confess I have felt trammeled," Long wrote. "If a minister devotes much of his time to [Blacks], and manifests much interest in their welfare, he may get the name of 'negro preacher;' and he passes by a crowd of miserable [white] loafers, he will hear one say, 'That man's got the nigger mania; he's just fit to preach to niggers!' and even his superiors in office may give him a few cold, discouraging hints."[14]

Long labeled as rank hypocrites those Methodists who supported missionaries to Africa but did nothing for Blacks in their own country. "I am trying to rebuke that sickly religious zeal that can cry over the condition of the negro in Africa, and yet have no sympathy for the unfortunate condition of those in America," Long wrote.

It would only get worse in Texas.

In the years ahead, racial segregation hardened in Texas into what became known as the "Terrell laws."[15] The Texas Legislature stripped Blacks of the right to vote, the law named for its legislative author, A. W. Terrell. Other segregation laws soon followed including requiring pulling down window shades on "colored only" railroad cars when passing through white towns.

><><

In early 1877, George learned who had torched the school building a year earlier.[16] The Dallas newspapers reported that a pair of "desperadoes"—two white brothers named Campbell—had been hung by a posse. "There came rumors that these men confessed to burning of a 'nigger' church in Dallas,"

George recalled in his journal. But that was not why the brothers were hanged. They were executed for killing a white woman.

In his travels through the Hill Country, George learned more about the Campbell brothers and their upbringing. The brothers had grown up on a plantation with about thirty slaves. Their mother, a widow, had been the slave driver.

"She rode her white pony over the fields with two revolvers in the holsters of her saddle," George wrote in his journal. "When she wanted to punish any of her men and women she would call two of her men and have them do the whipping while she stood by and held her revolver to make them do it thoroughly. In one instance she actually whipped to death a girl about 15 years old. I was told by the ex-slaves that had belonged to that plantation that they saw her shoot and kill two men in the field. Then she had a hole dug in the corner of the fence and had them tumbled in and buried. It was this kind of training that these young men had."[17]

After the Civil War, the plantation had fallen into ruin when the formerly enslaved fled. The brothers "knew nothing about work" and roamed the countryside "begging and stealing" before killing a white woman. They had been arrested, but vigilantes grabbed them before they stood trial.

"They gave the Campbell boys an hour to say their prayers, or to say anything they had to say. Among the things that they confessed was the burning of the Negro Church in Dallas." The brothers were hung from a railroad bridge. George also learned that the Campbell brothers had been paid by unknown leaders in the Ku Klux Klan to burn his school.

Forces more insidious than the Klan's torches threatened the school. Pastor Webster, who had courageously defied the Klan and stood against both white and Black separatists in the Methodist Church, fell ill and died March 14, 1877, likely succumbing in an influenza outbreak.[18] Webster had gone to the town of Mount Pleasant in East Texas to visit his children. "While at his mother-in-law's he was taken sick and never recovered," George recorded in his journal.

George wrote a long tribute to Webster for the Texas Methodist Church: "In the death of Bro Webster the conference has lost one her best and ablest ministers." He added a personal postscript in his journal: "We had learned to love him as a brother."[19]

The tributes, though, did little to help the school or church.

In September, Caroline Richardson kept the promise she made a year earlier. She and fourteen-year-old Emma traveled by rail to Dallas to join George and Owen and begin work at the school.[20] Emma arrived with a fever that dragged on for three weeks. She would be sickly much of the time she lived in Texas.

"Her mother nursed her," George wrote. Once Emma recovered from her fever, Caroline turned her energies to the school. Her workload quickly increased, and Caroline was appointed the "principal and preceptress" to manage the daily tasks of the school. Her administrative abilities far exceeded Owen's, who was still officially the president. Her talent for detail and organization freed George to get back on the road seeking new financial support for the school and do what he loved best: teaching, visiting congregations, and preaching.

Young Emma began teaching classes. At the end of the year, George wrote a tribute to his daughter in the school ledger: "Miss Emma Richardson—the assistant teacher has won the hearts of her scholars by her kindness and gentleness, and the interest she has always manifested them."[21]

As domestic life settled into a routine, George attended the annual West Texas Methodist convention "to look after the interests of the school." The new Black Methodist district was in a shambles with accusations rumbling about embezzlement by pastors and "such confusion that it was impossible to straighten out." The Methodist bishop overseeing the Texas congregations threw up his hands declaring, "that the West Texas conference was the most helpless conference he knew of."[22]

The Black conference was divided into three "mission" districts, and George was appointed presiding elder of one.

Events had moved so quickly, George wrote, that he'd had no time to "look up the condition of the field" before assuming the duties of presiding elder. This much he knew: the conference and its congregations were "torn to pieces." George also knew he faced a tougher challenge than just the embezzlement crisis: "I knew that a white Presiding Elder who would go among the colored people and live with them would be looked on with suspicion by all classes."

George set up his Methodist district headquarters in Austin, leaving

Caroline, Owen, and Emma at the school in Dallas. The arrangement lasted barely a year before "it was decided"—by whom he does not say—to move the family to Austin.[23]

Andrews Normal College of Dallas, Texas, closed. Resuscitating it in Austin would prove anything but easy.

>+><+<

We made a pilgrimage to Dallas, but it was all but impossible to imagine it as it was in the 1870s. St. Paul Methodist Church in Dallas, where the school once stood, is now surrounded by freeways and tall buildings. The wooden church building was replaced in the 1920s by a handsome brick church that still stands. No longer called "Freedman's Town," the neighborhood gentrified in the late twentieth century and was renamed the "Arts District."

The church is a block from the Dallas Black Dance Theater and only a few more blocks from the Dallas Art Museum. The Dallas Mavericks basketball arena is a mile away. There is little, if any evidence, of what the neighborhood looked like when George Richardson and Jeremiah Webster operated their school.

The church website noted how the city of Dallas ran roughshod over the church and its predominantly Black congregation in the development of the neighborhood.

"In 1988 the church voted to remain in downtown Dallas despite radical demographic and gentrification to the area. St. Paul was no part of the future of planning for downtown Dallas and what would become the Arts District."[24]

In staying, the St. Paul Church website proudly notes that it has become "one of the leading voices local and national on issues of race, injustice and community building." The legacy of Jeremiah Webster and my ancestor lives on.

While there, we went to the Dallas Art Museum for the opening of an exhibit of the works of Romare Bearden, a leading African American artist of the Harlem Renaissance of the 1920s and '30s. Bearden was born in 1911, the year George Richardson died. In his art, Bearden explored themes from the Bible, rural Black Southern life, and jazz clubs in Harlem. Jazz musician

Branford Marsalis created a musical album based on the exhibit, with titles from Bearden's paintings.

I could not help but feel the exhibit was a fitting tribute to the school that had once stood nearby even if only a handful of contemporary people were aware of the school's existence long ago.

GLORY BOUND

I am sometimes up and sometimes down
And sometimes level with the ground
But all the while for glory bound.

BLACK SPIRITUAL | 1870S

All of the contradictions of Texas—the good, the bad and the ugly—converge in Austin. Before it got the name, Spanish friars arrived there in the 1700s to build missions. Finding the place intolerable, they relocated to San Antonio.

Americans founded a new village in the same spot in 1837, naming it "Waterloo" probably because it sits along the Colorado River, not to be confused with the river of the same name that created the Grand Canyon. Two years later the settlement was renamed for the "father of Texas," Stephen F. Austin. Far from the centers of commerce and agriculture, the town's very remoteness made it an attractive choice for the state capital. In time, Austin would become the center of education in Texas.

The 1850 census recorded 629 people in Austin, with about one-third of them enslaved Blacks.[1] At the outbreak of the Civil War a decade later, the population had more than tripled. Probably more than one-third of the white families owned slaves.

Yet, while the rest of Texas voted to secede, Austin voted to stay in the Union. Many of Austin's leading citizens remained pro-Union throughout the Civil War, putting them at grave risk. Austin's leading Episcopal Church minister, Charles Gillette, was vocally pro-Union, ran afoul of his bishop, and was forced to flee for his life.[2]

After the war, Austin's population grew steadily. By the 1870s, Austin was booming as the western terminus of the Houston and Texas Central Railway, the only railroad line in Central Texas. Austin became more diverse with an influx of European settlers from Germany, Sweden, and Ireland. The first immigrants from Mexico also arrived. Newly emancipated African Americans composed more than one-third of the population.

Throughout the nineteenth century, other Texas cities attempted to grab away the designation of the state capital, but Austin turned back every such effort. In 1872, a statewide referendum settled the question: Austin would remain the capital. When the Richardsons arrived in Austin in 1878, a magnificent granite state capitol building would be under construction within a few years.

Austin was not just the political capital of Texas but the intellectual capital of Texas as well. The cornerstone to the first building at the University of Texas was laid in 1882. The first school for Blacks in Austin was founded in 1875 when the Congregational Church established Tillotson Collegiate and Normal Institute to educate African American women teachers.[3] The school was named for its founder, George Jeffrey Tillotson, a minister from Connecticut.

The Richardsons and the Methodists would be not far behind.

As George Richardson told the story in "Recollections of My Lifework," the official reason for moving his Methodist school to Austin was more Blacks resided in southern Texas than in northern Texas.[4] He also mentioned that the Dallas school was too close to another Black Methodist school, Wiley University in Marshall, about 150 miles east of Dallas. He maintained that the two schools were in an endless rivalry for scarce resources from Northern Methodists. George also felt that Austin as the state capital would be more visible and more centrally located than Dallas. Finally, he wrote, his work with small Black churches was increasingly in the Hill Country surrounding Austin.

"We had come to realize that the present location [Dallas] was in many respects unfortunate," George wrote.

But there was another reason for the move that George did not mention in his journal. His son, Owen, in his memoir written in 1937 near the end of his life, gave a different—and probably more accurate—version of the closure of the school in Dallas and its relocation to Austin: Black pupils had publicly upstaged white pupils in an exhibition of learning skills.

The incident began innocently enough—at a May picnic on a clear beautiful Texas day. With a "colored band" playing music, Owen wrote, their students displayed their academic prowess by singing and reciting speeches from memory, a skill known as declamation. "I trained the pupils in dialogue and declamation," Owen wrote. "The dialogues were suited to the pupils in the lower grades, as were the readings. Three young men declaimed 'The Charge of the Light Brigade,' Lincoln's Speech at Gettysburg and the 'Maniac,' a temperance poem. The pupils were enthused."

Everyone at the picnic was Black except for the white teachers—and a reporter from the *Galveston News*. As Owen recalled, the news story was favorable—too favorable. The newspaper reported that the Black pupils "excelled" considerably more than the five white schools whose declamations the reporter had attended.

"We thought the reporter meant well," Owen wrote, "but his comparison of the colored pupils [to those] of the white schools was disastrous to our educational efforts." Blacks had shown up the whites.

The consequences were immediate. The city of Dallas required that teachers pass a rigged examination that the teachers at the Richardsons' school could not possibly pass. The city of Dallas succeeded where the Ku Klux Klan had failed: the teachers were dismissed, and the Andrews Normal School was forced to close and leave Dallas. The doors were shuttered in May 1878.

Caroline packed up and headed back to Minnesota with Emma to rejoin her two younger sons, Frank and Mercein, neither of whom were doing well running the family farm. Caroline would do whatever she could do to help her youngest sons restart their lives and close the farm. Whether she would return to Texas was an open question.

There was one bright spot in the year: Owen married Clara A. Milne, one of the teachers at the Dallas school.[5] Owen had met her at a Christian revival meeting. "She was distressed over her sins, but failed to find relief," Owen wrote. After seven nights of revivals "light broke into her soul." She went home "laughing all the way." For several days after, "she had spells of prolonged laughter. Some of her friends feared that she was losing her mind."

Clara assured her friends she was quite sane but filled with religious fervor. She asked a Methodist pastor—his name is not recorded—how she could live into her newfound faith to help others "find the joyful experience she was enjoying." The pastor suggested she teach at the Dallas "colored" school, and she "joyously" accepted.

Owen's mother played the matchmaker. Clara had called on Caroline and discreetly inquired about Owen's "Minnesota fiancé." Caroline informed her that Owen was quite unattached, and the connection was soon made.

Clara and Owen were married on May 2, 1878, a few days before Caroline and Emma returned to Minnesota. "We were alone and very happy," Owen wrote.

Clara's commitment to the education of African Americans was at least as strong as Owen's—maybe even stronger—and her devotion to the cause proved crucial to the ultimate success of the family project: rebuilding the school, this time in Austin.

But the marriage of Owen and Clara was difficult with the birth of their only child, Carrie Mary. Her first name was the same as Owen's sister who had died as an infant, and her middle name came from Owen's other sister, Mary Emma (who went by Emma). The new baby was physically, and probably mentally, disabled.

〉━〈

By mid-1878, the school in Austin existed only in the imaginations of George, Owen, and Clara.

They had no buildings, nowhere to live, no teachers other than themselves, and hardly any money. Methodist Church authorities officially changed the name of the school to the "West Texas Seminary," but a piece of paper was all there was to show for it.[6] Making matters worse, George's health wavered once again. "When my wife started away she had a feeling that she would not see me alive again."[7]

Replanting the school combined with new responsibilities in the Methodist conference "had been too much for my strength," George wrote in his journal. "I had been building up [my health] ever since I came to Texas till the past winter. Now it appeared that I had lost all I had previously gained."

The winter and spring of 1878-1879 was discouraging. George's health sank when riding his circuit but strengthened when home and in a classroom. He never seemed to notice the pattern in himself, or if he did, he did not confess to his journal that his stamina was better suited to the classroom than the saddle. His compulsion to live on horseback pushed him back on the trail throughout his life.[8]

The Hill Country around Austin is dry and scrubby, prone to scorching summers and flash floods. The soil is poor and better suited to grazing than crops. Black settlements dotted the Hill Country but were confined to the worst of the lands and the mosquito-infested river bottoms. It was not easy country to travel, the roads often impassable. In a letter to Clara, George wrote: "The water is deep enough to come to the top of the wheels so we did not care to try it. Shall be obliged to camp here till tomorrow."⁹

On his first tour of his new territory, George was accompanied by a Black preacher, Isaac Smith. The pair took a train and then a stagecoach to Gonzales, about seventy miles south of Austin. They bought horses, saddles, and bridles for thirty dollars for their journey deeper into the Hill Country.

"The May sun was very oppressive, and it had been a long time since I had done any horseback riding," he wrote. "About noon I came as near having sun stroke as could be and avoid it. I became faint and thought I should fall off from my horse. I steadied myself the best I could and slid down and crawled into the shade of some mesquite brush."¹⁰

Reaching their destination, George Richardson and Isaac Smith stayed with a formerly enslaved African American family. Upon emancipation the family had become relatively prosperous with a one-thousand-acre ranch. "I mention this in particular, because it was not always my good fortune to find such a place to rest."¹¹ The prosperity of his host family was living proof to George that the emancipated could do well if given the chance.

George and his guide saddled up and visited more Black settlements and churches. He noted that those who could own land were doing better than Blacks working at menial jobs in the towns.

"I found in these frontier settlements that the colored people were buying land and making homes of their own and they seemed a more enterprising class of people than the colored people in the towns."

Returning to Austin, George rejoined Owen who was busily reestablishing the school.¹² The first step was finding a building. The African American Wesley Methodist Church, located on a hill at Ninth and Neches Streets, was willing to rent rooms for the school. The Richardsons took the offer and called the newest incarnation of their school "West Texas College."

Owen and Clara found a house for rent where all of them could live. Owen and Clara were the first teachers when the school opened in October 1878 at the Wesley Church.

Next they needed students. The public schools, George wrote, were significantly better in Austin than in Dallas, even for Blacks. "We were glad to find this state of things, nevertheless it made it more difficult to fill up our conference school," he wrote. "Under these circumstances our school filled up slowly."[13]

The Richardsons had help. Austin's Black Methodist pastors, particularly Charles L. Madison of the Wesley Church, began funneling pupils to the school. Madison's wife became the third teacher, and he became a pupil. She taught the same lessons to her husband at night that she had taught children during the day. We found in George's collection of "cabinet cards" a photograph of a Black pastor, likely Madison.

George began looking for a permanent site for the school. He found six lots—about an acre and a half—and purchased them for $1,350 with a down payment of $400 from church collections.[14] As it turned out, the lots were never used for the school, and the property is now Zaragosa Park on the east side of Austin.

Besides launching the school, George continued with his responsibilities as an elder of the sprawling Black West Texas conference. His territory was enormous, including huge swaths of Central, South and East Texas. The conference was subdivided into four districts; George led the district stretching from San Antonio to Austin and south toward the Gulf Coast; Madison, his friend from the Wesley Church, took the Black Methodist churches north from Austin to Dallas. A white bishop, Gilbert Haven, presided over all of it. George wrote that at their annual convention they got a "great uplift" from Haven's sermon when he declared "great faith in the colored people in their ability to throw off the degrading effects of slavery."[15]

George sought financial support for his Austin school at the annual Methodist gathering. The West Texas Methodist Conference had little resources of its own, and so approved a resolution pleading for financial help from the Freedmen's Aid Society.[16] The national organization had been founded in the Civil War as an alliance of Methodists, Presbyterians, and Congregationalists in the North to assist the freed slaves in the South. The West Texas conference pledged to turn over control of the school to the society if funds were forthcoming.

But they weren't.

Owen never got over the slight for the rest of his life. The Richardsons' school—later to be named Samuel Huston College—remained in the control of the West Texas Methodist Conference into the twentieth century until it merged with Tillotson College, founded three years before the Richardsons arrived in Austin.

The Richardsons' school had competition for resources with another Black Texas college controlled by the Methodist Church, Wiley College in Marshall, in the so-called Black Belt of East Texas that was heavily populated by African Americans who had migrated from the Deep South. The Methodist Church steered most of its funds for Blacks in Texas to Wiley College. The Richardsons found that frustrating, pointing out to national church leaders that Marshall was three hundred miles from Austin and one hundred miles east of Dallas, to little avail.

The situation was further complicated when Wiley College offered Owen a job.[17] Pastor Frank Moore, chairman of the Wiley Board of Trustees, came to Austin and met with Owen and Clara. His offer came with a salary and a comfortable house. Owen was inclined to accept. "The last year had been extremely exhausting," Owen wrote in his memoir. He put the proposition to Clara, "hoping she would say, 'we will.'"

She replied otherwise.

"Brother Moore," she told the visitor, "Marshall is three hundred miles from Austin. Very few of our pupils would be able to avail themselves of the advantages of Wiley. . . . I believe God wants us here."

Owen was disappointed but stayed in Austin. Whether his heart was with the school remained to be seen.

>⟶⟵<

In January 1879, George set forth to do what he knew best—saddling up and heading out on the trail to visit Black Methodist churches of the Texas Hill Country. He purchased a team of two horses and a wagon, and filled his rig with books. If Black sharecroppers and their preachers couldn't come to the school in Austin, he would bring the school to them.[18]

"My son used to call me the Traveling School," George wrote. The books weren't cheap—typically five dollars per volume. "I was not flush with money enough to furnish the books without pay," so he also became a traveling bookstore. George ordered the books wholesale from a New York publisher, and then sold the books at a retail price on an installment plan. The profits went to the Austin school and a credit line with book publishers. Nonetheless, George still needed to loan funds to his pupils out of his own pocket so that they could purchase books.

George's circuit was twelve hundred miles round-trip, taking him south-west to San Antonio, west to Fredericksburg, east to Mount Pleasant, and as far south as Corpus Christi. It was an enormous territory. Mostly he stayed with Black families. "I determined from the beginning to live with the people I served."[19]

Reaching these outposts took ingenuity. For one such trip he purchased a horse, rode to a town on his circuit, and then sold the horse when he got home. "I sold him for what he cost me, making my trip cheaper than it would have been by railroad, provided it existed."[20]

George's journal reflects his enjoyment of the hospitality and the cama-raderie with the African American preachers and congregations he visited. But he admitted he had a tin ear for their music. He much preferred the old Wesleyan Methodist chestnuts to the expressive lyrics and tones of African American gospel music. George could be downright condescending about it, writing that Black music didn't reflect "the highest state of grace to which the Christian might attain." Yet, in time, he grew enamored of the Black spirituals and recorded in the journal the lyrics of what he called the "plantation songs."[21]

His hard-won experience as a Minnesota circuit-riding preacher had taught him to tread lightly before trying to change his congregations. It took a year for him to win their trust. "I could suggest some improvements in their Sunday Schools, in their class meetings and revival services that they would hardly have accepted the year before."

George wrote glowingly in the journal about the Black preachers he en-countered.[22] Mack Henson, pastor of a congregation in Victoria, a settlement 125 miles south of Austin, was described by George as "eloquent." Henson would become one of the leading voices for civil rights in the region of the late 1800s. Another pastor, A. R. Norris in San Antonio, deeply impressed George with his leadership abilities. "I think he came as near getting out of the ruts of the slavery times as any man on my District." George saw to it that Norris would be appointed a presiding elder in Austin.

But George also found most of his preachers badly overworked and several in poor health. "Bro Davis has the idea that most of them had, that the best preaching was the kind that tore their throats to pieces the fastest."

He acknowledged that likely would not change.

George forged a lasting friendship with one preacher in particular: Henson. "He had the ability to move the church forward faster than any man in my district," George wrote. "I got some of my very best inspiration while I was preaching to [his] congregation." The day would come when Henson served as George's personal pastor.

His route through Texas took him to Mount Pleasant, three hundred miles northeast of Austin. For George, the trip to Mount Pleasant was more than a congregational visit; it was a pilgrimage. Jeremiah Webster, his partner in building the school in Dallas, was buried there. A guide took him to Webster's grave. "It seemed to me a very sacred spot. I could almost make it seem real that the angel Gabriel had received a special commission to watch over that sacred dust."[23]

Writing in his journal years later, George came close to acknowledging he sought forgiveness from his dead friend for abandoning the Dallas school. "All the intensity with which he labored to build up our school came back to me while I stood at his grave," he wrote. "I remembered how he seemed almost crushed as he stood by the smouldering [sic] ruins of his church, which we used for our school, and his intense delight when we decided to rebuild in the very face of our secret foes. . . . I think now, though I did not realize it at the time, that he overworked that year, and that hastened his death."

Many of the settlements where George traveled were in the heart of cattle country and the men—white and Black—were cowboys. Unlike on the plantations, there was no racial segregation on the range. Cowboys camped, ate, and worked together. "This sort of equality with their masters made the negroes in the cattle business superior to those in the cotton plantations."

<hr/>

By the fall of 1879, attendance at the Austin school had grown significantly, but so had the work and the expenses. The Wesley Church charged $5 a month in rent. The Richardsons still owed $900 on the six lots they had purchased for a future building site. "The assistance we got from the Freedmans [sic] Aid Society was very small," George wrote. "I found it necessary to put into the school all the money I could spare from my district work to keep it running."

Owen pleaded for funds in letters and telegrams to Richard S. Rust, the founder of the Methodist Freedmen's Aid Society, but did not get a response. Rust funneled all the Methodist funding into Wiley College in Marshall, far to the north and did not favor building a school in Austin. Owen's lack of respect for Rust did not help.[24]

Richard Rust was born in Massachusetts in 1815—nine years senior to George Richardson.[25] As a young student at Phillips Academy in Andover, Rust was bitten with the antislavery fervor of his region. He founded an abolitionist society at the elite school and was expelled in 1834 after refusing a faculty order to disband his society. Rust found his way into an experimental racially integrated preparatory school, Noyes Academy, in Canaan, New Hampshire. Local residents feared the integrated school would lead to interracial dating and "African huts" and they burned it down. Rust escaped with his life, but he was more committed than ever to abolitionism and equal education for Blacks. He eventually graduated from the Methodist Wesleyan University, and in 1841 was licensed as a Methodist preacher.

Rust served several churches and schools throughout his long life and was the founding president of William Wilberforce University in Ohio, established in 1856, the oldest historically Black college in the country. The school was named for the English political leader whose work led to the abolition of the British slave trade.

Rust is credited with helping to establish fourteen African American Methodist schools in the United States and he kept a tight grip on where to put them. Rust no doubt viewed the Richardsons as freelancing in Austin with no official sanction from any Methodist official organization.

Rust struggled with how white Methodists were miserly donors to Black colleges. Even calling them colleges was a stretch. "Because of the inferior quality of instruction in the public elementary and secondary schools, it was necessary for the Negro colleges to expend considerable effort in remedial work," wrote Texas historian Lawrence D. Rice. "Nevertheless, the colleges attempted to supply all of the educational needs for Negroes. This simply spread their efforts in too many directions with their limited funds, facilities and faculties."[26]

If Rust's problem was lack of an official imprimatur from the Methodist Church, George knew how take care of that. In December 1879, the West Texas Methodist conference passed its strongest resolution yet endorsing the Austin school, and for good measure, requested $1,000 from the Methodist

Freedmen's Society.[27] But Owen lacked his father's savvy in Methodist politics, and his persistence with Rust backfired. "My need seemed so great I telegraphed Dr. Rust at his headquarters in Cincinnati. In about a week, I received a note, 'Do not send me another telegram.'"[28]

Yet there were glimmers of hope.

The school got a visit from Joseph C. Hartzell, the editor of the *Southwestern Christian Advocate*, based in New Orleans.[29] He couldn't offer immediate help, but he had broad influence in the Methodist Church. It also helped that Hartzell was a bishop and had wide respect from the veterans of the abolitionist movement. During the Civil War Hartzell and his New Orleans church remained solidly aligned with the Northern Methodists and the Union antislavery cause. Hartzell was not in lockstep with Rust on the topic of Black schools.

During his visit to Austin, Hartzell was impressed with the Richardsons' efforts and pledged he would find financial help but it would take time. Two years after his visit to Austin, Hartzell succeeded Rust as president of the Methodist Freedmen's Aid Society.

Caroline Richardson returned to Texas in the fall of 1879, bringing with her Emma, now sixteen, and the Richardsons' youngest son, nineteen-year-old Mercein. Two other sons remained in Minnesota farming and going to school. "My wife had succeeded in closing out our affairs in Minnesota so we had torn up the bridges behind us and our work for the future was in Texas."[30]

Her return marked a crucial turning point for the school.

~ 21 ~

THE GILLETTE MANSION

A man is measured by his mind, and not by his sinewy arms;
The man with a mind will be on top, in the city or on the farm.

JOHN MASON BREWER | 1922

The Richardson household in Austin had grown to seven when Clara's sister, Jennie Milne, joined them as housekeeper.[1] The household was soon eight; Clara was pregnant, with her baby expected in early 1880. The family had outgrown their living quarters.

George discovered a house they could rent from the estate of Charles Gillette, an Episcopal priest who founded St. David's Episcopal Church in Austin.[2] The congregation was founded before the Civil War primarily with Northern immigrants to Texas and Gillette remained adamantly pro-Union. After refusing his bishop's order to recite a prayer for the victory of the Confederate Army, Gillette was forced to resign in 1864. His congregation feared for his life, and so Gillette abandoned his Austin house and moved to Ohio, never to return.

After the war, Gillette became the first the secretary and general agent of the Commission of Home Missions to Colored People—the Episcopal Church's organization paralleling the work of Rust's Methodist Freedmen's Society. Gillette raised funds to build Black schools in Maryland, Virginia, and the Carolinas—bastions of the upper-crust white Episcopal Church. Gillette died suddenly in March 1869.

Gillette's Austin home remained empty, and his family would not allow it to be occupied by the Texas Episcopal diocese. Many in Austin thought it was haunted by Gillette's ghost. As George Richardson wrote in his journal, "The stories of strange sights and sounds spread like smallpox among the white and colored people of Austin, and the house was abandoned."

The house was large—eight rooms—and built of concrete and brick. Gillette designed it for a seminary, with the lower floors for classrooms, and the upper floor for living quarters for his family. George found its size and antislavery pedigree perfect for his school. Gillette's family agreed and rented him the house for fifteen dollars a month. "We dignified it with the name Gillette Mansion, which the new name relieved it of some of its odium," George wrote.[3]

The Richardsons no longer needed to rent church Sunday school rooms at Wesley Church. Gillette's house became the first building solely dedicated to the school that would become Samuel Huston College, and later Huston-Tillotson University. The Richardsons occupied "Gillette Mansion" for the next five years.

An accident at Gillette Mansion forever haunted Owen and Clara.[4] In December 1879, while Owen was away from the house shopping for winter clothes, Clara slipped on the icy porch and hit her head. She was pregnant and near term. George rushed to help her. The injured Clara was carried inside, and Caroline cared for her until she recovered from what was probably a concussion.

Clara gave birth early, with Caroline serving as midwife to the birth of her first grandchild, Carrie Mary. The baby was born with severe disabilities, which Owen blamed—fairly or unfairly—on the fall, and on the school. "On January 17, 1880 our daughter was born, defective of sight and nerve control of her hands. She never walked until she was three years old. Her affliction was the greatest payment that we made that the West Texas Conference School should become a college," Owen wrote.

As she grew, Carrie's mental disabilities became more evident. But her grandfather, George, remained optimistic. While on his circuit visiting churches in the Hill Country, George wrote to Owen, "I think she will come out all right." In another letter to Clara, he wrote: "I am very glad baby Carrie has found out she has got some legs and can use them."

Sadly, little else is written about Carrie in the surviving letters or memoirs. Carrie died in 1920, at age forty. What little can be gleaned is she was institutionalized as an adult with physical and learning disabilities. Her father outlived her. Owen made no mention of his daughter's death in his memoir written seventeen years after her passing. He and Clara had no other children.

><><

George and his friend, Black pastor Mack Henson, were elected as alternate delegates representing Texas to the 1880 Methodist national convention in

Cincinnati.[5] They went north with a singular goal: "an opportunity to help the school by explaining our situation to the different officers of the Freed-man's Aid Society."

The Methodist national convention, or General Conference as it was called, lasted a month in Cincinnati, and George lodged in a boardinghouse. That he and Henson were alternates, and not delegates, worked to their advantage; they were not tied down to daily floor sessions or committee meetings but could work the rooms and make their case for supporting the Black school in Austin.

George wrote that he held "long talks" with Rust and Hartzell, and others who were committed to cause of education for the formerly enslaved. "I think I impressed them with the importance of our school at the Capital of the State of Texas."[6] Rust's opposition to the Austin school began to melt.

George was so single-minded at the conference that he forgot to write home on the occasion of his marriage anniversary. His silence elicited a sharp rebuke from Caroline: "Have you remembered that this is the anniversary of our marriage, or have you been so busy listening to the great celebrities that you have forgotten about it?" Caroline wrote. "I have written twice a week except once when I was so unwell that I had to be excused."[7]

She lightened up at the end of her letter, relaying news about their grand-daughter: "Monday Morn Baby Carrie's four month old today, her Mama has just weighed her. She weighs 15 lbs, and she is just so precious as ever."

A few weeks after the close of the Cincinnati Methodist conference, Rust visited Austin and brought with him a check for one hundred dollars. To the Richardsons it was a fortune, and more importantly a vote of confidence.[8]

Rust also brought major news: Samuel Huston of Marengo, Iowa, a Meth-odist abolitionist, pledged the staggering sum of $10,000 for the Austin school (Owen put the donation at $12,000, while another historian puts it at $9,000).[9] In today's dollars, the pledge would be worth more than $200,000.

The school was immediately named for Samuel Huston, about whom little else in known. In the years ahead, the Texans pronounced his name "Houston," probably mixing up Iowa's "Samuel Huston" with the legendary Texas figure whose named was spelled differently and who opposed Southern secession but was not an abolitionist.

On his inspection visit, Rust pronounced as inadequate the six lots George had bought for the school on the eastern edge of Austin. Rust's conclusion was unfortunate because the lots George bought were in a beautiful location and larger than where the school ended up. Rust probably considered it too far on the outskirts of Austin. The lots are now Zaragoza Park in the heart of an Austin multi-ethnic neighborhood.

Rust told George to sell the lots, and then Rust set about to find a better location for the school. George was in no position to argue. Rust purchased five acres "which was centrally located for the colored population of Austin," George recorded in his journal. Owen put in his memoir that the land cost $1,500, purchased from a Black family pleased to have it devoted to a school. The site became the permanent home of Samuel Huston College until the mid-twentieth century when it merged with nearby Tillotson College. The site purchased by Rust was below a hill, just east of what is now downtown.

Although Rust had come to the rescue, his friction with Owen still simmered. Soon after Rust departed, Owen resigned from the school he and his father had founded.[10] Whatever words were exchanged between Owen and Rust were not recorded. It might be that the price of Rust's support was Owen's ouster.

The elder Richardson put the best face on it that he could, writing in "Recollections of My Lifework" that Owen wanted to pastor a Black church. "I said to Bishop Haven I believed he would try his hand as Pastor of a colored congregation if he was needed."[11]

But Owen's conflict with Rust spilled forth onto the pages of George's journal. "My son Geo. O[wen] Richardson had put in four years trying to build up our conference school and had received but little support from the Freedman's Aid Society. It had taken everything the school could pay and everything I could spare from the income of my district to keep the school going. He felt that his work was not appreciated, and resigned."

Owen was assigned to Ebenezer Methodist Church in Marshall, the town of Wiley College, hundreds of miles from Austin. Clara was given a faculty position at Wiley. "My son was on the ground just as soon as he could possibly move," George wrote.[12] If anyone saw the irony of Owen's new assignment given his previous objections to Wiley being the favored location for Methodist largesse, no one mentioned it in their memoirs.

Owen's pastorate in Marshall was brief and unhappy. He dealt ineptly with Black resentments that a white pastor had been assigned to what was becoming a prestigious post among African American pastors. Owen did not have the deft touch of his father and little talent for maneuvering through conflict. His father later wrote that his son was heavy-handed. Both George and Rust visited Marshall offering Owen encouragement and advice, but to little effect. "My pastorate of Ebenezer church was very arduous," Owen later wrote.[13] Within a year, Owen was back in Austin as president of the family school and would henceforth be listed as the first president of Samuel Huston College.[14]

"The welcome we received in Austin was hearty," Owen recalled in his memoir.[15] The school was finally on a solid financial footing with "all the business tangles straightened." Joseph Hartzell, now head of the Freedmen's Society, visited the school and was considerably more encouraging than Rust. Hartzell assured the Richardsons of the continuing support of the Freedmen's Aid Bureau, though funds from the Huston estate were now tangled up in a probate dispute. In the summer, Owen rode his father's circuit for a few weeks so his father could take a break.

In June 1882, one year after his return to Austin, Owen quit the school again, this time with the stated purpose of finishing his oft-delayed college degree.[16] His younger brother, David—my great-grandfather—was at Carleton College in Northfield, Minnesota. Mercein had also departed. Their younger sister, Emma, was soon to start at Hamline University in St. Paul. Owen left Austin for Evanston, Illinois, to enroll in the Methodist Garrett Biblical Institute (later renamed the Garrett-Evangelical Theological Seminary). Owen's wife, Clara, and their baby daughter stayed behind in Austin.

Caroline was appointed acting president of Samuel Huston College.[17] She would bear the college on her shoulders longer than her son, and with more skill and steadiness. But her name has never appeared on the roster of presidents.

✍ 22 ✍

ALLEYTON

Deliver my soul from the wicked.

PSALM 17: 13 | KING JAMES VERSION

While Caroline managed the school in Austin, George traveled through his enormous Texas circuit teaching and organizing Methodist Black churches. His journal listed fifteen settlements in his territory, stretched over hundreds of square miles.[1] His circuit was geographically larger than all of his previous circuits in Minnesota, Wisconsin, and Illinois combined.

"Much of this District lay in the flat unhealthy portion of Texas," he wrote. "I was obliged to carry medicine with me all the time, and even with that precaution I did not avoid serious spells of sickness."[2]

He rode by horse and wagon—or "hack" as he called it—and his travels were not without mishaps. One of his two horses died while on the road. George somehow reached all of his appointed rounds with the surviving horse pulling his wagon full of books and provisions along the rutted and dusty roads.

Although he was white, George Richardson felt accepted by the Black Methodists he served. "They had come to regard me as their personal friend." Writing in his journal from the distance of three decades, he remembered that this friendship was warmly mutual. It is worth noting that George Richardson almost never wrote kindly about white preachers, considering many of them drunkards, bigots, fools, or thieves. His few exceptions among the white pastors were Chauncey Hobart, a handful of Army chaplains from his Civil War days, and the Presbyterian pastor who buried his infant daughter.

By 1882, George had been in Texas for seven years and presiding elder for six of those years in his Black district—a long tenure by Methodist standards in a church system accustomed to moving preachers every two or three years. He considered 1882 his best year yet.[3]

The annual Methodist conference in December was more like a rally than a church meeting. Bishop Thomas Bowman addressed the crowd, giving a "deeply emotional" sermon so much so that "it was difficult to suppress the shouts of the congregation so that he could proceed." George wrote that the conference adjourned with the determination to make 1883 "the best year ever known." To read George's words more than a century later is to hear him at his prime, filled with the spirit, and bathing joyfully in his work.

But he was still in the Texas of the post-Civil War Reconstruction era. White resentment seethed, and Blacks did their best to survive in an environment barely removed from slavery. George was living and working on the edge of a volcano—and it was hard to keep preachers in place before they gave up or were harassed into leaving—or worse. On one of his tours of his churches, George confided to Owen about his frustrations. "I am very much distressed over the work on this circuit," he wrote in a letter to his son.[4] "If I can keep my man here I can do them some good, and the light will slowly reach them."

His own life would soon be in danger.

In the summer of 1883, George ventured onto the trail to visit Hallettsville, a small Black settlement in the densely wooded flatlands about 120 hundred miles southeast of Austin.[5] "The membership was but a little over 100, and all poor," George recalled. Blacks in Hallettsville were barely surviving. Some from the town had emigrated to Liberia, the American Black colony in Africa. Many had returned to the United States and ended up destitute in New York. Even so, residents of Hallettsville continued to apply to the American Colonization Society for assistance in getting to Liberia.[6]

The Black Methodist congregation's small wooden church had been destroyed in a windstorm, and George secured a donation to have it rebuilt.[7] He went to the town to supervise reconstruction and boost the congregation's morale. He camped next to the construction project for a month, well into October, until the new church was finished. "On dedication day we had an immense crowd," he wrote. "It was a day of victory. That small membership, in their deep poverty, had the best church in the District except one."[8]

As he was about to depart Hallettsville, word came that the white residents of Boxville, about twenty miles away (renamed "Speaks" in the twentieth century), had taken up arms because of a rumored "nigger rising." Their paranoia was sparked when a white man had murdered a Black man, and the white murderer had gone unpunished. The whites feared that Blacks would seek their own frontier justice—as most certainly the whites would have done to Blacks if the situation were reversed.

The whites barricaded their women and children in the post office expecting an uprising at any moment. Meanwhile, white vigilantes roamed the Black settlements searching their cabins for guns. A few Black men had been arrested and taken to Boxville and interrogated.

There was one more sobering development: the whites blamed the Methodist circuit preacher—George Richardson—for stirring up the Blacks. "Somebody had been making the Negroes believe that they had a right to take care of themselves. Who could it be that put these unsafe aspirations in the heads of the Negroes!" George wrote years later in the journal. "There was that white Presiding Elder who had been teaching the Negroes that they ought to educate themselves and their children if they ever expected to be anybody."[9]

There was no uprising. Blacks were terrified. As the storm gathered, George wrote to his daughter-in-law Clara, and that letter survives.[10] "Threats were made to hang me if I came into that country again. The colored people were all called before the 'Squire' and examined one by one," he wrote. "To hold still and not turn and run, when I was within 20 miles of the field of strife, was the part that tried my nerve—I confess I was nervous some."

As George was about to leave Hallettsville, he was warned that a white posse was searching for him so "that I ought to be put out of the way."[11] Jackson Caesar, one of the Black pastors in the area, overheard a few whites talking about how to "put that white Presiding Elder where he won't make us any more trouble." The whites knew George's whereabouts because he had written ahead to Pastor Caesar, and the white postmaster had read his mail. The white postmaster was said to even be leading the posse. Pastor Caesar somehow evaded the whites to send a warning to George that he needed to hide. "I heeded his warning and saved my life."

Compounding his fright, George had recently visited with one of his pastors who was sick and had "blotches." As he was about to leave Hallettsville, the town marshal intercepted him and told him he had been exposed to smallpox. The marshal ordered George to leave town immediately. "I felt sure that the people who were seeking my life would attack me while I remained at the county seat, but I knew that they might have someone watching me when I was leaving town, and this would a good opportunity for them to come upon me when I was alone and carry out their murderous purpose."

George's route back to Austin was likely blocked, so he hid along the banks of Texas's Colorado River near the small Black settlement at Alleyton at the crossroads of what had been a Confederate Army encampment. He was still about one hundred miles from his home base in Austin.

Near Alleyton, the river is wide and shallow, meandering through thickly wooded flatlands. George slipped into the woods near the riverbank and was instantly invisible only ten feet from the road. "I stopped in an out of the way place, without a human being nearer than five miles that I knew of," he wrote in his journal. He described his hideout as in the "thick timber and brush in the river bottom."

He slept inside his wagon. "These were lonesome days." He worried that the white vigilantes would find him or that he might die of smallpox alone in the woods. "The prospect of being sick with a loathsome disease away from any human help was not comforting," he wrote. "When I lay down in my hack for the night, a little tremor came over me. 'I am in the hands of my enemies, and I may not see the light again.'"

"Just then the passage came to my mind as forcibly as though spoken with an audible voice 'The angel of the Lord [en]campeth round about them that fear him and delivereth them.' I said to myself if that if the angel of the Lord camps here I am safe."

As his exile stretched into November, a Black postal courier—his name is lost—brought messages to his hideout in the woods. The postal worker had scars on his face from smallpox, and so was immune from infection. He and George shared crackers and coffee each time they met. "He passed my camp every day, about noon, and every day I had lunch for him." His new friend promised to fetch a nurse if he got sick and took his letters each day. Among the most touching is a letter George penned to Caroline, which years later he copied into "Recollections of My Lifework":[12]

> I had a good breakfast this morning—sat down on the ground to eat
> with my heart full of thankfulness, and thanked the Lord not only for the
> comforts, but the luxuries of life—potatoes and bacon from Kansas—Java
> coffee—Cuban sugar—Illinois bread—New York cheese—Texas grapes and
> Michigan apples—Surely thou preparest a table before me in the presence
> of my enemies—my cup runneth over. After eating I got up into the hack
> and read the 23d Psalm. Just as I had finished that, a little breath of wind
> turned the leaves of my Bible, and opened to the 17th Psalm, which I read

through very carefully—and felt great comfort while reading, and great satisfaction in committing my ways to the Lord in prayer.

In the King James Bible that George read, the psalm declares God will protect the righteous from their enemies who surround them: "Keep me as the apple of the eye, hide me under the shadow of thy wings; From the wicked that oppress me, *from* my deadly enemies *who* compass me about."[13]

Ten days into hiding, the postal carrier brought word to George that there was no smallpox outbreak, and the white vigilantes had given up looking for him. George emerged from his hideout and made his way back to Austin, doubly relieved at escaping the mob and not having the deadly disease. George gave Boxville a wide berth on his way home and was never to return.

Two months after his return to Austin, George was reassigned to the San Antonio district. Why he was reassigned is not stated in the journal but no doubt his narrow escape and the threats to his life figured into the decision. If George argued with the transfer, he did not record it. Indeed, George was delighted to move to San Antonio where he had previously served. "The preachers and people were glad to see me back."[14]

The congregations in George's new district spanned another enormous Texas territory, from Mount Pleasant in East Texas, south to Corpus Christi on the Gulf of Mexico, and west to San Antonio. Sadly, word came that Pastor Caesar, whose warning of the vigilantes had saved George's life, had died shortly after George was transferred.

He was soon back on the road. Today much of the territory he covered by horse and wagon is a vast sea of oil derricks, pumpjacks, and giant twirling windmill generators.[15] In George's time, he would have traveled across an empty and arid brown landscape, rarely seeing another human being until he got to the next town. In a letter to Clara, he wrote of the loneliness of his life as a traveling preacher: "This would be lonesome work for me if I was not in constant communication with my wife and children. But when I know and feel every one of my children are watching the progress of my work with deep and prayerful interest it lightens the burdens and cheers me on."[16]

In time, two Black pastors who had helped restart the school in Austin and with whom he was close, Mack Henson, and Charles Madison, would take the leadership positions in the vast territory that George served. George wrote with pride that they were "the strongest preachers in the conference."[17]

><><

Visitors from the North to the Austin school were common by the mid-1880s, but they were not always welcome among those who had labored in the fields of emancipation for decades. One such visit from a northern Methodist matron sparked a breach between the George Richardson and his longtime mentor Chauncey Hobart.[18]

The conflict began when a Mrs. Lathrop came to Texas on a brief lecture tour. She was there just long enough to consider herself an expert and conclude that Methodist efforts to build schools for Black people were futile. She told Hobart that emancipation "was a great mistake" because Blacks "were fast degenerating into barbarism and heathenism." Or at least, that is the version of her report that came back to George Richardson.

Whatever she said, her report shocked Hobart, who wrote a letter to George with a series of questions including: "Am I right in supposing there is not an individual among them [Blacks] twenty years old that has not forfeited his or her claim to a life of virtue?" Was Mrs. Lathrop right? Were Blacks depraved immoral savages and emancipation a mistake?

George was furious—and incredulous at Hobart's about-face on the cause to which he'd dedicated his life and family. Hobart was on the receiving end of a five-page reply from his former protégé: "You were my friend from the first of our acquaintance," George opened his letter, "and when I was down in my finances and health, your friendship never wavered. I owe more to you than to any other human being that I had strength to rally again."

Then George blasted Northerners who came south on a "flying trip" and presumed to understand "the situation perfectly." Mrs. Lathrop had stayed only with aristocratic white families, "and such attention seemed to turn her brain." He felt that she'd renounced her own previous abolitionist position and "now felt that the sympathy was due the dominant race." He told Hobart that he knew more about the Black people of Texas than did Mrs. Lathrop—and he certainly knew more than any white visitor from Minnesota. "It may be largely in my imagination, but I do imagine that I have a stronger hold of the ministry and membership in the bounds of this conf. than I ever had of any people before."

George also told Hobart that his daughter-in-law, Clara, had heard one of Mrs. Lathrop's lectures. "My little gritty daughter-in-law felt that it was an outrage to let such sentiments go unrebuked, and before she knew it she was on her feet and her tongue was going as though it was loose at both ends. She told them that she had been in the South 8 years, and most of the time had worked for the colored people, and had failed to discover the marks of degeneracy her sister [Mrs. Lathrop] had discovered in a few days."

George complained that Hobart had only heard Mrs. Lathrop's viewpoint and then proceeded to give him a lesson on the injustice of slave owners and marriage laws. If Hobart was concerned with the sexual "morals" of the ex-slaves, he should remember that the slave owners did not allow legal marriage among the enslaved people they owned. "There was no marriage law," George told him. "The breeding of slaves was the most profitable part of the business in the border states. There was no sense of shame and no consciousness of crime in doing that which was legitimate and necessary to the whole system."

With emancipation, George wrote, the ex-slaves could now marry. "History does not record the instance when God has done so much for any people as he has done for this people, and the results are in proportion to the labor bestowed."

George told Hobart that, unlike Mrs. Lathrop, he had gotten to know many Black parents, and they were as devoted to the moral upbringing of their children as anyone else. He reminded Hobart that moral virtue among whites was just as questionable. "There are places in Tex—and I presume it is the same in other states—where moral insensibility still hangs around like your old winter."

As for Mrs. Lathrop, George wrote: "Please don't send sister Lathrop to lecture for the Colored people—some of them are ahead of her."

Though it was an angry letter, George also gave a glimpse into his own motivations for working with Blacks. George told Hobart that he had found fulfillment working with Blacks in Texas like he had never felt working in the white settlements of Minnesota. His postwar illness and depression were gone. "I am stronger now than I was ten years ago," he wrote. "I don't know of any richer harvest field for me than I am in now, and I am willing to let the Lord and the colored people of the South have the balance of my life; for this part of my life is so much clear gain."

How Hobart reacted to this letter is not known. Curiously, George did not record the incident in his journal. But he copied his letter into empty pages in Caroline's diary. The fact that George kept a copy of his letter to his former mentor suggests the breach was irreparable.

><><><

Not long after my father died in 2004, Lori and I drove the route of George Richardson's enormous Texas circuit south of Austin.

My ancestor traveled muddy roads by horse and wagon. We drove on paved highways and interstate freeways in a rental car.

His maps were poor, and he needed guides. We used a GPS device triangulating satellites orbiting the earth.

He slept on the ground under his wagon—the wood slats and an oilskin his only protection from rain. We stayed in hotels and the homes of friends.

He ate dry biscuits and drank water. We ate barbecue and drank beer.

We continued south on the highway, roughly parallel to the road George would have traveled, to the town of Luling, where the annual "Watermelon Thump" was in full swing—a county fair and summer harvest festival rolled into one. A sign at a local motel said, "Welcome Thumpers." We stopped for barbecue. The First Methodist Church, a 1960s-era building, is located near the center of town, while newer churches are located farther out. The main street of Luling is along an east-west railroad spur. We turned east onto Interstate 10.

Flatonia was our next stop, a town that has prided itself on maintaining its nineteenth-century flavor and buildings. We stopped in the city museum and inquired if they knew where the "colored" Methodist church might be, and we were pointed to the right place. We found the church, although the original building was long ago replaced by a small modern structure. We also found the stately white Methodist church, built in the 1880s. We cruised around Flatonia and found more buildings from that era, including the newspaper and an old hotel. It was easy to picture George Richardson rolling into town in his horse and wagon.

A few miles away we drove along the Colorado River near where George hid when vigilantes sought to kill him. The river is a wide, shallow stream meandering through thickly wooded flatlands. We parked our car and poked our way into the woods, trying to imagine what his hideout would have looked like. The woods are still thick enough that a person could remain invisible only a few steps from the road.

Back in the safety of our car, we came to Alleyton, on the eastern boundary of George's circuit. Of all the places we visited, Alleyton is probably the least changed from George's time. It is a tiny Black settlement with gravel roads and small houses. There are two small churches—both Baptist—in the center of Alleyton. Electrical lines and automobiles were all that distinguished it as a modern town. A historical marker nearby marks Alleyton's importance as a supply and munitions depot for the Confederate Army. No mention is made on the historical marker of who lived here, or how Blacks fared during the war or Reconstruction.

We did not see people—they were indoors because of thunderstorms. Perhaps some of the residents were descendants of those George served. I was tempted to knock on a few doors, but it was beginning to pour, and I could hear thunder rolling in not far away. We headed for the interstate.

⟶ 23 ⟵

CAROLINE

When you're ready for your relatives, the true grandmother will appear.

JAMES D. HOUSTON | *BIRD OF ANOTHER HEAVEN*, 2007

Caroline Fay Richardson had fended for herself most of her adult life, but in all that time she had never kept a diary. In her late fifties, she resolved to begin recording the events of her life, writing in her diary at least once a year on her birthday.

On her fifty-eighth birthday—October 4, 1883—Caroline made her first entry. "I really have no time to write, but then I have determined that I will occasionally snatch a little time from my household duties and domestic cares to scratch in this book," she wrote.[1]

Her time was taken up not just by "domestic cares." She was serving as acting president of the Samuel Huston College so that her oldest son, Owen, could finish his college education and her husband tend to the churches in his sprawling circuit. Caroline recorded her health was good and that her sons were out of her household. Only her youngest, Emma, was still at home with her in Austin.

Caroline had come a very long way in the decades since taking a riverboat with her new husband up the Mississippi River into the Midwestern frontier. She confided to her diary that she had learned many lessons over many years, "some vexing and annoying, some heart-rending and saddening—other times disappointing and grieved over the short comings of those that we had thought could be depended upon."

When I began retracing my great-great-grandfather's steps, I had no idea that my great-great-grandmother had kept a diary. There was never hint from any of my relatives that such a book existed.

We found it by accident.

A few years ago, Lori and I were visiting my Aunt Madge—my father's sister—who was living in an assisted living home in Redding, California, about three hours north of our home in Sacramento. She was a collector of family memorabilia, and her house was filled with papers, binders, nineteenth-century trunks, and boxloads of letters from family members dating back generations.

She had done considerable research into our family genealogy, particularly the family of George Richardson. I picked her brain many times and told her of my travels, phoning her at each stop. But she never mentioned Caroline's diary. With her health failing, she told me there were other documents in her house but wasn't sure where they were. On this particular visit, I asked her if I could go look for them. She agreed and gave us the keys to her house.

Moments after walking through the front door, we looked up at the stairwell and it was covered with books and papers on each step. Lori immediately spotted a large black hardbound notebook in the stacks on the stairs. The corners were frayed, revealing the thin brown wood of its cover.

"What's this?" Lori said, picking it up.

When we opened it, we discovered it was Caroline's diary. It felt like Caroline was saying from the beyond the grave: "If you are going to write my husband's story you had better get my story in there, too." But her book was much more than a diary. Where George recorded the events of his life, Caroline recorded the words of her heart and her hard-won wisdom. After reading and absorbing her book several times, I've come to think of her as my "true grandmother."

In her first entry, Caroline expressed regret in not having written in diary until she was approaching old age. "I have often wished that I had occasionally at least put down the record of events as the years were passing. But my married life has been so full of labor and cares that it did not seem possible to find time to write in this or my old diary that I used often to talk till I changed from Miss to Mrs."[2]

The "old diary" of her youth was long lost.

In her new diary, Caroline looked back on her early years of marriage to the man she called an "itinerant." She reflected on how disoriented she had felt moving to the frontier of Minnesota. "It was all new and strange to me," she wrote.[3]

Yet she could confidently claim she was "strengthened" by her travels and "firmly believe that I made some advancement in a religious life." Caroline proclaimed she was willing to bear George's absences because their separation was the price of the Lord's work. Whether she fully realized it or not, she had grown in stature not only within her family but also among a widening circle of admirers and supporters, both white and Black. She had run households and schools and was the pillar of strength for everyone around her.

Caroline wrote that her husband was "kind and loving" and "invested our home with a halo." But she also recalled that when their first son was born, George was away on church business. He was gone a lot.

While writing her birthday diary entry for 1883, her husband was away once again.[4] She had received a letter that day from George containing a twenty-dollar bill. She enjoyed a birthday dinner cooked by Hamile, who Caroline described as one of her "sisters." Hamile was probably an African American woman working at the school. Caroline wrote that her birthday meal was "abundant," and mentioned that she had gone to the funeral for "Carrie A.," the daughter of one of her friends. She closed the diary entry with a prayer: "Blest Comforter—seek those sad, weary mourning hearts tonight. The soothing balm must come from thee."

She also made diary entries on her husband's birthdays. On November 26, 1883, Caroline wrote: "Yesterday was my husband's birthday—fifty-nine years old—once I thought when a person had entered their sixtieth year they were quite old. But I have been gradually outgrowing that idea for some years. I know he is gray and bears some other marks that youth has passed away—but I never think of him as old without a special effort."[5]

Caroline's hair was thinner and cut shorter than it had been in her youth, but she reflected that her family had a "quite remarkable" ability to retain their youthful looks and vigor. She noted her husband's family was similarly long-lived and vital. "I am thankful my husband is strong enough to labor on in the Master's great harvest field."

But she was beginning to feel her age. "Time has dealt very gently with me. Tis true I am sometimes rheumatic and have lost most of my teeth. Through the skill of the dentist my looks have not suffered as much as my feelings. I was always slow eating—now I am slower."

George was often away on his birthday. "Is it wrong of me," she wrote in 1886, "to hope that his labors will be so arranged that he can have some comfort of his home?"[6] She was lonely. "I'm afraid I shall grow old if I have to live so far from my children."

Caroline also remembered the fright she felt when her husband—whom she referred to as "Mr. R"—was hiding from white vigilantes. "The Lord not only preserved my husband from the fury of the rain and hail, but on one occasion from the fury of an <u>excited mob</u>."⁷ The underlines in her diary are hers.

She recounted how "a gang of men went out on the road Mr. R. would have come, with ropes to hang him." Caroline remembered the letter she received from his hideout, and how Psalm 17 had comforted him in worst hours of fear. "He says the impression was that every word was written for him, and for that occasion. His prayer was a talk with an almost visible Savior. The angel of the Lord <u>did camp</u> round about him that night, and he slept sweetly and safely."

Unlike her husband with his prolific pen, Caroline found it hard to write about herself. She was far more private. Indeed, during the Civil War, George nagged her to write him more often. But whatever she lacked in prose she made up for in poetry. With her verse she gave us a glimpse into her heart—and her heartaches.

"I have long contemplated copying some of my fugitive verses in this book, not because I suspect them of possessing any great merit. But they are the creatures of my imagination and consequently I have quite a strong affection for them."⁸

She filled her pages with poems, copied from scraps of paper (now lost), the verses she had written decades before her marriage. She still had the poems written in her teens and twenties from the 1840s, and signed with her maiden name, Fay, as she did with this one from 1844:

> Gentle songster of the spring
> Let me hear those notes again
> Come and sit in the old oak tree
> And warble out that tone to me.⁹

A year later, when she was twenty years old, Caroline wrote another poem titled "Kindness."¹⁰ She copied it into her diary three decades after writing it, dating it October 4, 1845:

> 'Speak kindly' whether friend or foe
> Not asking who they be
> It is enough for thee to know
> They need thy sympathy

Then freely give it unto all
Wherever you may be
Thy Father's bounties never cease
But still descend on thee.

Another poem recorded in her diary, titled "A Dream," was written in May 1862 in the depths of the Civil War.[11] Her words spoke of how she missed the tenderness of her late father, but also hinted at her loneliness during her husband's absences.

My Father's face was smiling, and always on me shone.
Only my would be lover, sought our quiet home.
My heart was well nigh breaking, I woke in faltering tone.
I can never bring a shadow, upon my early home.
The hum of infant voices, broke strangely on my ear.
My husband bending o'er me said, take the baby dear.

Her poems and diary entries are reminders that Caroline lived in a world where death was an ever-present, uninvited guest. Death came from war, disease, accidents, vigilantes, bandits, and bad luck. In October 1861, her younger sister, Eliza, died at the age of thirty-two, leaving behind a husband and two young sons. Caroline pasted into her notebook a note that Eliza had sent her in 1845 when Eliza was fifteen years old.[12] Caroline called it one of the "little epigrams" the two sisters wrote for each other when they were young.

My sister there hast cheered full many an hour
When sickness o'er me threw her dreaded shower
Then there rejoiced with spirit, glad and free
Thy kindness all is cherished in my heart
That kindness felt and not portrayed by art.

She shared with her Austin students another of her youthful poems, "Life A Dream": "This life is all an empty dream; that shortly will be o'er." Her poem, however, sounded similar to a popular Charles Wesley hymn, "Come, Let Us Anew Our Journey Pursue," and her students pointed it out.[13]

"Some of the students disputed the originality of my compositions," she wrote in her diary. In her defense, she gave them another of her poems.

"The following feeble effort silenced them so that I never heard any more of their fault finding."

The poem that silenced them was about a "stormy night."

> I sat me down this stormy night
> To write a composition,
> My mind is gloomy as the night
> I have no disposition.

She also used her poetry to express her politics (a topic her husband avoided in his journal). In a poem titled "A Prayer," she castigated President Andrew Johnson as a "traitor" for his reversal of Lincoln's commitment to emancipation.[14]

> He, who should guard our ship of state
> Is kneeling at the Southerners gate,
> Kneeling, to idols made with hands,
> Bartering freedoms glorious lands,
> This hand upraised with tyrants rod.
> . . .
> "He whose eye doth never sleep,
> Bids you labor, watch and weep.
> And with strong untiring hands
> Stay the traitor of our land.

She also wrote an ode to abolitionist Owen Lovejoy after his death in 1864:[15]

> Though no flag is draped above him
> And no muffled drum is heard
> He has fought as truly—bravely
> As one who bears a sword.

Caroline also wrote passionately about the evils of slavery and racism. Her commitment to emancipation transcended politics—for her, it was a religious cause. As a young wife—pregnant with her first child—she had helped her husband spirit an enslaved young woman to freedom. Her commitment to emancipation did not end with the Civil War. As the acting president of Samuel Huston College, what had begun as an abstract principle in her youth—emancipation—was now fully her life's work. Only her children mattered more to her.

Caroline wrote a remarkable essay in her diary about the white caste system of the South.[16] She titled it "The Time of The Exodus"—a reference to Moses leading the Hebrew slaves out of bondage in Egypt. For her, the emancipation of African Americans was the same holy cause. Her hand-written essay is undated, but judging by its placement in her diary, it was probably written in 1886.

Her perspective on race appears more nuanced than that of her husband, reflecting her depth of understanding of the systematic racial politics of Texas and the economics of sharecropping. She castigated Texas legislators for allowing the planter class to keep the formerly enslaved in a state of permanent "serfdom very little better than the former bondage." She protested that Blacks were blocked from buying land in choice places. In those locales where Blacks could purchase land, they were gouged with usurious interest rates—24 percent—twice the interest rate on mortgages for whites.

"And from all we can gather," Caroline wrote, "this harsh and oppressive treatment has not been haphazard or isolated character, but the result of a deep laid scheme. The plan seems to have been so to impoverish their laborers as to make them helplessly dependent, to check by tyrannical repression the normal impulse of advance, to arrest the people through their elementary needs at a capriciously chosen point in their progress, and to fix them in it."

Caroline maintained that white claims of Black laziness were nothing but ruses to justify racial oppression. She noted that Blacks were prosperous in those places where they had been able to purchase fertile farmland. Yet even in those locales Blacks were subject to endless intimidation and "have no security that their cows, horses or sheep" would be safe from stealing by whites. The truth was that African Americans could not expect white lawmen to help them when whites robbed them.

She pointed to the absurdities of the racial caste system. White women could travel on the railroad in first class with Black servants, but white men could not travel in first class with their Black servants. Blacks traveling on their own were confined to steerage.

And those were just the preliminaries in her essay. The political issue that most vexed her was an 1879 Texas law ending public expenditures on the education of Black children.[17] "It is easy to see that these articles are legal descendants of the old slave code, in which the child was to remain in the condition of the mother."

Caroline concluded her essay expressing her outrage that Black women had no legal rights—even if raped. "A colored woman can gain no legal redress for any outrage where a white man is concerned. She has no character before the law and no rights that a white man can be compelled to respect. But let a colored man be guilty of the same crime for which his sister can get no redress, if his victim is white there will be no waiting for the slow process of law in case, an outraged community will execute him without judge or jury."[18]

><><

While serving as the acting president of Samuel Huston College, Caroline carried a full teaching load and managed the large household at Gillette Mansion. She hosted a revolving cast of family members and guests. Living under her roof were her husband (when he wasn't out riding his circuit), daughter Emma, and Jennie Milne, the sister of her daughter-in-law Clara. Richard Rust and Joseph Hartzell came and went. By now, Clara and her daughter, Carrie, had departed for Evanston to be with Owen while he finished his studies. Caroline was the glue holding everything together.

The family nearly dissolved in 1881 with a crisis involving Emma, who was then eighteen years old.[19] What exactly happened is not clear—no one recorded the details in any diaries, letters, or memoirs that can be found. All that George wrote is that Emma was "an invalid." To help her recover, George took Emma and Caroline on a meandering camping trip of six weeks south to Luling, and then northward to the headwaters of Texas's Colorado River in the hills near Lubbock, about four hundred miles from Austin.

"A trip of six weeks was a benefit to us all especially the invalid," George wrote.[20] But if Emma had a physical illness, why such an arduous trip could have helped her is not clear. Emma was already small and thin before whatever malady befell her.

Getting her out of Austin may have been the point.

According to my Aunt Madge, the story passed orally through the generations has it that Emma had fallen in love with one of the students at the school—a *Black* student. Whether true or just gossip can no longer be determined, though there is plausibility to the story. Although her parents were progressive for their time on racial issues, interracial romantic relationships were almost certainly beyond what they could accept—if only for the danger this could pose for Emma, the Black student, their families, and the continuing existence of the school. They were not naïve about the reality of the penalties for violating the racial caste system. A Black man discovered having sexual relations with a white woman likely would have been tortured, castrated, and lynched. Emma's life might also have been in danger, and certainly she and her family would have been forced to leave Texas. In the few letters of Emma's that can be found, she made no mention of a physical ailment in these years, nor of any romantic relationships.

What happened after the six-week trip, no one recorded in any of the letters or diaries known to exist. A year later, with school out for the summer, George took Emma on another long trip camping trip through the Texas Hill Country, this time accompanied by Clara and her two-year-old daughter, Carrie. "We were in no haste to get anywhere," he wrote.[21] The camping party slept on wooden pallets shoved underneath their carriage each night to protect them from rainstorms and the bugs crawling on the ground.

Caroline skipped the summer trip, instead going north to the Dakota Territory to visit son Mercein, who had begun farming on his own.

A few years later, with Emma's crisis apparently behind her, Caroline confided to her diary her anxiety about her daughter.[22] By this time, Emma had gone to Minnesota to be a student at Hamline University. Caroline suspected that her daughter would take a different path from the "natural duties" of womanhood—and that was fine with Caroline.

"Our daughter—our regular pet baby girl Emma—was 22 years old the 27th of last April," Caroline wrote. "What line of work Emma will take up is still among the things unknown. I am ready to concede for most of thoroughly good women the natural duties that come of love, and marriage, home-making, wifehood, and motherhood is woman's highest sphere." But, Caroline wrote, maybe not for Emma.

Caroline noted that Emma was still searching for her life path. "I would not for a moment detract anything from the grand-helpful-world-wide work accomplished by a few unmarried noble women," she wrote. "They were perhaps left . . . on purpose to do a work that had they been encumbered with house-hold cares, husband and children, they would never find time for. My precious Emma's future I place in the hands of 'Our Father' asking that she may be guided into the right path—and that her life may be eminently useful in whatever field her life-work may lie."

Emma remained unmarried throughout her life, though later in life she mentioned living with a woman named Louise. Was Emma gay? There are hints, but they are only hints.

She was not the only member of the family struggling with life's challenges in the early 1880s. Owen, the oldest, admitted in his memoir that he was a mediocre student at Garrett seminary. He complained that the other students were much younger—and sharper—than himself. "The youngsters learned more readily than I did."[23]

Owen flunked Greek, the curse of many a seminarian before and since. He was floundering emotionally and, most of all, missing his family. "I became much discouraged," he wrote. After the 1882 term ended, Owen returned to his mother's household in Austin. He was unsure whether to return to Garrett for another term. "My son was now wholly at sea," George wrote.[24] "He had severed his connection with our colored school at Austin, and as yet he had not found a situation where he could go on with his Education or ministerial work."

To clear the air, George invited Owen, Clara, and her sister, Jennie, to accompany him on a trip to visit one of his Black congregations, in Oakland, Texas, about one hundred miles southeast of Austin. They readily agreed to join him. On the trip, "we talked over the situation," George wrote.

They stayed with a Black family—and got another lesson in the risks of violating the racial rules in Texas. As Owen and Clara were walking home one evening from a church meeting, they were confronted by "a white man who considered it a crime for white folks to be entertained by colored people. The man declared he would kill them," George wrote. "He gathered up some stones or brickbats and followed them, but their colored friends just gathered around them and escorted them to their rooms."[25]

At the end of the trip, Owen agreed to return to Evanston to complete his studies. His wife and child stayed in Austin until he got settled in Evanston, and then they joined him. Owen was done in Austin.

〉✕✕✕〈

Caroline confided to her diary that she felt the stigma from whites because of her work with Blacks. She knew she would never fit into white society in Texas—and she didn't care. "Many of the most refined and educated ladies left their homes in the North, and went into the Towns and settlements in the South to teach the Negroes, when they knew they would be regarded by the Southern whites as more debased than the emancipated slaves."[26]

She also understood the stigma her husband faced.

"A goodly number of ministers left good positions in their own conferences to preach Christ to this class of the Lord's poor, with the full knowledge that they would be ostracized by Southern society. The prejudice against them was so strong that it became necessary very often to accept the hospitality of the Negro cabin rather than the comforts of Christian homes among the whites. My husband was among the first to face these obstacles and give himself to the work of elevating the Freedmen in Texas."

George, in fact, preferred the "Negro cabins."

Caroline wrote an essay that George later transcribed into her diary titled "Kind of Work and Remarkable Protection," about the challenges of educating Blacks in the South. The essay is undated but was probably written in 1883 after George had escaped from white vigilantes in the Hill Country.

Caroline made no mention of her own work, but indirectly explained her motives and those of other white women working among African Americans during the Reconstruction era. "The Negroes had been a race of slaves for 200 years," she began. "The war resulted in saving the Union and in emancipating four million of these human beings without preparing them for the responsibilities of freedom and citizenship."

Whites, she argued, bore a heavy responsibility for ensuring that the formerly enslaved had the tools and education to thrive in freedom. "They must be educated," Caroline wrote, "they must be taught purer morals, they must have broader and nobler ideas of religious obligations and religious life, or their presence as freemen would endanger all the institutions of civilization in the South. The Northern Army had freed them, and Northern philanthropy and Christianity must care for them.[Underlines hers]"

As George navigated his Texas circuit, he was increasingly alarmed about the flood of moonshine soaking the Black settlements.[27] Moonshining may seem an innocent vice in our age of opioids and methamphetamine, but in the nineteenth century, homemade booze was a lethal scourge of both white and African American rural communities. The sugar for illegal distilleries was abundantly available from the sugarcane fields of South Texas, and moonshining proved a ready source of income. Racial boundaries were permeable when it came to alcohol; whites were readily willing to buy white lightening from Black moonshiners.[28]

The cause of Temperance was not new to the Richardsons. The entire family had signed a "Family Pledge" on July 6, 1870: "We agree to abstain from the use of tobacco and all intoxicating liquors as a drink."

Meanwhile, the school in Austin was running out of money. Rust's promised benefactor, the estate of Samuel Huston of Iowa, still had not come forth with promised funds, and the teachers couldn't be paid. Classes were suspended in 1884, not to resume for another year.[29]

Without the school to manage, Caroline began accompanying George on his rounds in his district. He gave her a speaking role at "the most prominent hour of the Sabbath" during worship services. "Her themes were temperance and purity and improvement in homes," he wrote his "Recollections of My Lifework," underlining words for emphasis.[30] The work was exhilarating but exhausting; both Caroline and George became sick during one of their trips. Caroline fainted during a presentation and had to be helped to bed. Her illness hung on for several weeks.

Her health worried George. "Ma has been unwell for two or three days," he wrote Clara.[31] "She was a little better last night and gave her 'Home' lecture very much to the satisfaction of the good people of Browns Chapel. I think her talks are not lost." He also wrote to Owen, admonishing him to get his rest—advice he might well have given himself: "If you replenish the mind by exhausting the body you are destroying your ability to do good."[32]

In 1885 the Methodist Freedmen's Bureau leaders met in Austin with the goal of reopening Samuel Huston College. They had secured enough donations from the north to pay teachers, and part of the Samuel Huston bequest came through. Indeed, enough funds were raised to not only reopen the school but to begin laying the foundation for a permanent building. Caroline went back to work in the school in the fall term and was paid a salary for the first time in her life.[33]

✄

When the college was on summer break, Caroline returned to the road with George, lecturing about temperance to mostly Black audiences and congregations.[34] Caroline's talks in 1885 and 1886 were well attended, and she was recruited by the Woman's Christian Temperance Union to travel the state promoting the complete prohibition of alcohol. She even traveled alone on several of her trips, including to Fort Worth, a city not known for being friendly to banning alcohol.

Years later, George recorded her travels in his journal. "When the hour for the meeting came a carriage waited on her to the Negro church and waited until the close of her lecture, then took her back to the family that entertained her, or to the Depot if it was time to leave for her next engagement," George wrote.[35] "She gave about six weeks to this kind of work and lectured every day, and on Sunday, two or three times, She did this without any remuneration except her travel expenses."

In December 1886, Caroline wrote a detailed report about her work for the West Texas Methodist conference.[36] She had traveled 138 miles by horse and hack, 530 miles by railway; gave talks in twenty-three congregations and organized two women's auxiliaries. She reported listening to nine children recite their school lessons and distributed twenty dollars' worth of mission goods. She started a small mission school, with a teacher named Ida Norris instructing fifteen pupils, until "summarily closed by scarlet fever."

Another school that she had started, in Milford about 150 miles north of Austin, had eighty-five pupils, "some of these were orphan children." She obtained paid "subscriptions" for the schools and reported her work regularly to Dr. Rust's wife. Caroline collected contributions for the year of $26, with $7 sent to the Freedmen's Aid Society headquarters in Cincinnati. Her traveling expenses for the year were $20.45, and she collected donations toward her expenses of $7.05.

"One item more," Caroline added. She had managed to raise enough money to send one young African American woman to the Rust Industrial

Home in Holly Springs, Mississippi. "A mother's desire that her daughter should have the benefit of industrial training has been granted."

And that got Caroline thinking: the young Black women of Texas needed their own school in Austin. "Sleeping or waking I am dreaming, planning and thinking how we shall secure an Industrial Home in Austin for the training of our girls. If I could gather up some of our wasted resources my planning would assume reality," Caroline concluded in her report for 1886.

George and Caroline campaigned for a proposed alcohol prohibition law on the Texas state ballot in 1887. Blacks could still vote, and the Richardsons tried to win their support. Caroline brought charts to her lectures to illustrate "the effects of the use of intoxicants" on the body. "I have known her to hold her audience spell bound for an hour at a time, and a few times I have known her to draw her entire congregation to their feet," George wrote.[37]

But prohibition was a lost cause, and the ballot measure failed. George blamed his white temperance allies for overlooking Black votes. "The friends of Temperance made one mistake. They forgot that the vote of a plantation Negro counted as much as the vote of the Governor."[38]

><><

Caroline reflected in her diary about her work, but also lamented that she had lost track of most of her surviving siblings.[39] She feared they were dead. One of her brothers was running cattle in Colorado, but she knew little else about him and had lost contact. As for her four sons, they were long gone from her nest, and mostly out of touch. Still, she looked at the bright side.

"I have every reason to believe that they are good citizens—upright members of society—and best of all intelligent earnest Christians—willingly helping in all measures and means, that is for the advancement of the pure, the true the good in human society. When mothers are mourning over ungrateful or criminal sons—my heart goes out anew in thanksgiving that my prayers were heard, my weak efforts wonderfully blessed—that my sons are thus far a comfort and blessing to me, and their own families, the church, and the world."

On her sixty-first birthday, October 4, 1886, writing her annual birthday diary reflection, she reported having a "delightful summer through my husband's kindness, and the thoughtful care of my children."[40] Yet, she felt uneasy: "My 61st birthday although I have only goodness—loving kindness tender compassion to record when I think of my Dear Heavenly Father—but somehow it has been a very unsatisfying day—I am trying to feel reconciled to my circumstances and surroundings. I feel more and more assured that it is the little foxes that spoil the vines."

Who or what those little foxes were, she did not mention.

Caroline was tired, and others noticed. "She did not know how weary she was, and did not give herself the proper time to rest, but immediately took her place in the school," George wrote.[41]

Caroline worked steadily through the spring term at the Austin college and then went back on the road delivering temperance lectures in the summer of 1887. She returned to Austin in the fall and plunged back into work at the school.

A few days after her sixty-second birthday, Caroline felt unwell and she took to her bed for a week.[42] She was not up for writing a birthday reflection in her diary. When she began to recover, the town doctor pronounced that his services were no longer needed, and he departed. "She seemed unusually bright and cheerful," George remembered. That evening, though, she had a fainting spell and went back to bed. A woman from the school came to stay with her so that George could get some sleep.

During the night of October 22, 1887, Caroline Amelia Fay Richardson died.

~ *PART IV* ~

24

AUSTIN CITY LIMITS

Times without number I have learned that life is hard, as hard as crucible steel.
HOWARD THURMAN | *JESUS AND THE DISINHERITED*, 1949

The living legacy of George and Caroline Richardson is the school they founded in Austin.

Samuel Huston College survived—though only barely—after their time in Austin. The first building on the new campus was only partially completed when funds ran out. The school remained closed for a decade until the Methodist Freedmen's Aid Society found the money to reopen it and in 1900 appointed the school's first Black president, Reuben S. Lovinggood.

Lovinggood was born in the last year of the Civil War in the Blue Ridge Mountains of South Carolina.[1] He described himself as "mountain black" and learned the alphabet in a Methodist church Sunday school. At Clark University, a Black Methodist college in Worcester, Massachusetts, he majored in classics—Latin and Greek—and worked his way through school as a janitor.

At the time of his appointment as president of Samuel Huston College, Lovinggood was the chair of the Greek and Latin Department at Wiley College in Marshall, Texas—rival to the Richardsons' school in its early days. When asked why Blacks should study Greek and Latin, Lovinggood replied with a quote attributed to Confederate firebrand John C. Calhoun: "If I could find a Negro who knew Greek syntax, I would believe the Negro was a human being and ought to be treated as a man."

So Lovinggood did just that.

Under Lovinggood, students at Samuel Huston College would be required to take four years of Latin. When Lovinggood arrived, he found birds nesting in the rafters, and pigs and goats sleeping in the basement. On the first day of instruction in 1900, students sat on trunks. Furniture soon arrived, donated by the Austin Black community.

"The devotion of the colored people to the school was most touching from the very first," so described an official Methodist history of the school published in 1922, the same year my father was born.[2] "For many years wash-erwomen came Saturday after Saturday with their small earnings tied in a handkerchief to divide with the school."

The school that the KKK could not destroy, that Dallas had evicted from its city, and that was nearly extinguished by white Northern indifference, would never close again. And George Richardson would still be alive to hear about it.

But white supremacists still reigned in Texas. In 1928, the Austin City Council enacted a new city plan designating a "Negro District" on the East side of Austin.[3] The city forced all Black businesses, including Black churches, to relocate to the new "Negro District." The city's plan noted, "This will eliminate the necessity of duplication of white and black schools, white and black parks, and other duplicate facilities."

The order was enforced with the threat of cutting off municipal utilities. Samuel Huston College was already in East Austin, so it was spared the indignity of moving. But Wesley Church—the school's first home in the Richardson era—was forced to give up its prime real estate in downtown Austin and a white Baptist congregation moved in.

Nearly a century later, elderly alumni still talk of the trauma their parents and grandparents endured in the forcible relocation of Blacks to East Austin.[4]

⋙⋘

By the 1950s, there were two predominantly Black schools in Austin: Samuel Huston College and Tillotson Collegiate and Normal Institute. Both were strapped for cash. The trustees of the two schools voted in 1952 to merge and consolidate on the Tillotson campus on Bluebonnet Hill—the highest hill in East Austin. Alumni take it a point of pride that their campus looks down on the massive and powerful University of Texas.

All that remains today of the Samuel Huston campus is the foundation of an old building on a vacant lot. A windowless state office building occupies most of what was the Samuel Huston College campus. Off in a corner next to the parking lot is a Texas state historical marker: "The Rev. George W. Richardson founded a college in Dallas for the education of African American youth. . . . The school moved to Austin in 1878."

Lori's first reaction was, "Wait a minute: I'm the Texan and your family gets a historical marker?"

On another visit, we found the marker defaced with graffiti.[5]

Gillette Mansion was torn down years ago. Wesley Church, built with donations raised by Black pastor Charles Madison[6] that first housed the Richardsons' school, was torn down and replaced by a modernistic white Southern Baptist church. The cornerstone from the old church building is all that remains in the garden of the "new" Wesley Church in East Austin.

A short distance away sits the campus of Huston-Tillotson University. The surrounding neighborhood has a rough look, and the college campus is behind fences and gates. My ancestors would have approved of a sign at the gate: "No alcoholic beverages allowed." A guard screens everyone who enters.

Huston-Tillotson, now a university with graduate programs, has more than one thousand students, predominantly African American but with an increasing diversity of ethnicities and nationalities. The campus is compact; most of the buildings have a no-frills look. There are a few handsome buildings and a modern belltower. Nothing looks wasted.

On our first of several trips to Huston-Tillotson we were welcomed like visiting dignitaries. The college president at the time, Larry L. Earvin, arranged a meeting with pastors on a college advisory committee. They wanted to hear about George Richardson, about whom they knew little, although his photograph then graced the home page of the university's website.

President Earvin took us across campus to a reception in our honor hosted by college trustees, faculty, and alumni. On a table was a cake decorated with "Welcome Back Jim." Having never been there before in my life, I was humbled at this undeserved attention, and I told them the cake should have been decorated with "Welcome Back George."

At each stop on our campus tour, I was asked to tell the story of George Richardson and his family, and I happily complied. More than a few people noted my facial resemblance to my ancestor. I heard the proud history of Huston-Tillotson University: Jackie Robinson coached basketball and served as athletic director at Samuel Huston College in 1944–1945 before crossing the color line into Major League Baseball.

The faculty in the 1940s also included John Mason Brewer, a poet and a noted scholar of African American folklore. While we were visiting it so happened that Brewer's image adorned banners celebrating the school on lampposts in downtown Austin.

Alumni included Cecil Williams, who went on to become the well-known pastor of Glide Memorial Methodist Church in San Francisco.

In 1948, Howard Thurman, the leading Black theologian of the time, gave a series of lectures at Samuel Huston College that would put the Austin school into the spiritual and intellectual heart of the civil rights movement. Thurman delivered his lectures from notes, and later reshaped his lectures into a groundbreaking book, *Jesus and the Disinherited*, that had a profound impact on one seminary student in particular: Martin Luther King Jr. In later years, King packed the book with his clothes and took it everywhere on his travels.[7]

Thurman was invited to give the lectures by his friend, Karl E. Downs, the president of Samuel Huston College. Thurman later gave him the first draft of the manuscript that became his best known and most influential book.[8]

"American Christianity has betrayed the religion of Jesus almost beyond redemption," Thurman wrote.[9] In his lectures and book, Thurman reclaimed Jesus of Nazareth as a dark-skinned outcast, disinherited from the political power structure and persecuted by the Roman Empire. Thurman's meaning was clear: he was talking about not just ancient Romans but also about modern Americans and their racial caste system. "Many and varied are the interpretations dealing with the teachings and the life of Jesus of Nazareth," Thurman wrote. "But few of these interpretations deal with what the teachings and the life of Jesus have to say to those who stand, at a moment in human history, with their backs against the wall."

Thurman had met Mohandas Gandhi in India, and drawing deeply from that encounter, Thurman argued that white supremacy must be confronted not by violence, but by "loving the enemy" into change. "The religion of Jesus makes the love-ethic central," Thurman said. He did not suggest it would be easy. "This is no ordinary achievement."

Martin Luther King, Ralph Abernathy, John Lewis, and others were enormously influenced by Thurman, whose words delivered at Samuel Huston College continue to reverberate; there has been a resurgence of interest in his work in recent years.

As I walked around the Huston-Tillotson campus, many people shook my hand; one woman exclaimed, "roots are standing in front of me." The track and field coach stood up from behind his desk and vigorously shook my hand. He gave me a tour of the athletic department showing me pictures of Olympic athletes raised up by the college. I realized that at Huston-Tillotson, connecting with the past gives legitimacy and moral authority to the present—and provides a compass to the future.

With all of this attention, finally I said to someone, "I haven't done anything. I'm just carrying the name."

"You have done something," one of my new friends replied. "You are carrying the lamp inside you of your great-great-grandfather that will keep lighting the lamp of the college."

I could feel a spirit in the smiles and the stories of everyone I met. It was as if they were saying, "Tell your great-great-grandparents we are still here, we have kept the faith, and we are doing good work."

A year later, I returned to deliver the invocation at commencement. In the procession to the stage, the graduates stopped, turned, and formed a double column to shake hands with the faculty. As I walked behind the faculty, I shook the hand of every graduate that day. I have never felt so proud to walk in a graduation ceremony.

That Sunday, I was invited to tell the story of the Richardsons at St. James Episcopal Church, founded in 1941 by students, alumni, and faculty from Tillotson College.[10] In the 1940s, St. James became the only predominantly Black Episcopal Church in Austin. In the 1980s the church went through a period of introspection and decided to become multi-ethnic. A Spanish-language worship service followed, and the 2000s, the parish called its first white rector, Greg Rickel, who went on to become the Episcopal bishop of the Diocese of Olympia in Seattle.

Many of the current St. James members are associated with Huston-Tillotson, including alumna Ora Houston, a prominent leader in the Black community and a member of the Austin City Council. She proudly told me her church has "blown the lid off assumptions" by practicing "radical hospitality."

President Earvin retired in 2015, and I was invited to tell the story of the founding of the school at the inauguration of a new president, Dr. Colette Pierce Burnette. I sat on a stage with Ora Houston and other alumni, telling stories about the school and its history. On behalf of our family, we donated the ledger book showing the names of the first students at the school before it was burned in Dallas.

We also donated an original letter from Richard Rust to "Bro Richardson," dated May 9, 1882, that came with a check for purchasing property for a campus. "Close at the earliest time you can with credit and the good of the cause," Rust wrote.[11] His letter is the closest thing there is to a charter from the Methodist Freedmen's Aid Society for Samuel Huston College.

✨ 25 ✨

LILY

Thou has been faithful to thy family, friends and to God.

INSCRIPTION ON CAROLINE RICHARDSON'S TOMBSTONE | 1887

At the age of eighty-one, after many years of carefully recording his life story in his journal, George Richardson stopped writing.[1]

The event he could not bring himself to describe was the death of Caroline, his wife of thirty-six years, mother of his six children, and partner in the cause of Methodism, abolitionism, education, and temperance. The best he could muster in his first draft was to hand copy her obituary in the back of her diary.[2] He did not pick up his pen again for almost a year. The reason he gave for halting his writing was an injury sustained falling off a roof while building a new room onto his house. But it had been a year since that injury. Finally, on George Washington's birthday in 1906, George pronounced himself ready to write again.

Even twenty years after her passing from this earth, Caroline's death was still an excruciatingly painful memory. He had to ease himself into the subject, so he began his new entry in "Recollections of My Lifework" by first describing the room where he sat. His handwriting was shaky and the ink from his pen blotchy from lack of use.

"I am at my desk in the new room, with a comfortable fire, ready to resume my 'Story.' I have almost forgotten where I left off, but I remember that the last year of my Presiding Eldership was an <u>eventful year</u>."

But church affairs were not where he picked up the story. His next words were to recount the terrible details of Caroline's death in October 1887 and the numbness he felt in the days that followed.[3]

He told of Caroline's fainting spell, and how he had summoned the doctor who stayed for two or three hours before leaving again. Then one of the women teachers from the school had come to stay with her. Caroline seemed to rally. George drifted off to sleep until he woke up at 2 a.m., went to Caroline's bedside, "and found there had been a startling change." He quickly left her bedside to summon one of the women who had been attending to her.

When he returned, Caroline was dead.

"It was all so sudden!" George wrote. "She had not entertained the thought that the end was near, at least she had not said so. We had not talked over any plans that contemplated such a change, but the change came while I was away, and we had no opportunity to say goodbye."

His anguish filled three pages of the journal, "What I would not have given, for one word at parting, for one backward look when she was crossing that mysterious Border Land."

George wrote that Caroline's cause of death was "La Grippe." His description of her fainting spell and rapid decline is consistent with the symptoms of a strain of influenza known as the Russian flu that spread worldwide and came to North America in the late 1880s. It is considered the first modern influenza pandemic.[4]

"I was all alone," George wrote. "But strangers were kind and sympathizing." Owen was away at college at Northwestern in Evanston, Illinois. George sent him a telegram, asking him to notify his brothers and Emma, who was a student at Hamline University in Minnesota. "I had no thought of anything else, only that the precious dust would be interred at Austin," where one of George's friends had already dug a grave.

Then George received a telegram from his second son, David (who would be my great-grandfather), asking to have his mother's remains brought to Minnesota for burial. As far as David was concerned, Minnesota was his mother's home, not Texas. George consented to David's request. Though he had lived in Texas more than a decade, "I did not regard Austin as my home. No one of the family would be near."[5]

Her funeral would be in Austin. Other pastors in Austin took charge of the funeral arrangements, and an extraordinary, unprecedented event was about to unfold. "My wife had said to me only a short time before, that if she should die in Austin, she wanted the colored people to whom she had labored for eight years to have an opportunity to be at her funeral."[6]

Caroline's body was prepared by the women teachers of the college. Her funeral was remarkable by the standards of any age; both Blacks and whites sat together at Central Methodist Church on the afternoon of October 24, 1887. White pastors E. O. McIntyre of Central Methodist and W. H. Shaw of Cumberland Presbyterian sat with Black pastor Mack Henson. All three preached. It was to be the last time for decades that Blacks and whites sat together at a funeral in Austin.

The church was "well filled," George wrote. The pastors preached, but none were more eloquent than Henson. "The address of Rev. Henson moved the audience to tears when he spoke of the sacrifice Mrs. Richardson had made in giving her time, without compensation, to improve their homes and their habits, and at last to give her life for his people."

Her casket was loaded onto a train that night, bound north to Minnesota. George accompanied her remains. Owen boarded the train in Chicago and together they took Caroline to her final resting place in Red Wing, Minnesota. His old mentor, Chauncey Hobart, met them at the station in Red Wing. Owen had arranged for his father and his siblings to stay at the Hobart home. Another funeral was held, this time with Hobart presiding.[7]

The expenses for Caroline's burial, including transportation of her casket north, were beyond George's financial means. The Methodist Missionary Society paid all of the expenses in recognition of Caroline's service to the Methodist Church and to the "colored" community. More than likely Hobart arranged for that.

Caroline was laid to rest in Hobart's family plot on a wooded bluff near the Mississippi River in the Oakwood Cemetery in Red Wing. A gray granite marker was placed at her grave, inscribed with the dates of her birth and death, and the words: "Thou has been faithful to thy family, friends and to God."

Hobart himself would be buried just a few feet away.

During the many years of George's absences, Hobart likely had felt responsible for Caroline's wellbeing. George could not have afforded to purchase a plot on his own, and no doubt Hobart viewed it as an act of charity for an old friend, and possibly even as a peace offering. But George never recorded how he felt about his wife being buried in Hobart's plot.

In 1904, Hobart's remains were laid to rest. His elaborate Victorian red stone marker was flanked by the small tombstones of the two wives he outlived and towered above theirs and Caroline's nearby. Over the intervening decades, the inscription on Caroline's tombstone had weathered and was nearly obliterated.

On an unseasonably blustery summer day, we visited Caroline's grave.[8]

Numerous trees and branches had been knocked down and scattered in a recent storm, and another storm was on its way. I read aloud from George's journal the account of Caroline's death to a gathering of Richardson descendants. I blessed her tombstone with holy oil. It began to rain. We scurried to our cars and the wind began whipping branches and leaves around us.

After burying Caroline, George stayed in Minnesota for about a month before returning to Texas. He made no mention in the journal about his earlier conflict with Hobart, nor whether the two talked much during his grim visit to Minnesota. Whether the two reconciled is not known, but George made no further mention of his former mentor in his journal. Nor did George return to Minnesota for another twenty-eight years. He probably did not see Hobart alive again.

As for Hobart, he only made passing references in his memoir to George Richardson on the many lists of preachers whom he had hired and fired. Hobart made no mention of Caroline.

Decades later, George expressed regret at having forced Caroline to leave Minnesota. In a letter to his children in 1891, he wrote: "Your own mother had those intense longings for an earthly home, which were partially satisfied with our home at County Line. With all its drawbacks of mortgages—failing health and failure of crops it was for the time home to us. I never knew, till after she found her heavenly home, what it cost her to leave it. Some scraps in her diary show what a sacrifice it was to her."[9]

He also hand-copied her obituary into the back of Caroline's diary. The authorship is unknown, but it has the unmistakable echoes of his writing. "When her husband would have sunk under his load, her brave heart and words cheered him on," the obituary reads. "After coming to Texas her time was more fully given to others besides her family than it had ever been before. She taught in the institution for colored children and youth for several years."[10]

It's not known whether it was published, but such obituaries were commonly read aloud at funerals.

><><

Bereft, George returned to Austin in December 1887 but did not stay long. He was emotionally exhausted. Reminders of his deceased wife were everywhere. "When I came back to look around the country where my wife had traveled with [me], the sense of loneliness seemed to crush me. I seemed powerless to take up the burden again."[11]

George resigned as presiding elder of his Black Methodist district and gave up leadership of the school. But within a few days, he had second thoughts. George considered whether "I should have remained with my colored brethren," he wrote. "There was one thing that gave me much anxiety as I was leaving"—the college.

There were only two teachers left, and financial support from the Freedmen's Aid Bureau was still sporadic. "Now that all of my family were out of the school I feared an utter collapse and all we had done would go for nothing."[12]

On a Sunday night late in December 1887, only a few months after Caroline's death, "I became so distressed over the condition of the school that I prayed and agonized all night," he wrote. "As the morning dawned I felt the comforting assurance that Samuel Huston College would <u>live</u>, but it might be suspended for awhile."

Samuel Huston College remained open for another year-and-a-half before instruction was suspended in June 1889. The tangle over Samuel Huston's estate took several more years before all the funds came through and a permanent building could be constructed. Joseph Hartzell, the president of the Methodist Freedmen's Aid Society, came to Austin to sort out the mess and offered to make Owen once again president of Samuel Huston College. Hartzell sweetened the deal by offering Clara a music teaching position.[13]

But Owen felt that the salary wasn't sufficient, and he declined to accept. Without Owen and Clara, the fate of the school was uncertain. The Richardson family involvement in Samuel Huston College was sadly at an end.

>⊷⊷⊷<

George Richardson left Austin forever in early 1888 and headed north to the Texas Panhandle, a colorless dusty plain with more cattle than people.[14] If anything could revive George's spirits it was an adventure. He signed up as chaplain to the cowboys on the sprawling Matador Ranch with its 125,000 head of cattle.

George arrived by railroad in Clarendon, a new town near the tracks. George brought everything he owned, and everything fit inside his wagon, and the wagon fit inside a boxcar. Clarendon had few buildings and there was nowhere to store his goods, "so I had them piled up on the open prairie under a tent." He took a room above a saloon, which he soon regretted. "I felt the odor of liquor would not be a good atmosphere in which to prepare sermons." He moved his quarters into the back office of the town's doctor.

George was soon preaching to anyone who listened. He purchased a large second-hand tent that became his portable church and piled it into the back of his wagon. He purchased a team of two horses for sixty dollars and began roaming the Panhandle in search of new converts among the cowboys. He called his horses "Billy" and "Charley," the favored names of many a Methodist preacher's horses.

George set about to evangelize the cowboys on the massive Matador Ranch—all 150 cowboys spread out on the range. The absentee owners lived in Scotland. "It was part of their policy to care for the morals of their cowboys." The owners put George on the ranch payroll. He soon organized a Methodist "class" of fifteen cowboys. They met and worshiped in a large mess hall. Attendance grew to about seventy-five. The ranch owner banned alcohol, winning George's approval. "The more reckless kind of men had left the ranch."

George rode his 430-mile round-trip circuit in his wagon, pulled by Billy and Charley. When he could not find lodgings, George slept in the wagon. It took him four weeks to make the circuit. He tried to construct a church building but needed help. He sent for his oldest son.

Owen and Clara were soon on their way to Clarendon.[15] No mention is made of their daughter, Carrie, who by then was likely institutionalized. When Owen and Clara found George, he was still living in a tent. The progress on the church building, Owen recalled, was "the lumber was on the lot." All of his father's efforts had gone into riding the range to win converts.

Owen found two carpenters to help build a house and finish the church. He described it as a "box" measuring roughly fourteen-by-twenty feet that the three of them moved into. That summer, Owen expanded the box to include a kitchen, and by December it was windproof and secure for the winter.

Among the more endearing tales told by Owen in his memoir is about Christmas 1888. The Richardsons hatched a plan to have an "evergreen Christmas" in Clarendon, complete with a Christmas tree and the greening of their new, small church.[16] When it was pointed out that there were no evergreen trees for hundreds of square miles on the Texas Panhandle, Owen talked with the railroad office. A train hauling a load of Christmas trees from the Rockies to Fort Worth was due to pass through Clarendon. Arrangements were made to have the conductors toss a tree off the train on its way through town, and as planned, the train dropped a sixteen-foot fir with extra branches for decorating. The church was trimmed with the utmost of secrecy. Meanwhile, cowboys, ranch hands and families on the Panhandle were invited to come to Clarendon to celebrate Christmas.

"Some of the families came one hundred twenty miles, camped overnight on the way to the celebration," Owen wrote. "The surprise was complete. The appreciation of the visitors was magnificent."

George continued riding the range, preaching in ranch mess halls, living in his wagon, or sleeping under it in bad weather. Owen also traveled a circuit that took him away from Clarendon four days a week: Thursday through Sunday. Arriving in a cowboy camp, "I changed my cowboy suit for my clerical suit," Owen wrote.[17]

Later that year, Owen returned briefly to Austin for a Methodist conference. Hartzell came with news that the bequest from Huston's estate had finally settled, and he once again offered Owen the presidency of Samuel Huston College.[18] Owen initially accepted but balked again at the low pay. Hartwell withdrew the offer. Whether George Richardson was even aware of Owen spurning the offer, he never recorded in his journal. Owen returned to the Panhandle and remained on the Texas Range another two years.

Emma, age twenty-six and a teacher, spent her summer break in 1889 with her father on the Texas Panhandle.[19] "Her presence for fifty days made the summer pass pleasantly and rapidly," George wrote, "but when she returned to school, I was more lonely than ever."

While Owen and Clara did their best "to make me comfortable," George decided it was time he had his own home. "I decided to marry again." He was sixty-five.

From the tone in his journal, his decision to remarry sounds more convenient than romantic. Nor does he mention any previous connection to his new wife. "After some correspondence with Rachel Elizabeth Silver of Halifax, Nova Scotia, we met at Fort Worth Texas, and were married Sunday November 17th 1889."

Everyone called her "Lily," and at age forty-four, she had not previously married.[20] She was closer in age to George's oldest son than to George—only seven years older than Owen. One of five children, Lily was born and reared in Nova Scotia. Her father had been a druggist and had moved his family to Hastings, Minnesota, and died not long after. To support the family, Lily taught at the school in Hastings. She lived with her mother for most of her life.

But she was not a mail-order bride. Lily, in fact, had a long connection to the Richardson family. Census records show that she had been a school-teacher in Minnesota in the 1860s–1870s, living near the Richardsons' farm at County Line. She was, indeed, the Richardson children's teacher. From the descriptions in Owen's memoir, she was more than their teacher—practically their second mother. Owen wrote that "Miss Silver," as he called her, had been both nanny and tutor—and he was much indebted to her for helping him to become eligible for college.[21]

"Our school [in Minnesota] was her first attempt at teaching," Owen wrote in his memoir. "She was a fine scholar and an excellent teacher." When she finished teaching the Richardson children, Lily moved back to Nova Scotia.

Owen played the matchmaker with his father and Lily. "I knew her to be a woman of more than ordinary strength of character—thoroughly consci-entious, and firm in her convictions of duty." He noted, however, that her physical health was fragile.

Soon after Lily arrived in Texas from Nova Scotia, Owen presided at the wedding. "The next day we commenced housekeeping," George wrote.

Joining the newly married couple, he noted, was "the aged mother of the bride who was to make her home with us." The three moved into a small box house that Owen had built for them next to his box house.

That George was devoted to Lily is clearly evident in his journal and letters he wrote his children. But from the start, Lily could not keep up with the demands of his circuit riding. With chronic asthma, Lily did not have the physical stamina to accompany him on his four-hundred-mile round trip, nor was she comfortable sleeping under wagons on the Texas range.[22]

George concluded it was time to leave Texas. He sold his small house in Clarendon, finished his church work, and prepared to move as far west as he could go: California. There were many more congregations—and many more scrapes—ahead for him and Lily.

Yet Caroline remained forever in his dreams.

~ 26 ~

WILD GEESE

I feel it in my bones like wild geese in the Spring.
GEORGE RICHARDSON | LETTER, MARCH 3, 1891

Dunsmuir, California, was established in the 1880s in the shadow of Mount Shasta, at the foot of a dormant volcano near the headwaters of the Sacramento River about three hundred miles north of San Francisco. A later generation coined the town motto: "Home of the Best Water on Earth." By the twentieth century, Dunsmuir was known primarily as a premier trout fishing destination.

But in the late-nineteenth century, Dunsmuir was known not just for its water, but for the railyard where steam locomotives could be repaired after hauling loads up and down the steep grades in the rugged Cascade Mountains to the north. Railroads in California were the most powerful political force in the growing state—and that made Dunsmuir the largest town in California north of Sacramento. Dunsmuir was not even ten years old when George and Lily Richardson moved there in 1890.[1]

Nearly one century later, three generations of Richardsons held a family reunion in a Dunsmuir park to celebrate George Richardson's arrival on the Pacific coast. The Minnesota branch of Richardsons joined the Pacific coast branch for the reunion. Big freight trains rumbled past the park where we picnicked, but the railroad was no longer king and the town tiny.

At the time, Lori and I were preparing to be married. As we sat by the banks of the Sacramento River, we talked about having our marriage ceremony right there (with a little fishing on the side). Our wedding plan was scuttled when relatives pointed out there were not enough hotel rooms for our guests in Dunsmuir.

In the fall of 1890, George accepted a temporary preaching position in Dunsmuir. He didn't have much choice. There were already more Methodist preachers in California than positions so this was the best he could do. George and Lily departed Texas—never to return—taking a train to California.

For the first time in their lives, they saw the snowcapped peaks of the Rocky Mountains and the Sierra Nevada. "To us the scenery was grand beyond description," George wrote.

The people of Dunsmuir "received us very cordially" but there was no parsonage for them to live in. He rented a house in town. "I soon found that the weariness I had experienced in Texas was passing away. I gained in flesh & strength."

George made his headquarters in Dunsmuir. "The people of Dunsmuir were from everywhere and were mostly Railroad men. I visited the men in their homes and in the shops, and was soon on good terms with most of them, and they gave me good congregations for the size of the town."

Compared to his vast circuits in Texas, the Dunsmuir circuit was small and easily manageable. He started a Methodist congregation in Mott in a small church building that had been abandoned by the Episcopalians. A few years after he left, the entire town, along with the church, burned down in one of the wildfires that continue to plague the region.

Caroline, and the sacrifices she had made, was not far from George's thoughts. He wrote a letter in March 1891 to his children, telling them that their mother came to him in his nightly dreams standing at the house at County Line, Minnesota.[2] "I was with you all again and with us the one whose memory holds the most sacred place in our hearts." Sunday afternoons "brought back a train of sacred memories."

He acknowledged that Lily knew of his feelings about his deceased wife. "And just here I want to say that your present mother is not jealous on account of the sacred regard you have for your own mother. That night at family prayer she thanked God that she was connected with family who had felt the moulding [sic] power of such a Christian mother. She has said often that she doesn't expect or desire to 'take her place.'"

As much as George enjoyed Dunsmuir, the church posting was temporary. The mountain winters were as harsh as in Minnesota, and Lily had difficulty with the climate. George was soon making inquiries about employment to the milder Willamette Valley in Oregon to the north.

"I would have been well satisfied to remain in California if I could have been admitted into that conference, but I did not wish to remain as supply," he wrote in "Recollections of My Lifework." It is also plausible that his past ministry among Blacks hindered acceptance by white Methodist authorities in California.

In his letter from Dunsmuir to his children, George alluded to his life-long restlessness. "We have a comfortable house and a kind hearted people to serve, but I feel it in my bones like wild geese in the Spring, I must seek a home."

George accepted a position in Tillamook, on the chilly, isolated Oregon coast.[3] To get there required either rough ride in a stagecoach or ocean steamer on the choppy sea. "I should have been very reluctant to have ac-cepted this charge," he wrote in his journal. "I simply accepted Tillamook to get into the conference."

Besides preaching in Tillamook, George had two other "preaching places" in the area. The roads along the rough Oregon coast were too rutted for a carriage, so at age sixty-six, George was back on horseback.

Tillamook was not a happy experience for George and Lily. The climate was damp and cold—Lily suffered badly. The church building, the only one in Tillamook, held two hundred people and was shared by three competing denominations. George soon was crossways with the other two.

That building was torn down long ago. In our travels, we found the cor-nerstone of the old church, planted in the garden of a modern Methodist church in Tillamook. We arrived on a summer day, and it was truly cold, windy, and damp. We did not linger.

Owen and Emma—the two children closest to George—soon arrived to help their father and new stepmother.[4] Emma graduated from Hamline University and took a teaching job in Cheyenne, Wyoming, 1,200 miles to the east. When school was out in June 1892, she joined her father and Lily on the Oregon coast for the summer. Meanwhile, Owen had left Texas for a preaching job in La Grande, in northeast Oregon not far from the Idaho state line.

By July 1892, George began looking inland for a new preaching post. "My wife was suffering so much with asthma, that we deemed it best that she should go to Idaho to find a dryer climate."

George and Lily continued moving in the Pacific Northwest, accepting more short-lived positions including in Idaho. Yet life as a circuit riding Methodist preacher was beginning to catch up to George. "I sometimes found that the sage brush road was too tiresome for me, and I would take the main road to the nearest station and go the balance of the way by railroad."[5]

On his sixty-ninth birthday—November 24, 1893—George wrote a revealing reflection on a blank page in Caroline's old diary.[6] Perhaps he had read Caroline's birthday reflections and felt inspired by her example to write one of his own. "Twenty years ago I did not expect to live till this time." He observed that he began to "rally" when he went to Texas. "I never expected to continue beyond 70 in the 'effective relation.' If I am strong as I am now I may continue another year or two."

He acknowledged his spiritual struggles with his "communion with God." His life was "full of interruptions" and so he resolved "to leave no means untried" for "greater spiritual power." The key, he wrote, was "greater patience in my home."

George and Lily worked in Idaho's Bruneau Valley for a year. But at the end of 1894, the Methodist elders transferred him once again to a new circuit, this time based in Oxford, in the southeast corner of Idaho.[7] The town was closer to Salt Lake City than to Boise, and it was full of Mormons. The location made it nearly impossible to win converts for the Methodists. To add to the difficulty, the railroad bypassed Oxford.

George dutifully packed his household goods and went ahead to Oxford to find a place to live. What he found stopped him in his tracks. The town was nearly deserted. "I found only one Methodist family, and they were not backward in telling me they were sorry I had come. What there was left of the town was Mormon." The task felt impossible, and George was not shy about saying so.

George telegraphed the freight agent to hold his goods. He asked the Idaho presiding elder to be relieved and was granted permission. "I found we were thrown out on the prairie without any support. I had been given some hard appointments in the course of my ministry, and never flinched, but I thought this was more than I could stand."

George and Lily moved to Boise where Owen was now preaching.[8] They lived and worked in Boise for three years, the typical length of an appointment in the Methodist system. At the end of the annual Methodist conference of 1895, Owen was appointed to Haines, Oregon, while George was appointed to St. Anthony, in the eastern corner of Idaho, near Yellowstone National Park. George considered the appointments as punishment.

"This was an entirely new field—no members—no church—no parsonage. The Eastern portion of Idaho was largely settled by Mormons," George wrote. "In this open sage brush country I was tossed out almost beyond civilization with only $175 missionary money. I felt there was a special cruelty about the whole business. I wondered what I had done, or failed to do, that I should thus be thrown away."

George conducted funerals in nearby outposts, reaching them by sleigh in the winter of 1895–1896. "It dawned on me gradually that my hair was gray, and that I was 71 years old," he wrote in his journal. "I made the trip without freezing but I suffered very much with the cold."

⟩⟩⟨⟨

George Richardson had yet more adventures in him.

In the summer of 1896, Owen joined George, Lily, and her mother, who was by now living with them, on a trek to Yellowstone National Park.[9] Clara, who was in poor health and had been injured in a wagon accident, stayed behind.

George wrote two lengthy letters to his other children about their trek through Yellowstone. George copied the letters into blank pages in Caroline's diaries, and the originals were preserved in his papers.[10] His account is a remarkable description of Yellowstone at the close of the nineteenth century when it was still remote and all but unknown to the vast majority of Americans. The park had been open for less than a decade.

"I know you would like to see Yellowstone National Park with your own eyes, and hear the groaning and heaving of the geysers and cataracts with your own ears," George wrote, telling his readers he would serve as their eyes and ears in more letters.

The party set forth on July 27, 1896, traveling by horse and hack. The second day it rained, and the cart nearly slipped off the road on steep hill. It took three days to reach Yellowstone. They were among 4,659 visitors who reached Yellowstone that year; by the twenty-first century, more than 3 million people visit Yellowstone annually.[11] The party purchased a guidebook for 50 cents at the Fountain Hotel, then the premier lodge in the park (the hotel was torn down in 1927). They did not stay in the hotel but camped.

The Richardson party wasted no time exploring the geysers and lava beds.

"I felt a strange sensation as though I were on the verge of the bottomless pit." They visited the Fire Hole Basin and Hell's Half Acre, and camped next to boiling springs, which George described as "blubbering like a pot of mush." On Sunday, the Richardsons held a family prayer meeting near the Lone Star Geyser, about three miles south of Old Faithful. Owen boiled eggs for supper in one of the hot springs.

"Mosquitoes and flies were fearful," George reported. The adventurers escaped the bugs by staying inside their tent. "I smoked them out of the tent the best I could, and Mother [Lily] smoked them out of the hack and closed the curtains as tightly as possible and we were able to get some sleep."

The party explored the Grand Canyon of Yellowstone on August 4. "Our ride beside the Yellowstone River was delightful. Owen caught trout for dinner, which we cooked and ate by the roadside while the horses were feeding in the luxuriant grass." Yellowstone's Grand Canyon reminded George of his "imaginings" of Hell. "In a wild side-cave there were groanings and heavings as though some chained demon were making superhuman efforts to get free."

George wrote that they could not get enough of Yellowstone. "All day was spent sight-seeing," he wrote on August 5. "And yet we were hungry to see more of this wonderland. We were thoroughly exhausted with our walking and climbing, and our exclamations of oh! oh! Beautiful."

Exhausted but exhilarated, the Richardsons departed the national park on August 10. "I said goodbye to this vision of beauty with a feeling that I shall never see its equal this side of heaven." On their way out of Yellowstone, they stopped at the park post office and were delighted to find a letter from Emma. "Weary and surfeited we took up our march for home."

Owen returned to his pastorate in Haines, Oregon, and found his wife, Clara, in failing health. He served another three years until he could no longer ride his circuit because of her health. Their daughter was in an institution, and his debts mounted. He began selling tonic water in Adams, Oregon. His church pastor days were behind him.[12]

But George carried on with his flocks.

By his count, his work on the eastern edge of Idaho had yielded exactly fourteen new Methodists.[13] He set about to build a proper Methodist church building in St. Anthony. He sold the parsonage and two lots to finance the project. A new presiding elder in his district "was a great help to our new enterprise." By 1897, membership had grown to twenty-five. Lily taught school eighteen miles away. Lily saved her salary so that they could buy a home when he retired. With deep snows, they saw each other only once that winter—and when they did, they knew it was time to retire.

George and Lily decided to move to Denver.[14] How they settled upon Denver as their final home, he did not record in his journal. Before leaving Idaho, they tried to sell their horses—their most valuable possession—but no one would buy. So, he loaded all of their household goods in their horse drawn hack and set forth overland from Idaho to Denver. George was seventy-three.

They departed Idaho in September 1897—late for travel in the Rocky Mountains where snow has been known to fall in early September. The trip was 940 treacherous miles, taking them forty-five days following a route that now roughly tracks modern US 20 and Interstate 90. The first part of their journey took them through Yellowstone. "At Billings we left the River valley and <u>climbed</u> and <u>climbed</u> and <u>climbed</u> the mountains by a blind road."

To find their way, George often walked ahead of the horses. They camped twenty-seven nights and found lodging in homes on seventeen other nights. In Parkman, Wyoming, George was invited to preach on a Sunday before getting back on the trail. On October 1 they were blasted by high winds while following the road along a ridgeline. They barely made it.

"A sudden storm came up and it seemed as though the hack would be blown over. The horses turned their back to the storm and stopped feeding. I brought them up to the leeward side the hack and blanketed them the best I could, and stood between all night rubbing their legs to keep them from freezing. I could not put up our tent in such a wind." He covered Lily with blankets in their wagon. "I have had some rough storms in Texas, but this was the worst night I ever experienced."

George and Lily reached Denver on October 18, 1897, and checked into a hotel. They got off the trail just ahead of a blizzard. The next day, they set about finding a place to live in their new city, renting a house on Julian Street. "Now at the age of 73 years, when I could no longer meet the responsibilities of an itinerant minister, I had found a place to rest. My satisfaction with having a home was unbounded."[15]

Emma soon joined them.

↣ 27 ↢

EMMA

Thou hast proved mine heart; thou hast visited *me* in the night;
thou hast tried me, *and* shalt find nothing.

PSALM 17: 3 | KING JAMES VERSION

As I worked on this book, I became increasingly fascinated by Mary Emma Richardson, the youngest of Caroline and George Richardson's children and my great-grand aunt. I hoped to find her own words from a diary or journal, but all we could find were a few letters and brief entries she made at the end of her father's journal. The details of Emma's life remained tantalizingly just beyond the horizon. Nonetheless, a few facts about her could be gleaned from what we found.

Emma was born on the upper midwestern frontier during the Civil War. Her father was absent for most of her childhood. As a teenager in Texas, Emma experienced firsthand the war's aftermath and the crushing oppression of the Southern racial caste system. She was a young adult during the so-called Gilded Age, which was anything but gilded in the frontier towns where she lived. She taught in schools, traveled by rail in the western United States, and cared for her father in his final years. Although struggling with poor health throughout her life, Emma lived into old age, surviving through two world wars, multiple pandemics, and the Great Depression. She died ten years before I was born.

I wondered: What was it like being a young white woman from the North and a teacher in a school for African Americans in the South? How did she make her way in life free from the domestic expectations of her age, never to have a husband and children? What motivated her? What was her story?

A few of Emma's letters turned up, written in midlife to her favorite niece, Florence, who was married to a college professor in Kansas, and to her brother, David Fay Richardson (my great-grandfather), who lived on an apple farm in Oregon. The letters were found under piles of papers and in shoeboxes in my Aunt Madge's house in California. We also found a few photographs and records from her life, including college transcripts. From these scraps of paper, Emma's voice began to emerge. She could be chatty and droll: "I have just returned from church where the attendance was small, owing to a drizzling rain that has kept up since before I opened my eyes," she began one of her letters.[1]

Emma was meticulous and detailed. She enjoyed showing off her colorful, fashionable clothing. But there was one fact about Emma Richardson that loomed far larger than any other: her lifelong penchant for education.

⸻

Hamline University, the Methodists' jewel of higher education in the upper Midwest, was founded in 1854 in Red Wing, Minnesota, when George Richardson was a young preacher.[2] He had, in fact, turned down an offer to teach math when the school was new. The first classes were held on the second floor of the town's general store. Named for a Methodist bishop, Leonidas Hamline, the school was the first university in Minnesota. From the start, women were admitted as students.

Besides developing as a steamboat port on the banks of the Mississippi River, Red Wing was also the center of Chauncey Hobart's universe and the unofficial headquarters of Methodism in the region. George and his family lived in Red Wing in the 1850s when he was an itinerant preacher under Hobart's charge.

In 1869, Hamline closed, and its building torn down. Hamline reopened in 1880 in Saint Paul, the state capital. Three years later, Mary Emma Richardson entered as a student, one of six women in her class of nine. Emma was twenty years old. She entered college already experienced as a teacher at her family's school for African Americans in Texas.[3]

Unlike her brothers, Emma was a natural and dedicated scholar. She earned a bachelor's degree from Hamline in 1888 with high marks in math, physics, German, Latin, and history. She had taken courses in biology, botany, Greek, international law, "Calculus and Surveying," and "Evidences of Christianity."[4] She never had a grade lower than a B or a mark lower than 87 (in calculus). Emma matriculated nine days before her oldest brother, Owen, who graduated (finally) from Northwestern University after many years of struggling to finish.[5] Owen had flunked Greek; Emma had earned a B.

Emma later earned graduate level credits in education at the University of California in Berkeley in 1921, and again in 1923, which made her the first of many in the Richardson family to attend Cal or one of the UC campuses, including my sister and me.

Emma had a flair for clothes. As a child she adored a pink dress sewn for her by a neighbor.[6] As a college student, a photograph of her class in the Hamline archives shows her in a dress of many folds with embroidered flowers down the front.[7]

Another photograph taken at Emma's Hamline graduation shows her with eight classmates wearing mortarboards.[8] Standing in the back row, Emma is wearing a long black dress with metal buttons down the middle; her hair is in a bun, tucked under her mortarboard. Another woman in the class photograph is smiling, but Emma looks all business. She has a long face like her father's, and her gaze is sharp. She was the shortest in the row and thin. Her father later wrote that she weighed only about one hundred pounds.

A Hamline biographical sketch for the Alumni Association described her as "delicate."[9] Many years later we discovered a light tan dress in a trunk that had a fitted waist measuring less than twenty inches.

Her nieces always marveled at her clothing, and it was a point of pride for her that they noticed.[10] Florence was especially dazzled by how Emma dressed, although the older generation of Minnesotans had their reservations. Florence wrote, "Aunt Emma shocked Mother by her extravagant clothes. I'll never forget Mother's expression when Aunt Emma showed her some beautiful changeable tan and blue taffeta she had purchased for the *lining* of her new suit."[11]

Florence's sister Ruth described Emma as having "good form" with "beautiful golden hair without a grey in it." Ruth also admired Emma's taste in clothes. "She dresses very tastily and prettily."

Emma enjoyed the attention, once writing to Florence, "I feel quite spiffy in my new silk dress, new navy blue hat, with the shape of a toad stool with a bunch of flowers forming the crown, new white shoes."[12] Among the photos from her later years shows her under a hat with plume feathers at the top. In another photo, Emma is in a floral-patterned dress. The drab clothes of the era did not suit her.

After graduation from Hamline, Emma returned to Texas to take a position as a tutor at Texas Wesleyan College in Fort Worth—the first of many teaching posts she would hold.[13] Emma was as restless as her father. By the time she retired in 1930, she had lived in Wyoming, Texas, Oregon, Illinois, Minnesota, California, Colorado, and the Dakota Territory. She never set foot anywhere east of Wisconsin her entire life and did not put down roots until in her forties, and only then because she became her father's caregiver in Denver.

Emma could poke fun at herself. When she filled out a Hamline University Alumni Association questionnaire for a class reunion, she answered a question about earning postgraduate degrees: "That of spinster." To the question, "When, to whom were you married," she wrote, "Never to nobody."[14]

Emma was devoted to her father to the end of his life. She finished his journal for him.[15]

⋙⋘

Emma Richardson was thirty-four in 1897 when her father and stepmother, Lily, settled in Denver. Emma had been a teacher for nearly a decade and was then teaching physics at South Side High School in Minneapolis.[16]

"Truth to tell, I have not been making history or anything else very rapidly this past year," she wrote in a letter to the Hamline Alumni Association. Emma complained she was chronically ill with sore throats and headaches and that she could not gain weight. When school was out for the summer, she went to Denver to stay with her father and stepmother. When her father set eyes on her, he thought she was "a thoroughbred invalid."[17]

The rental home in Denver was soon crowded with visitors and family members. Besides Emma, "Mother Silver"—Lily's mother—arrived from Omaha. George's third son, Frank, also moved in "for his health." Little else about Frank is recorded in the family records except that he left about three months later.[18]

George soon purchased a four-room house for $700, and they moved in on New Year's Day 1898. A photograph, taken that summer, shows George, Lily, and Emma sitting on the front lawn. More family photos in front of the house followed in the years ahead, including photos of my grandfather, Russell, as a child and later as a teenager.

Besides finding a new home, George and Lily also sought a new church. They began attending Asbury Methodist, a large ornate Victorian brick church built by well-to-do Denver Methodists. The building and its upscale congregation stood in sharp contrast to the small frontier wooden churches of Minnesota, the shanties of Black settlements, and the cowboy tents on the Texas range where George had toiled most of his adult life.

George volunteered as an assistant pastor at Ashbury, and his income was supplemented with donations from the congregation. "I did not come to Denver expecting any [financial] support, and the work I did was better for me than to sit in the house and do nothing. I am more thoroughly attached to Asbury for the work I have done."

George and Lily settled into housekeeping. "We both loved flowers, and our garden was a 'thing of beauty' during the summer months," he wrote in the journal.[19] "We both were literary in our tastes, and our long evenings were the brightest part of the year. In short, it was <u>home</u>, with all that the word means."

In 1899, George officially transferred his Methodist ministerial license back to the Minnesota conference. Why he did that, he did not say, but it probably had to do with qualifying for a pension from the conference where he had served the longest. He had no intention of returning to Minnesota other than for short visits.

At the turn of the new century, George traveled by rail to Minnesota to visit his sons, David, Frank, and Mercein. By then, David—who would be my great-grandfather—had become a furniture storeowner in Northfield; the occupations of Frank and Mercein are not known, but they probably were farmers. George attended the annual Minnesota Methodist conference and found his colleagues cordial, but he knew only a few. He had been gone for thirty years. "The members were strangers to me." He made no further mention in his journal of Hobart, who died not long after. George returned to Denver immediately following the close of the conference.

George had one more adventure in him. He took a train to Los Angeles in 1904 to attend the Methodist national convention.[20] His official reason for going was to advocate for friends in Idaho who wanted to redraw church boundaries with Oregon. George took a circuitous route to Los Angeles; stopping in Sacramento, and then traveling south by rail to visit Emma, who was then teaching school in Tulare in the Central Valley farm belt of California.

Emma had moved to Tulare two years earlier from Minnesota, George said, "for her health" and to escape the harsh northern winters. Emma lived on the 160-acre family farm of one of her mother's brothers, her Uncle Alfred Fay. In a twelve-page letter written on the Fourth of July 1904, George recorded the details of his adventure in California and how he slept through the stop at Tulare where Emma waited for him. "Emma called hurriedly, 'Is there a gray haired, one armed man on the train?'"[21]

The train began rolling south toward Los Angeles without him getting off. "Stop that train," she shouted. "The train moved out of sight of the Depot, then stopped and put me off on the open prairie. I was just awake from a sound sleep and half dazed. I began to walk back to town carrying the two valises."

Two men riding in a buggy came by and brought him back to Tulare. Meanwhile, Emma sent a search party looking for him. He finally made it to Alfred Fay's home, "I was never more completely exhausted," he wrote. "I was too tired to eat or sleep. Emma worked over me till midnight giving me a warm bath and ginger tea."

George stayed with the Fays and Emma for a week. It had been two years since he had seen her. "I found her well and strong." She now weighed about 129 pounds, he wrote. Emma told her father that a practitioner from the Christian Science Church had started her on the path to health, though she remained a Methodist. George reflected, "whether the Lord has affected a cure without the ordinary remedies, or with them, we will thank him for your restoration."

After staying a week with Emma and the Fays, George boarded a train for the Los Angeles Methodist conference where he wrote a newspaper article for the *Pacific Christian Advocate* with the byline "By a Visitor." He clipped it and pasted it into "Recollections of My Lifework." "I had a chance to visit with ministers and laymen from all parts of the world. It was a period of my life worthy to be remembered forever."

George succeeded in straightening out the church border dispute between Oregon and Idaho Methodists, but he was otherwise unimpressed by the plodding pace of business. In his newspaper dispatch, George wrote how the Methodist conference dithered over a proposal for financial assistance for disabled Civil War veterans.

"Days were spent in long-winded, hair-splitting discussions over the 'Rules of Order' and other matters just as important, but there was not time to provide for the disabled soldier." The proposal came to a vote on the last day of the national conference "when the haste to adjourn made it impossible to secure the proper legislation, and with a wave of the hand it was brushed aside for another four years."

During the recesses, George saw old friends from the Methodist conferences where he had served—and he was especially delighted to see Joseph Hartzell, who was now a bishop. In his letter to his children, George also mentioned seeing E. O. McIntire "who was your mother's last pastor" and had preached at her funeral in Austin.[22] Seeing him "afforded me great pleasure." McIntire now lived in Los Angeles.

"There were many men and women from all parts of the world, whom I had personally known, or of whom I had read—that made this place a <u>reunion</u> on grand scale, and a fitting type of the general <u>homecoming</u>. My satisfaction was unbounded. I shall never regret going to the General Conference."

At the close of the conference on May 19, 1904, George returned to Tulare for another ten days with Emma. He was invited to preach at the local Baptist Church and was introduced as a "young minister from Denver, Colorado." He was almost eighty. "So of course I had to be as young as I could."

From Tulare, George went north to Oregon to visit Owen and his family.

Two months later, Emma went from Tulure to Denver to be with her father and stepmother. Her father was delighted. "It was a pleasant surprise."

George celebrated his eightieth birthday in November 1904 with his daughter Emma and his second wife Lily by his side.[23] He had lived nearly forty years longer than he thought he would when, at the close of the Civil War, his health and morale were in shreds.

Emma helped Lily organize a birthday celebration. He received as a present a photographic portrait of all of his grandchildren in Minnesota. "I cannot describe my emotions—all my grandchildren right before me. All beautiful and true." Among those in the photograph is my grandfather, Russell, at the age of nine. "I had always regarded myself rich in my children, but here were 'new editions' of the Richardsons 'revised and improved.' Here were eleven pair of loving eyes right before me—eyes that spoke of bright hopes for the future."

Emma left Denver soon after Christmas and went back to Minnesota for a teaching position in Morton, about one hundred miles west of Minneapolis. Her niece Florence Richardson was a teacher in the same school. Emma and Florence formed a lifelong bond.

Her nieces and nephews adored her. "No matter what time of year Aunt Emma arrived, she brought little gifts for us all," Florence wrote. "Her visits were greatly anticipated by us all. Mother inveighed even Father into doing all sorts of renovating and repairs 'before Emma comes.'" Another niece, Ruth, wrote in her diary that Aunt Emma was "good to all of us" and "kind of a second mother."

Florence wrote her own memoir in 1943, inspired not by her grandfather's journal but by the essays and poetry of her grandmother, Caroline. Florence had inherited from Emma "a few family heirlooms and treasures" including Caroline's dairy. "Reading her writings," Florence wrote, "has given me such insight into her charming personality and unselfish character that I've been wondering if I, too, might not make a contribution to the family lore."

And, Florence wrote, she wanted her own children and grandchildren to know something of her Aunt Emma "whom I have known as long as I have known my parents."

>×-×<

In his sixties and seventies, George had rarely complained of any aches or pains. In his eighties, he still felt strong, and he immersed himself writing his life story in what became known to his family as "the journal." His son, Mercein, wrote to him: "We can't detect from your letters that you are growing old; in fact I don't believe you are, in mind. And judging from the things you do, you seem to have vitality enough to carry you along for a number of years yet."[24]

But in July 1905 George fell off his roof while trying to build a study where he could finish writing "Recollections of My Lifework." He broke his only wrist and injured his back. His accident laid him up for months. Lily needed help caring for him, and Emma was in Minnesota. When Emma got word of the accident, she hurried to the depot. "A train was due in an hour," George wrote, "and Emma was at the Depot, ready for a 1000 mile trip."[25]

With Emma's help, Lily nursed George back to health, although he never regained full use of his remaining hand. "My wife had been my right hand for 16 years. For this three months she was my right hand and left hand both." He got a sympathetic note from Hartzell. "I was melted into tears."

When he recovered, Emma returned to Minnesota and her teaching post. But six months later, George suffered another accident by tripping over the coal bin outside his house. He broke a rib. It took George a year before he resumed writing the journal. "At this date (July 26–1906) nearly a year after the injury I have not the perfect use of my hand." That summer, his granddaughter, Florence, came to visit and painted a watercolor of the garden view from his study. The painting was placed as the frontispiece of "Recollections of My Lifework."

Florence's painting depicted more than she probably intended about how narrow her grandfather's world had become.

George and Lily decided to sell the house on West 26th Avenue and move closer to Asbury Church; their house sold for $1,450—twice their purchase price. They bought a "double house," or what is now called a duplex, and rented out one unit for $17 a month. The new house on Caithness Place was three blocks from Asbury Church.

The deed was put in Lily's name, which resulted in later difficulties. "I expected my wife would outlive me by a number of years, and I wanted the source of her livelihood to be in such shape that she could handle it." Lily was twenty years younger than George, so it was not an unreasonable expectation that she would outlive him. But Lily, whose health had been frail throughout their marriage, was also declining.

Lily had been sick for a week, no doubt exhausted by caring for George. She was confined to bed most of the day but was able to come to the dinner table and to the family altar for evening prayers. "I discovered something unusual and hastened to her, but a gasp or two were all the signs of life that remained." On March 17, 1907, five months after moving to the new house, Lily died.[26]

A doctor later told George that she had "heart failure"—probably a heart attack. "I was stunned and bewildered," George wrote in his journal. "During the ten years we were neither of us free from bodily suffering. She was the greatest sufferer. Her asthma, which had been aggravated on the Pacific Coast, was a constant affliction," he wrote. "Our sufferings bound us together closer than ever. I knew it then, but I realize it more since she is gone, that she lived for me. [underline his]"

He notified Lily's family in Omaha, and Emma immediately set forth once again from Minnesota to be with her father. An obituary in a local newspaper, inserted into George's journal, described Lily as "intelligently religious, believed in the Bible from Genesis to Revelation—never doubted that Jesus was the Son of God." The obituary recounted their time on the "the plains of Texas," in the "lumber regions of Northern California and Oregon" and "the mining camps" in Idaho—"the out-of-the-way neglected settlements."

Lily's funeral was held at Asbury Church. Five preachers spoke. "The Pastor read the Obituary, which paid a generous tribute to her and to her work. I have inserted this tribute among these pages," George noted.[27]

They were the last words George Richardson wrote in "Recollections of My Lifework." Emma would have to finish the journal for him.

><><

Lily's remains were placed under a large granite tombstone in Fairmount Cemetery on the outskirts of Denver. "Elizabeth S. 1844–1907" was inscribed on the lower half; the upper half was left blank for George's name when the time came. George included a black-and-white photograph of the tombstone in the journal, the only photograph in his book. The tombstone was surrounded by trees and flowers.

Emma wrote a touching ten-page postscript in her father's journal about Lily's death.[28] "I came to Denver to help Father through the trying ordeal," she wrote. "It was Father's request that I write of his last days and of the funeral services. So I begin where his Journal leaves off with the death of my stepmother."

In what she labeled the "appendix" to her father's journal, Emma described his health as "good for his age, but each year he grew frailer." He was increasingly confined to home. "He attended church very regularly the first two years. The third year only twice, and the last year he did not leave the grounds."

Emma moved permanently to Denver to live with her father. Emma found a teaching job in Denver at North High School, where she taught math for another eighteen years. As Emma later recalled, she "began housekeeping (my first experience) in the cozy home where my stepmother had died."

However, their house was ensnared in probate court along with an exhaustive list of small items including Lily's spoons and broach pins.[29] Lily's will had left the house to her sisters with the idea that she would outlive her husband. Awkwardly, George had to sue his in-laws to win clear title to his house. "Unique, in that it covers the smallest bequests ever made in a will filed in the probate court," the *Lincoln (Nebraska) Star Journal* reported, "will hold the record for a long time as being the oddest document of its kind ever drawn."

Emma straightened out the mess.

Emma wrote a weekly letter to her family in Minnesota. Those that can be found bear her unmistakable humor and her love of life and learning. She admonished her nieces and nephews to get a solid education. In 1907, upon the twelfth birthday of her nephew Russell, who would become my grandfather, Emma wrote "You are certainly to be congratulated on 12 years well spent; at the same rate 10 more will finish your education and fit you for some useful place in life."[30]

George and Emma returned for a visit to Minnesota in 1909, staying in Northfield with Emma's brother, David.[31] It was to be George's last trip to Minnesota. A photograph shows four generations of Richardsons: George, with a long white beard; his son, David, dapperly dressed with a neat mustache; and David's daughters Florence and Ella (my grand aunts).[32] The photo also shows two baby boys in baptismal gowns—George's great-grandsons, Harold and Paul.

"Father simply had to go see his first Great-grandchildren," Emma wrote.[33] He baptized the two babies, and the ceremony was covered in the local newspaper. George also posed for a formal portrait at a studio in Northfield. He got haircut for the occasion. Emma and George then returned to Denver.

Owen visited Denver not long after. It was to be his last meeting with his father with whom he had shared so much.[34] By 1909, Owen's wife, Clara, had become an invalid, and Owen could no longer travel much. He was the postmaster in Adams, Oregon, where he had been the Methodist pastor. The position did not pay enough for him to care for Clara, so Owen sold insurance on the side. The days when he could have remained a college president were long behind him. He rounded out his meager income with an annual pension of $150 from the Methodist Church.

The Denver duplex was sold in 1910, and George and Emma moved to 3421 Stuart Street, about a mile from Ashbury Church. They could get to church by trolley car. "Father greatly enjoyed the change, and for a few months gained steadily," Emma wrote. But in January 1911, her father caught the flu. He recovered slowly. In May he began to decline. "It was not a disease, simply a fading away," Emma wrote.[35]

The spring and summer of 1911 saw a steady stream of relatives arriving in

Denver to pay their respects to the patriarch of their family. George's sixteen-year-old grandson, Russell (my grandfather) visited in June and stayed for the summer. "His grandfather was very fond of him, and used to lean on his strong arms for his little walk around the house and garden. He used to say to everyone who came in, 'Russell is such a good help.'"

A snapshot shows the family sitting in front of the house on Stuart Street with George in the center. He is wearing a long, heavy morning coat that might well have been the same coat he wore in his Civil War portrait a half-century earlier. Another photo, probably taken the same day, shows him walking in front of his house. The photographs are the last taken of George Richardson.

Emma purchased a small foot-peddle pump organ. One of her friends, Lois Russell, who was also a Denver teacher, moved in with them and played church music. "Father was very fond of her, and she usually played & sang for him an hour every evening," Emma wrote.

"He slept much in his reclining chair, but till almost the last he retained his interest in everything—the church periodicals & daily newspaper, church, city & national affairs. He was dressed & in his reclining chair till almost the last. His mind was clear, & he was cheerful and contented, quietly waiting the summons 'Come up Higher.' But the last two weeks dragged heavily, he was so anxious to go Home."

George Warren Richardson died quietly at home on August 8, 1911, at 4:45 in the afternoon. Emma was with him.

><><

George Richardson's funeral was held at Asbury Methodist Church in Denver with a phalanx of pastors serving as pallbearers. "The funeral was simple," Emma wrote. "Father had made all the arrangements some two weeks before his death." A silk American flag was draped over George's coffin,[36] and his ashes were buried next to Lily at the Fairmount Cemetery in Denver. Decades later, Emma's ashes were placed there, too.

Emma copied into the journal the flowery eulogy of Pastor James Harris, the former pastor of Asbury Church, who lauded George for his "self-sacrificing labor in the toils of the early ministry."

But no mention at his funeral was made of George's participation in the

Underground Railroad, or his service in a Black Union regiment in the Civil War, or his founding of a school for African Americans in Texas. The cause that drove George Richardson for most of his life—the emancipation of African Americans—had already begun to fade from the memory of white Americans.

The congregation at Asbury Methodist Church concluded the funeral by singing the hymn "How Firm a Foundation, Ye Saints of the Lord"—the same hymn that had been sung at the funeral of Confederate general Robert E. Lee: "When through the deep waters I call thee to go; The rivers of sorrow shall not overflow."[37]

Whether Emma caught the irony of singing that hymn—linking her father, the abolitionist, to the defender of the "Lost Cause"—she did not mention in the final entry in her father's journal.

⬦

When George Richardson was on the road visiting his congregations, he carried with him a five-by-seven-inch hardbound notebook covered in brown leather with a gold crest on the cover. Stuffed into saddlebags, year after year, the cover was scratched and frayed. The notebook was one of the treasures passed along from Emma to her niece Florence, then to my Aunt Madge, who gave it to me.

On the first few pages, George recorded the names of the officers with whom he served in the Civil War, and under their names the states where they came from—Missouri, Iowa, Illinois, Indiana, and New York. He used the same the notebook to record the marriages of Black soldiers and their "contraband" wives.

In the back of the notebook George wrote outlines of his stock sermons, numbering them. He kept track of where and when he delivered each sermon so he would not repeat himself to the same congregation. In "Sermon No. 22," George told his listeners that the blessings of heaven were theirs on Earth before they died.[38] "We need not wait till death."

He admitted that with so many trials in life, he often found it difficult feel to feel such blessings. He then asked his listeners, "How can this be accomplished?" Where to start? Then answering the question for himself:

"Commence from the point where you now stand. Go on."

⌖

Lori and I arrived in Denver on a drizzly cold spring afternoon after two days of driving the interstates across the endless prairie from Minnesota. We stopped in Omaha for the night before another long day on the road to reach Denver.

We had been on the road for two weeks, following the trail of George Richardson and his family across the South and Midwest. We had walked into the Slaughter Pen south of Nashville and found the nearly obliterated remains of Fort Pickering in Memphis. We had explored old churches, graveyards, and homesteads. We looked for lost letters from the Civil War at the Abraham Lincoln Presidential Library in Springfield, Illinois. We had been to the site of churches and schools in Dallas and Austin. We'd walked across windswept farms in Minnesota and found Caroline Richardson's grave, her tombstone weathered by a century's worth of harsh winters.

We were now at the end of a journey that had begun at a family picnic many years earlier on the banks of the Sacramento River in Dunsmuir. By the time we reached Denver, most of those at that reunion had died, including my father.

We followed our GPS to the ornate gates of Fairmount Cemetery that had once been on the outskirts of Denver but was now in a suburb. Metropolitan Denver had grown around it. Looking at graveyard maps on the internet we were uncertain whether we could find the Richardson plot. The cemetery contained eighty-six thousand graves.

When we arrived, we met our Colorado hosts Ann Imse and Robert Tonsing, journalist colleagues and friends of many years. Ann had combed the records of the dauntingly large old cemetery to locate the Richardson family plot. Our rendezvous point was the "Ivy Chapel," a gothic-revival building with flying buttresses in the heart of the cemetery. Ann and Robert had gotten there ahead of us and scouted possible locations. They had narrowed the search to a few yards right in front of the chapel. We started walking, umbrellas in hand.

George Richardson's gravesite was in "Section 6" next to a gravel road crowded with tombstones. "RICHARDSON" was etched in block capital letters on one side of the tombstone, and on the other side, "George W. 1824–1911" above "Elizabeth S." There were no flowerbeds like those that had surrounded in the tombstone in the black-and-white photo in George's journal. Mary Emma Richardson's name was inscribed in small letters on a narrow side.

Just as it did when we found Caroline's grave in Minnesota, the skies opened, and it began to rain. I said a silent prayer and left a small pebble from the Sea of Galilee in a crevice under the tombstone. I had carried the pebble in my pocket for many years. It was time to let it go.

Later that day, we found Asbury Methodist Church where George ministered in his final days, and where his life was celebrated at his funeral. Our friend, Ann, discovered the street names had been changed in the early twentieth century, presenting a navigational challenge finding the church—but find it she did. Asbury Church had ceased to serve as a Methodist church long ago when the neighborhood had become a slum. We found gunshot holes in the windows.

The red stone church building was sold and resold, but it still stands as a spectacular reflection of Victorian church architectural sensibilities. No longer called Ashbury or Methodist, it became a nondenominational evangelical church called "The Sanctuary Downtown" catering to young urban professional families. After our visit, the building changed hands again and became an event center called "The Kirk of Highland."[39]

George might not have appreciated the amplified guitar music in the nondenominational church, but he would have smiled at the evangelical ethos. We were given a tour by the pastor's wife. The woodwork, railings, and chairs were much as they had been when George and Lily Richardson were regular in their attendance, but the original pulpit was gone.

Later that day, we found the house on Stuart Street where George Richardson had died. Not much had changed from how it appeared in century-old family photo albums.

Our journey following my ancestor's trail was at an end.

⁓ 28 ⁓

SEAS AND STARS

Oh, that each in the day of His coming may say, 'I have fought
my way through; I have finished the work thou didst give me to do.
CHARLES WESLEY | "COME, LET US ANEW, OUR JOURNEY PURSUE," 1750

Emma lived in Denver for the rest of her life, teaching mathematics and history at North High School until she retired. She taught the children of my father's generation. After selling the house on Stuart Street where her father died, Emma got a place of her own. When school was out for the summer, she visited her relatives in Minnesota, Oregon, and California.

During the First World War, Emma attended a patriotic rally in Denver at the municipal auditorium that seated fourteen thousand. "I wouldn't have missed it for anything," she wrote in a letter to her brother David.[1] "Hundreds stood through the long program. The singing by that vast audience, led by our new $80,000 organ, of 'America the Beautiful,' Star Spangled Banner, Keep the Home Fires Burning, & Over There, etc. was thrilling."

Emma kept up correspondence with her nephew in the Navy, who one day would be my grandfather. "Where is Russell?" she inquired of her brother, David. She was thrilled to get a letter from another nephew on his way to France, but not from Russell.

In the summer of 1918, as the World War raged, Emma nearly died in a cholera epidemic after her return to Denver from one of her periodic trips to Minnesota. She would live to see the Second World War. To the end of her life, Mary Emma Richardson placed a flag at her father's grave on Memorial Day.

After his father's death, Owen continued serving as postmaster in Adams, Oregon.[2] When Clara's health improved, she became assistant postmaster next to him in the Adams Post Office. Owen and Clara took in wayward teenage boys, with mixed success. Owen made no further mention in his memoirs of his own daughter, Carrie, or her death in 1920, though her death was recorded (probably by Emma) on a genealogical chart in the back of the journal.[3]

When Clara died in 1932, Emma invited Owen to move in with her in Denver, and the two bought a house together. They did not always see eye-to-eye. He did not care for Asbury Church and found another Methodist church more to his liking. Emma kept her membership at Asbury, but more often than not, accompanied her brother to his church.

Owen wrote his memoir while living with Emma, and she helped him with the chapters on Samuel Huston College. As Emma later put it, they did so to "clear up the dim past history." A note in her papers mentions that they based their history of the college largely on their father's "Recollections of My Lifework." Owen died in 1939, one year after finishing his memoir.

Emma stayed connected to the college. In March 1943, she wrote to Stanley E. Grannum, president of Samuel Huston College,[4] expressing her appreciation for a "fine account" of the school's history she had read in the *Christian Advocate*. She included photographs of her parents, her brother Owen, and his wife, Clara. "I wondered if you might not be pleased to have the pictures of those who dreamed of it and gave eighteen years of service and sacrifice in laying the foundation upon which the later donors have built."

Those pictures can still be found in the Huston-Tillotson University library. Enclosed in Emma's letter was one more item: a check to the school's "victory campaign." The amount was smudged out in her copy of the letter. All she asked in return was a college catalog.

Near the end of her life, Emma wrote a will. She sold her house to her favorite niece, Florence Street, for a dollar plus "love and affection." Emma sent a box of her father's handwritten letters written during the Civil War to Florence, who was married to a professor at Pittsburg State University in Kansas. Typed copies of the letters resurfaced in the summer of 2014, and the originals resurfaced a year later in my aunt's home.

Emma died on October 1, 1943. The Samuel Huston College catalog was still in her papers mingled with her father's papers. With Emma's death, interest in Samuel Huston College disappeared in our family.

George's second son, David Fay Richardson—my great-grandfather—prospered for a time as a furniture store owner in Northfield, Minnesota. He had no connection or interest in the school in Austin. He never saw it or visited his parents when they lived in Texas.

Dave, as he was known, graduated from Carleton College in Northfield, and was prosperous enough to send his own children to college. He married

Clementine Watson and they reared three daughters and two sons. The youngest was my grandfather, Russell. His brother, Fay, was given as his first name the maiden name of his grandmother, Caroline. The brothers were inseparable as young boys. As an adult, Fay settled in Minnesota and reared a large family. Years later we reconnected with his daughter, Jeanette, who helped us locate graveyards, homes, and churches—and connected me with more second cousins from Fay's lineage.

Owen wrote a letter in 1937 to his brother Dave, praising him as a good father and faithful Methodist.[5] "For years your achievements have made me almost envious," Owen wrote. "I am certain that the Recording Angel has filled many pages with credits for your unselfish endeavors." However, Dave hit the economic skids in mid-life.[6]

He swapped his furniture store in Minnesota for a farm in Sutherlin, Oregon, where he made a modest income apple farming. Dave tried to write a memoir in 1938, but never completed it. He died in October 1943, eight days after his sister Emma died. Frank, the third son, whose health was never good, died in 1921. Earl Mercein, the last of their generation and the youngest of George and Caroline Richardson's children, died in 1947 at the dawn of the nuclear and television age.

The children of George and Caroline Richardson were born during the time of slavery and civil war. They grew up on farms and traveled mostly on foot or by horse and wagon. Train travel was a rare luxury. They had witnessed the upheavals of war, emancipation, Reconstruction, the settlement of the West, world wars, and at least two economic depressions. They lived through staggering cultural, religious, political, and technological revolutions.

My father and grandfather saw more of the world than their ancestors. They were both fascinated by the sea and sky. They had learned how to read the stars aboard us Navy ships in the middle of world wars, finding their way across the oceans with charts and sextants. They knew the names of dozens of stars and constellations. Long after their seagoing days, they could stare at the stars for hours and point out this star or that, and they wanted me to learn them, too.

Their love of the sky was in their bones. On the night before a raid in Mississippi, Chaplain Richardson had laid on the ground for an hour "where I could study astronomy very well."[7] Tucked inside his notebook were two pages of sketches he drew in a grungy mosquito-infested Civil War fort of the phases of a solar eclipse in October 1865. He mailed another set of sketches to Caroline.

I wondered what my ancestor imagined when he was looking at the stars, and what he imagined those of us who came after him would see.

⊱⊰

By trying to see through my ancestor's eyes, I hope my own eyes have become sharper. My own discomfort—outrage, really—at seeing Nathan Bedford Forrest Park in Memphis had everything to do with knowing that one member of my family knew Forrest for the butcher he was. I knew this because George Richardson wrote it down.

The Richardsons, and many others like them, saw the hand God in the battles to bring freedom to the enslaved. The Gospel of Jesus, George preached, was "heaven's Emancipation Proclamation."[8] He meant it literally.

"Salvation is abundant. Salvation is free," he preached. "If we have tasted the water of life, can we be content to allow others to perish without it?"

To George and Caroline Richardson, the fight to end slavery was more than a political cause. It was a religious calling, and worth sacrificing comfort, riches, and even their lives. Ending slavery was inseparable from the war to save the Union. Yet, we make a mistake if we equate his evangelical fervor with the right-wing politics and sexuality culture wars of our own time.

The Civil War-era Richardsons were not the only faithful people of their time attempting to atone for the sin of slavery. In our travels, we came across the stories of other families who worked tirelessly to abolish slavery, build schools for the emancipated, and defy the terrorism of white supremacists. Many died trying.

After the war, George and Caroline did something more; they carried the holy cause of emancipation forward not with guns but with school buildings and books. Perhaps George can be faulted for not confronting the social or political structures of his time, and he often failed to see how those structures severely held back the previously enslaved and his work. Judging by her words, Caroline saw this more clearly than he did. But together they did what they could, where they could, when they could—and they trusted that would be enough. They somehow knew others would come after them taking up the mantle of their cause.

Author and journalist Isabel Wilkerson, in her extraordinary book, *Caste*, details how the racial caste system has permeated our national life at every level for generations. "And yet, somehow, there are rare people," she writes, "who seem immune to the toxins of caste in the air we breathe, who manage to transcend what most people are susceptible to. From the abolitionists who risked personal ruin to end slavery to the white civil rights workers who gave their lives to help end Jim Crow and the political leaders who outlawed it, these all-too-rare people are a testament to the human spirit, that humans can break free of the hierarchy's hold on them."

I like to think that my ancestors are among those "rare people."

George Richardson's vantage point was not from the perch of a lofty famous preacher, or a political theorist, or a professional theologian. He saw life from the saddle or a wagon on the trail where souls and emancipation were won. He knew life was tenuous and temporary but believed that faith and salvation were eternal. By writing what he saw, he could teach those of us who came long after. "We are all journeying," he preached in 1862 during the darkest days of the Civil War.[9] "The instability of earthly things teaches us this great truth that here we have no continuing city."

An Episcopal priest friend of mine, Michael Cunningham, is fond of saying that "faith must have feet." Those feet must be sturdy and real to be true and meaningful. I have thought of those words many times as I have reflected on the life and work of my great-great-grandparents, George and Caroline Richardson, and their children, especially Owen and Emma. Their faith most assuredly had feet. When their faith faltered, as surely it did, they picked themselves up, dusted themselves off, and tried again.

The torches of the KKK could not stop them. The City of Dallas could not stop them. The segregationists in the Methodist Church could not stop them. My ancestors changed lives. They took the hard road with risks to their lives and cost to their comfort. Sometimes sleeping under a wagon was comfort enough. They knew they could not do everything, but they knew they could do *something*. In one of his sermons, George Richardson implored: "We excuse ourselves by saying we cannot do as much as some, therefore we will do nothing."[10]

✿ 29 ✿

CHARLOTTESVILLE

The conventional Christian word is muffled, confused, and vague.
Too often the price exacted by society for security and respectability
is that the Christian movement in its formal expression must be
on the side of the strong against the weak.

HOWARD THURMAN | *JESUS AND THE DISINHERITED*, 1949

Why is equality so assiduously avoided?
Why does white America delude itself, and
how does it rationalize the evil it retains?

MARTIN LUTHER KING JR. | *WHERE DO WE GO FROM HERE*, 1967

The evils that George and Caroline Richardson confronted in their day are still very much with us in ours.

Their descendants—my parents' generation and my generation—would be caught up in the conflicts and causes of our time: civil rights, Black power, and Black Lives Matter; feminism and gay rights; terrorism and the wars in Vietnam, Iraq, Afghanistan, and Ukraine; environmental degradation, global warming, and economic injustice; the Covid-19 pandemic; political chaos and right-wing insurrection—in short, all of the turmoil that has tumbled forth out of the twentieth and into the twenty-first century.

Looking back, I realize I've been living most of my life at the intersection of these conflicts through journalism, politics, and religion.

As a career choice, my becoming an Episcopal priest in midlife did not make a lot of sense to many of my friends in journalism. Truth be told, I had moments when it made no sense to me, either. My only explanation was that the tug of something deep inside me—call it the yearnings of the heart or the call of the Holy Spirit—was leading me to places I never imagined I would go.

I had thought as a teenager I would follow this path later in life, following the example of Carl Gracely, the middle-aged seminarian in our suburban parish. As improbable as it still seems to me, it happened. When I made my departure announcement to my colleagues, even some of my journalism friends told me (in hushed tones) that they went to church, too. Something about the hard-edged ethos of newsrooms did not easily lend itself to such admissions.

I was ordained a priest at the dawn of this new century, yet I never felt I had left journalism. For me, both vocations have the same mission: bringing truth and light into the shadows of narrowness and despair. Both vocations have richly formed me and sharpened my awareness of both God's presence and the evils of our age.

As I continue trying to make sense of my work as a priest, I frequently reach back to my years as a newspaper reporter. What I learned then about people, poverty, and politics indelibly shapes how I see the world. Among my hardest and longest assignments as journalist came in 1980 when I covered the Ku Klux Klan. What started as a one-week assignment stretched into six months when the Klan emerged as an unexpected force in California politics.[1]

The KKK had made resurgence in Southern California, and its epicenter was the white working-class town of Fontana, about sixty miles east of Los Angles. Fontana was the birthplace of the Hells Angels motorcycle club following World War II. But in the late 1970s, the massive Kaiser Steel foundry had closed, and the run-down white neighborhoods of Fontana looked not much different than the run-down Black neighborhoods of East Riverside near where I lived.

Fontana became fertile ground for angry young white males with drug habits and criminal records. My reporting showed that the Klansmen were mostly dangerous to each other. One had gone to prison for murdering another Klansman. The KKK seemed a disorganized rabble of dopeheads fighting each other, unable to cope with the changing demographics of Southern California. Parading in the streets in their white robes and taunting the police, the Southern California Klansmen became a spectacle for the media, and we bit. They made for good television and newspaper copy. But the Klan was hard to take seriously as a political force.

And then came Tom Metzger, their grand wizard from a small town in the avocado country northeast of San Diego.[2] He was short with slick black hair. He described himself as a television repairman, and we soon learned he had a knack for sound bites. Barely noticed by the media until primary election night in 1980, Metzger won thirty-three thousand votes and the

Democratic nomination for a Congressional seat representing the rural swaths of Riverside, San Diego, and Imperial counties.

Metzger had no chance of unseating Republican Claire Burgener, the seven-term incumbent in the overwhelmingly lopsided Republican district. But it didn't matter. Winning was not the point for Metzger. His goal was shredding the political order, and that he did. Metzger got a flood of media attention and stunned the sleepy San Diego Democratic Party, which was forced to disown him.

I ended up spending the summer and fall of 1980 on the road, following Metzger to campaign events and doing my best to cover a fringe candidate who had secured a major party nomination and knew how to play the media. In November, Metzger won forty-six thousand votes in the general election but was handily defeated by Republican Burgener, who won nearly three hundred thousand votes. That same election sent Ronald Reagan to the White House, and Tom Metzger was soon forgotten. The media moved on.

Had I been a better reporter at the time, I would have asked why Metzger won forty-six thousand votes. Metzger had made no secret of his Klan leadership and his racist views. He appealed primarily to white rural and working-class males alienated from the Democratic Party—"Reagan Democrats," as the media called them. Metzger, indeed, benefited from Reagan's strategy that ultimately upended the center-left coalition that had propelled Democrats into power since the New Deal.

Two years after his run for Congress, Metzger ran again, this time statewide for the United States Senate, and again as a Democrat. But the political story that year was former Governor Jerry Brown, who easily won the Democratic nomination for the US Senate but lost in the general election to Republican Pete Wilson, the mayor of San Diego. Metzger had won seventy-six thousand votes from Californians in the Democratic primary, but the news media—myself included—didn't much notice.

As a force in politics, these voters were not going away. The seeds of Donald Trump's rise were sown in those seventy-six thousand votes.

〉━━✕━━〈

In 2008, the year Barack Obama was elected president, I accepted a call as the rector—the senior pastor—of St. Paul's Memorial Church in Charlottesville,

Virginia. I had been a priest by then for seven years. The idea of moving anywhere east of Reno was not in my game plan. But after hearing how the congregation was committed to engaging with social justice issues in a tangible way I accepted the position. I ended up shepherding this Southern progressive congregation for seven years.

Our congregation was active in a community-organizing project called IMPACT, drawing together Christian, Jewish, and Muslim congregations to solve issues in poor neighborhoods, which were primarily Black, Latino, and immigrant. We housed homeless people inside our church buildings for the night during the winter and raised money for schools in Africa. We pioneered marriage equality in our region, hosting the first same-sex wedding in an Episcopal church in Central Virginia. Yet, as a westerner—and worse, as a Californian—I did not always fit into Charlottesville or the South. I moved back to California in 2015, feeling I had accomplished what I could do.

Two years after I left, "Charlottesville" entered the national lexicon not just as a place but as an event.[3] Although I was on the other side of the continent, it felt like a gut punch in August 2017 when angry young white men invaded Charlottesville, carrying tiki torches and rendering Nazi salutes on the lawn across the street from the church I had led. My emotional connections to Charlottesville were deeper than I realized.

The young white supremacists descending on Charlottesville were there ostensibly to protest the removal of a statue of Confederate general Robert E. Lee. But they came looking for a fight. They were the offspring of Tom Metzger's cause.

On that first night of their invasion, the neo-Nazis rallied in front of a statue of Thomas Jefferson on the grounds of the University of Virginia, choosing the spot to celebrate Jefferson as a slaveholder. Unbeknownst to them, they stood in front of statue created by a Jewish artist depicting Jefferson holding a book upon which the word God is inscribed in the languages of the world's major religions, including Allah and Yahweh.

Just across the street, inside my former church, people had gathered to pray and hear from Black intellectual Cornell West. I heard later from friends of how they felt trapped and terrorized, fearing for their lives if they left. They departed through a back door, walking in small groups for mutual protection.

The next day, three people lost their lives. A white supremacist drove his car into a crowd, killing a young woman and injuring others. Two police officers died when their helicopter crashed after monitoring the protests from the sky.

Congregation Beth Israel, the only synagogue in Charlottesville, asked for police protection. None came. Neo-Nazi websites called for it to be burned. The congregation hired an armed guard.

"For half an hour," said the congregation's president Alan Zimmerman, "three men dressed in fatigues and armed with semiautomatic rifles stood across the street from the temple. Several times, parades of Nazis passed our building, shouting, 'There's the synagogue!' followed by chants of 'Seig Heil' and other anti-Semitic language. Some carried flags with swastikas and other Nazi symbols."

A few days later, President Trump said there were "some very fine people on both sides."

Why was Charlottesville at the epicenter of this? It was certainly not the only Southern town with a Confederate War statue. In fact, Charlottesville's Lee statue had come under a fair degree of mockery in recent years. The yearly Gay Pride festival was held at the foot of the statue and old Bobby Lee was annually draped in rainbow flags.

The neo-Nazis chose their target well. Charlottesville is an embodiment of the contradictions around race in American life. The town is primarily associated with Jefferson, the author of the Declaration of Independence who penned "all men are created equal." Though he expressed his belief that slavery would somehow fade away, he was a slave owner to his dying breath.

Jefferson's home, Monticello, sits on a hill overlooking the town. The design reflects his ambivalence about slavery, hiding the enslaved workers in the undercroft and tucking the "Mulberry Row" slave quarters off to the side and out of view of the front entrance. Jefferson's imprimatur is everywhere in Charlottesville. The University of Virginia was not only founded by Jefferson, but also designed by him. Slaves built it. Among Jefferson's unique architectural innovations at the university are eight-foot-high wavy brick walls that kept the slaves out of sight, again reflecting his contradictory feelings about slavery.

In the nineteenth and twentieth centuries, Charlottesville was segregated like other Southern towns. The scars are still noticeable. The Jefferson Theater, now a venue for rock bands, has a balcony where the "colored" were allowed to sit.

Charlottesville went through the convulsions around integration in the 1950s, joining other Southern communities in "massive resistance" against desegregation court orders for public schools. Charlottesville's schools closed rather than integrate, and nearly all the white churches were complicit by allowing their buildings to be used for whites-only schools.

One of the few exceptions: my church, St. Paul's Memorial, whose rector at the time, Ted Evans, labeled cooperation with segregation as "evil." He would not allow his church building to be used for an all-white school, and he was forced out by his bishop. The congregation stood firm in support of Ted Evans's stance, especially a group of young parents who joined the church because of his courage. It would be years before the rest of Charlottesville caught up.

By the time I arrived in Charlottesville in 2008, those young parents of the 1950s had become the elders of my church—and they were just as committed to the cause of their youth. By then, several had served on the city council and as mayor.

In recent years, Charlottesville has had Black, Sikh, and Jewish mayors, and the city voted solidly for Barack Obama—twice. President Obama was a regular visitor, bringing with him foreign dignitaries on visits to Monticello.

Yet with all of its progressive ethos, neighborhoods are still defined by race, and there is still a wide economic disparity between the white community and the communities of color in Charlottesville.

The 2017 incident in Charlottesville forced me to once again ask how far we have come, and how far we have left to go. A new generation brought forth the slogan "Black Lives Matter," confronting entrenched white supremacy, brutal police conduct, and unequal justice. The faith communities of Charlottesville—Christian, Jewish, and Muslim—pulled together to confront the Nazis when they invaded the town. That was no surprise. They had been working together for years.

But the white supremacist invasion of the Charlottesville of 2017 was also something else: the precursor of the deadly insurrection and attack on democracy at the US Capitol in January 2021, with Trump supporters tromping the halls with Confederate flags, defecating on the floors, and taunting Black police officers with racist slurs. Five people, including officers, died, and 140 others were injured.

After a four-year court battle, the bronze statue of Robert E. Lee was finally removed in 2021 from its perch in Charlottesville. The city council voted to donate it to a local African American heritage center that proposed melting it down, and turning it into "a new work of art that will reflect racial justice and inclusion."[4]

The arguments over Confederate statues fester. In the summer of 2021, the state of Tennessee removed the statue of Nathan Bedford Forrest from its state capitol building. The lieutenant governor of Tennessee, Randy McNally, announcing his opposition to the move, declared, "The woke mob means ultimately to uproot and discard not just Southern symbols, but American heroes and history as well."[5]

The issues of race and justice confronted by my ancestors are still with us—and won't let us go. Who we think of as heroes still matters.

✣ 30 ✣

REMEMBERING

Let my vindication come forth from your presence;
let your eyes be fixed on justice.

PSALM 17: 2 | BOOK OF COMMON PRAYER

Framing justice as something done to white people who have no intention of
denouncing their power is an idea too radical for many white people to consider.
But the gospel is radical. And racial. And we would all do well to ensure that race
and all that lives around it is always, honestly, part of the conversation.

OLUWATOMISIN OREDEIN | FEBRUARY 23, 2021

I am left with the same question I began with in this exploration of the
memories of my ancestors: how could a family so committed to the emancipation and liberation of the enslaved forget so much?

The story of George and Caroline Richardson faded into the distant
memory of our family. Our ancestors painstakingly recorded their memories,
but their words sat on shelves for nearly a century, unread except by few. Yet
they had hoped otherwise.

Was this a benign amnesia borne from ignorance, or was this a manifesta-
tion of the malignancy on our national soul masquerading as polite neglect?
I once thought it was the former but now realize it was the latter.

Of course, it is easy to see how memories faded as new generations came
forward and older generations died off. Others married into the family,
bringing with them their own religions, politics, and prejudices. Situations
and locations changed. Men left the farms, went into business, and their
wives climbed the social ladder—the *white* social ladder. The Republican
Party of our ancestors' upbringing, forged in the cyclone of abolitionism
and civil war, became the party of industrialism and suburbanization. Their
schools, workplaces, and social gatherings were smothered by theories of
social Darwinism and the fake science of racial eugenics. Forgetting the
cause of emancipation was easier than the work of remembering.

But the loss of memory in our family was more than this. We didn't just lose our memory—we buried it in a graveyard of white Christianity.

My family were mostly well-meaning church-going folk. They ate fish on Fridays, hushed their kids in church on Sunday, and cared for their neighbors in need. But they did not escape the ossification of middle-class white Christianity that served to uphold the rigidity of the racial caste system. For the most part, we thrived in it.

Many commentators have noted—to the extent that is a cliché—that the most segregated day of the week in America is Sunday. This has been so since European settlers first reached these shores. Not even the most ardent, religiously motivated abolitionists of the nineteenth century or the faith-filled civil rights activists of the twentieth could change it.

Indeed, as civil rights for Blacks expanded, so did the religious bastions of white privilege.[1] The predominantly white conservative and rigidly patriarchal Southern Baptist Convention became the largest Protestant denomination in the United States, and Jerry Falwell's Liberty University grew out of nowhere in 1971 to have an annual enrollment of more than one hundred thousand students a half-century later—more than double the state university where I went to school.

Author and pastor Michael Eric Dyson, in a powerful sermon at the Washington National Cathedral, noted a connection with the rightward swing of white Christianity and the insurrection led by white supremacists at the US Capitol that attempted to overturn the 2020 election.[2] "The gospel of Christ has been shamelessly exploited by angry white citizens who mask their bigotry in faith," he preached twelve days after the violence. "In the wake of this carnage, many citizens claimed that what occurred at the Capitol is not America. The sad truth is that, for many people, this is the only America they know."

The blood on the Selma bridge still looms large in our national soul. "Unity is the bridge; justice is the destination," Dyson said. "We don't celebrate the Edmund Pettus Bridge; we celebrate the brave souls who crossed it and the voting rights Black people won for doing so."

Black churches are still being burned, bombed, and worse with alarming regularity. On June 17, 2015, Dylann Roof, a nineteen-year-old white supremacist hoping to ignite a race war, walked into "Mother" Emanuel Church in Charleston, South Carolina—the historic flagship of the African

Methodist Episcopal Church. He took out his pistol and proceeded to kill nine parishioners, including the pastor.[3] All of the victims were shot multiple times. Roof was convicted of multiple murders and sentenced to death. He remained unrepentant.

In my Sunday sermon a few days after the murders, I noted the mental health of the gunman was an easier topic for whites than the gunman's racist targeting of a Black church: "This young man did not grow up in a vacuum. He learned his racial hatred somewhere—and from someone."[4]

The malignancy of racially segregated religion is not confined to conservative churches, and rears itself in nuanced ways that signal "keep out" to non-whites. Oluwatomisin Oredein, a Black Presbyterian pastor, writes searingly of leaving her progressive white church to teach theology in Texas because its *whiteness* overwhelmed everything about the church. "White belief operates first and foremost from how white people interpret themselves in a world of their making," she writes. "How they want to see themselves must be how they actually are. There is no accountability to different communities; there are no checks and balances—just an assurance and supreme confidence in the force of the white imagination."

All true. I have attended more church board retreats than I can remember where we filled the walls with large poster papers, listing among our goals becoming more racially diverse as a congregation. We always saw this in our own terms. Pooling our ignorance only served to fill larger pools of ignorance. We never paused to probe our underlying motivations or listen to the stories of those left out, let alone what it would mean to give up control of the gate to people not like ourselves.

We might talk of racial diversity or even racial reconciliation in our white churches, but rarely do we talk about racial justice. The words proclaiming justice in Psalm 17 are usually missing from our lips. As a white pastor, I've come to see how avoiding the topic of racial justice is the cancer not just on Christianity, but on the soul of our nation.

The tragic truth is that white Americans have never faced the barbarity of slavery, or its aftermath, and how powerful Southern planters fought a vicious civil war to preserve it. The South of George Richardson's time was not just a collection of states but a vast prison camp for the benefit of a landed aristocracy. The legacy of slavery—the walls of a caste system based on skin color—still permeates American life.

We could begin to break down those walls by acknowledging the painful—sometimes brutal—stories of our ancestors. We could listen to each other's stories from a place of openness and not defensiveness. These stories shape who we are, often in ways we don't see—and sometimes in ways we don't want to see. This is the legacy we carry with us.

We can also hear the stories of those, like my ancestors, who sought to break down those walls. We do not have to accept the excuse that people are "captive of their times." Our attitudes and actions are shaped by the world around us, but there were always those who saw injustice for what it was and followed a different path. This, too, is the legacy we carry with us.

I am acutely aware that I present my words from a place of privilege in that white caste system. I live in a safe neighborhood. I have never been excluded from anything because of the color of my skin. I don't know what it is like to be a Black parent who must teach their sons how to behave when pulled over in traffic by a police officer. When I've been stopped by a cop I've never feared for my life. I don't need to sleep in a bathtub at night to keep from being hit by a stray bullet in a drive-by shooting, a common practice in Riverside's barrio, Casa Blanca, when I covered the neighborhood as a reporter. I don't have to worry that I might be treated as a criminal when the police come to my neighborhood.

This malignancy on our national soul led to the police killing of George Floyd in Minneapolis in 2020. The nine minutes and twenty-nine seconds that Minneapolis police officer Derek Chauvin put his knee on George Floyd's neck, choking him to death, led to a national reckoning like none we have seen in a generation.[5] We learned again that the Selma bridge is everywhere, and always was, even in the Minnesota of the Richardson family.

Will we ever cross that bridge?

><><

When he was eighty-five—two years before his death—George Richardson went back to Minnesota to see his children, grandchildren, and great-grandchildren. He knew this would be the last time.

He delivered a sermon at Northfield's Methodist Church.[6] His cheeks were gaunt and his gray beard long. Dressed in black, the old itinerant preacher climbed into the Northfield pulpit that had once been his sole domain. Others had long since come and gone, taking his place. But he was here again, one last time.

It certainly must have crossed his mind that Caroline's grave was only a few miles away.

For his text, George Richardson used a passage from the Old Testament describing Jacob wrestling all night with a mysterious man who breaks his hip.[7] At the break of dawn, Jacob discovers he has been wrestling with none other than God. Jacob survives the match but comes away scathed with a permanent limp.

The Reverend Richardson then told his listeners how he had wrestled with God his entire life. He told of how, like Jacob, the wrestling match nearly crushed him: the loss of his right arm, the loss of a child, the loss of two wives and many friends.

He described bloody Civil War battles he had witnessed, wretched field hospitals and the soldiers who did not come home. "The infinities that confront me in this passage are overwhelming," George explained. He told of how he had seen so much—too much—and that despair had become his companion. "The visions of youth have failed of realization. Hopes have ended in disappointment. Cherished friends have vanished from our sight. Health has failed," he said. "We are weak and helpless."

But then he told of how he never felt alone, how an invisible force held him up giving him strength and a vision of a future not his own. From whence did he find this invisible force?

My great-great-grandfather's answer fills my soul with hope:

"His Almightiness in the form of love."

George Richardson inserted this watercolor painting by his niece, Florence Richardson, into his journal as a frontispiece. He described it as the view "from my study door to the street past the kitchen door" of his house at 2612 West 26th Avenue, Denver, Colorado, July 1906. Author's Collection.

ACKNOWLEDGMENTS

This book would not have been possible without the faith and work of my wife, Lori Korleski Richardson, who joined me exploring graveyards and battlefields, plowed through files at the Abraham Lincoln Presidential Library, heard my perplexities and frustrations, and supported this project in a thousand different ways. Her insights, ideas, and skilled editorial eye touched every page of this book. She has spent countless hours scouring the internet for details enriching this story and fact checking. This project has truly been a collaboration as we have lived this book together.

As we traveled across the country, I was constantly reminded of why it matters that we tell the stories of our ancestors—and why it matters we hear these stories. I am enormously blessed that my ancestors put their stories on paper and left them where we could find them. My greatest debt is to them.

I come from a family of writers—men and women—beginning with George and Caroline Richardson. Those who came after them also wrote their stories beginning with their oldest son Owen. And given that his sister Emma helped him (and was probably the better writer) we can surmise that many of the recollections contained in Owen's memoir are hers.

Not all were as skilled with words, but they gave it a try. David Fay Richardson, their brother and my great-grandfather, wrote about his days at Carleton College and running a furniture store, but he never finished his memoir. His son Russell, my father's father, made a stab at writing his journal, though he did not get past his service in the Great War. His daughter Madge—my aunt—pushed him forward. I helped him finish by taping a series of interviews in 1976, but I did not know enough to ask him the right questions.

Florence, his sister, wrote her memoir, inspired by the diary of their grandmother, Caroline. Their sister Ruth wrote hers, and it is a remarkable record of her early life in Minnesota and then in the rough settlements of Oregon in the early twentieth century, topics beyond the scope of this work. And, of course, my father wrote his memoir with his ancestor's journal on a shelf above his desk.

George and Caroline Richardson inspired all of them. To have this treasure of their words—written in their own hand—is a priceless gift beyond measure. That it took this long to read their words is shame on me.

I owe a huge debt to my aunt Madge Richardson Walsh, the keeper of family records and Richardson oral tradition. She spent decades tracing genealogies and annotating journals and memoirs. Her upstairs workroom in Redding, California, was filled with binders, papers, old books, and many of the primary sources used in this book. She was an unflagging supporter of this book project and read early drafts, pointing out where I had missed the mark and suggesting other lines of inquiry. She died in 2015, long before this book was completed. After my aunt's death, her daughter Caitlin unearthed more records and photographs in the workroom and gave them to me. Her generosity and ideas help shape this book.

Many guides and archivists in several states were enormously helpful. I am especially indebted to Genile Dennison, a graduate assistant at the Pittsburg State University in Kansas who discovered the existence of George Richardson's Civil War letters. Her many clues led to a stack of papers deep in my Aunt Madge's workroom where they were stuffed in a folder. I would have missed them except for Genile's descriptions. I am also grateful to Candace L. Hart, university archivist at Hamline University who provided digital copies of alumni records and other documents related to Emma Richardson and searched for other records on the Richardsons that ultimately eluded discovery.

I am in enormous debt to all of those who have read drafts at many stages, including my cousin Caitlin, and Jenny Weber, Bill Bergen, Ray Tessler, Suzanne Choney, Ilana Debare, Chris Bowman, Greg Richardson, Bernie Street, Kaji Dousa, Nicki King, Sands Hall, Elizabeth Rosner, and my talented Community of Writers group: Grace Anieza Ali, Nicki Glasser, Rachael Holliday, Lorri Holt, Stacey Powells Lyster, Mike Medberry, Christi Payne, Claire Walla, and Tobey Ward. Colleagues and friends Ginger Rutland and Neil Henry made enormously insightful suggestions for the final drafts. All of these readers have made this book better.

Many friends and relatives have encouraged this project over many years and served as my sounding board: Scott Harris, Karen Hogan, Sarah Allen, Ann Imse, Robert Tonsing, Margaret Engle and the Alicia Patterson Foundation, Jim Naughton, Rebecca Wilson, Laura Mecoy, Janet Vitt, John

Reid, Michael Curry, Lucinda Ashby, Barry Beisner, Megan Traquair, Mark Richardson (no relation), Don and Carol Anne Brown, Darla Morgan, Diana Butler Bass, and friends and relatives gone from us: Virginia Smith Sprague, Jeanette Richardson Nelson, and John Lewis. They have kept me going.

Lori and I extend our thanks to Linda Wallihan, who gave us the keys to her home in Sacramento for three months during a sabbatical while I wrote the first draft. Rich Zeiger, my friend and mentor of more than forty years, encouraged me and provided invaluable help with the photographs.

The students, faculty, and staff at Huston-Tillotson University are my inspiration. Their hospitality is beyond measure. I am especially grateful to President Colette Pierce Burnette and President Emeritus Larry Ervin for their support and friendship; and Ora Houston for her wisdom, hospitality, and encouragement.

I will be forever grateful to Michael Millman, senior acquisitions editor, of the University of New Mexico Press for enthusiastically embracing this project and his professionalism at every stage; James Ayers, editorial, design, and production manager; and to the other talented staff members who I never got to meet because of the COVID-19 pandemic. Special thanks goes to Bridget Manzella for her keen-eyed copyediting and wise suggestions.

Finally, thank you, dear reader, for traveling with me on this long family journey.

NOTES

Note to book epigraph: Luke 4:18, copied from a pocket Bible carried by a Civil War soldier. The American Bible Society published thousands of these small books in New York and distributed them to soldiers in both the North and the South. President Abraham Lincoln remarked in his second inaugural address, March 4, 1865: "Both read the same Bible and pray to the same God and each invokes His aid against the other." His statement was literally true.

Note to chapter 1 epigraph: Psalm 17 had a special significance for George Richardson when he was hiding from white vigilantes in 1883.

1. Letter from George Warren Richardson to Chauncey Hobart, April 8, 1886, copied into blank pages in Caroline Fay Richardson's diary (CAR Diary), 65a.

2. "We had learned to love him as brother," "Recollections of My Lifework" (GWR Journal), 183.

3. George Richardson wrote the first version of his journal on empty pages in the notebook his wife Caroline used for diary, poetry, and notes, titled "Mrs C A Richardson's Prose – Poetry and Selections," noted here as CAR Diary. A comparison between the two version shows it likely that the version inside CAR Diary is a draft and not a copy of the final version. Much of the draft is not narrative but a compendium of dated paragraphs that appear to be copied from George Richardson's diary, now lost. George Richardson pasted a table of contents into the front of Caroline's diary, but the page numbers conform to the polished version and not the draft inside Caroline's diary. The draft is 134 pages; the final version is 334 pages. He also hand-copied several documents into Caroline's diary with the final entry dated March 12, 1903 (CAR Diary, 165). The title page of "Recollections of My Lifework," noted here as GWR Journal, is dated December 15, 1905. That version also contains details about the deaths of Caroline and George, and his funeral in 1911, written by his daughter, Emma Richardson.

4. GWR Journal, 225–30; see also CAR Diary, 163–65.

5. Psalm 17: 2, Book of Common Prayer; Psalm 17: 1 and Psalm 17: 13, King James Bible.

CHAPTER 2

1. GWR Journal, 1–28.

2. GWR Journal, 1.

3. George Owen Richardson, memoir (GOR Memoir), 2.

4. GWR Journal, 332.

5. GWR Journal, 2.

6. GWR Journal, 2.

7. George W. Richardson, "Sketch of the Life and Work of Rev GW Richardson, written for a book by Rev Carmichael," inserted by George Richardson into Caroline Richardson's diary: CAR Diary, 70 (2).

8. GWR Journal, 2–3.

9. MacCulloch, *Christianity*, 755–65.

10. MacCulloch, *Christianity*, 761.

11. See "Siege" in GWR Journal, 41; term also used in GOR Memoir, 103.

12. GWR Journal, 4.

13. Blight, *Frederick Douglass*, 121–23.

14. GWR Journal, 5

15. GWR Journal, 6–7.

16. GWR Journal, 7.

CHAPTER 3

Note to epigraph: From *The Fire Next Time,* 43. Baldwin (1924–1987) was a prolific writer, playwright, and social commentator.

1. Russell Richardson, interview with the author, November 1976. Russell Richardson, letter to the author, April 18, 1976.

2. GWR Journal, 322.

3. David C. Richardson, "Autobiography," 1988 (DCR Autobiography), 95.

4. DCR Autobiography, 97.

CHAPTER 4

Note to epigraph: From Wesley's *Hymns for the New-Year's Day* (1750). Charles Wesley (1707–1788) with his brother, John (1703–1791), was a founder of the Methodist movement and possibly the most prolific hymn writer of all time. His hymns remain a staple, especially of Protestant worship, to this day.

1. GWR Journal, 6–8.

2. GWR Journal, 9.

3. GWR Journal. 9.

4. CAR Diary, 28a–29a.

5. GOR Memoir, 2.

6. CAR Diary, 7a.

7. GWR Journal, 6–8.

8. GWR Journal, 11.

9. GWR Journal, 13.

10. George Richardson is listed in the freshman class of 1848–1849, *Catalogue of the Officers and Students of Allegheny College*, 8.

11. GWR Diary, 14–17.

12. GWR Journal. 15.

13. GWR Journal, 21.

14. Letter from Caroline F. Richardson to George W. Richardson, Feb. 4, 1849, Author's Collection.

15. GWR Journal, 23.

16. GWR Journal, 24-25.

17. GWR Journal, 27. Marriage certificate in Author's Collection, May 16, 1851, signed by J. M. Snow "Minister of the Gospel."

18. GWR Journal, 28.

19. GWR Journal, 29–78.

20. CAR Diary, entry, Oct. 4, 1883, 40a.

CHAPTER 5

Note to epigraph: From *Darkwater: Voices from Within the Veil*, 29. W. E. B. Du Bois (1868–1963) was a prolific writer, sociologist, historian, and the most prominent Black civil rights activist of the early twentieth century. He was a founder of the National Association for the Advancement of Colored People (NAACP).

1. Broussard, *Black San Francisco*, 138.

2. Broussard, *Black San Francisco*, 138; Lincoln and Mamiya, *The Black Church in the African American Experience*, 95, 422; Richardson, *Willie Brown*, 47.

3. DCR Autobiography, i.

4. Richardson, *Willie Brown*, 140–41.

5. Jerald asked that I not use his last name.

CHAPTER 6

Note to epigraph: Pauli Murray (1910–1985) was a poet, lawyer, and civil rights activist. In 1977, she became the first Black woman ordained as an Episcopal priest. She had a lifelong struggle with her gender identity and sexual preference. Murray was added to the Episcopal Church calendar of saints in 2009. Her annual feast day is celebrated on July 1.

1. GWR Journal, 29–43.
2. Newson, *Pen Pictures of St. Paul,* 175.
3. Hobart, *Recollections of My Life,* 9, 333.
4. Hobart, *Recollections of My Life,* 303.
5. Hobart, *Recollections of My Life,* 335
6. Hobart, *Recollections of My Life,* 313–14.
7. Hobart, *Recollections of My Life,* 341.
8. McPherson, *Battle Cry of Freedom,* 8.
9. McPherson, *Battle Cry of Freedom,* 88–89.
10. For the apocryphal stories of Abraham Lincoln and Harriet Beecher Stowe, see Daniel R. Volare, "Lincoln, Stowe, and the 'Little Woman/Great War' Story: The Making, and Breaking, of a Great American Anecdote," *Journal of the Abraham Lincoln Association* 30, 1 (Winter 2009): 18–34, https://quod.lib.umich.edu/j/jala/2629860 .0030.104/--lincoln-stowe-and-the-little-womangreat-war-story-the-%20making ?rgn=main;view=fulltext.
11. GWR Journal, 29.
12. Newson, *Pen Pictures of St. Paul,* 176.
13. CAR Diary, 40a.
14. GWR Journal, 32.
15. GWR Journal, 33.
16. GWR Journal, 38.
17. GWR Journal, 43.
18. GWR Journal, 43; GOR Memoir, 5.

CHAPTER 7

Note to epigraph: John R. Lewis (1940–2020) was a civil rights activist, pastor, and politician. He represented Georgia's fifth congressional district in the US House of Representatives for more than thirty years.

1. The Rt. Rev. Barbara Harris was elected Bishop Suffragan of the Episcopal Diocese of Massachusetts in September 1988 and consecrated on Feb. 11, 1989, at a

service attended by 8,000 people. Throughout her ministry she was a strong advocate for the inclusion of all who felt left out of the church, especially Blacks and the LGBTQ community. She died March 13, 2020.

2. According to the Poynter Institute, a journalism think tank, the phrase "to comfort the afflicted and afflict the comfortable" comes from a fictional Irish bartender, Mr. Dooley, introduced to readers by the *Chicago Evening Post* on Oct. 7, 1893. David Shedden, "Today in Media History: Mr. Dooley: 'The job of the newspaper is to comfort the afflicted and afflict the comfortable,'" *Poynter,* Oct. 7, 2014, https://www.poynter.org/reporting-editing/2014/today-in-media-history-mr-dooley -the-job-of-the-newspaper-is-to-comfort-the-afflicted-and-afflict-the-comfortable/.

CHAPTER 8

Note to epigraph: Inspired by Lincoln's widely publicized 1863 letter to James C. Conkling, Caroline wrote her poem a few weeks later, recording it in CAR Diary, 26a. See epigraph for chapter 10.

1. Federal Writers' Project, *Galena Guide,* 9, 61.

2. White, *American Ulysses,* 135–40.

3. Chernow, *Grant,* 559.

4. GOR Memoir, 6–7.

5. GWR does not mention Cadwallader Washburn during his Galena years. But his son, Owen, wrote that his father "renewed his acquaintance with General Washburn" in Tennessee, and thus secured his position as chaplain to the Seventh US Colored Heavy Artillery Regiment in Memphis (GOR Memoir, 26–27).

6. GWR Journal, 44–49. Margaret Harshman appears in a small daguerreotype of the Richardson family, circa 1855. Inside the small case, a note in George Richardson's handwriting identifies her.

7. Henry Park is listed as justice of the peace in *Galena City Directory* (1854), 110.

8. GWR Journal, 46–48; Letter from George Richardson to Caroline Richardson, May 29, 1864, Cornish Collection, Folder 107, PSU.

9. GWR's first draft was written in the same notebook that Caroline used for her diary. He numbered his draft separately from the numbers she used. The entry on "Katie" is 30 of GWR Draft.

10. McPherson, *Battle Cry of Freedom,* 79–81; Brands, *The Zealot and the Emancipator,* 110–11, 114–16.

11. GWR Journal, 47–48.

12. GWR Draft, 70 (4). He used the name "Kitty" in this version.

13. *Galena Guide,* 59; White, *American Ulysses,* 139, 473.

14. GWR Journal, 49.

15. Oakwood Cemetery, Red Wing, Minnesota. "Rev Chauncey Hobart," Find a Grave, June 2, 2012, https://www.findagrave.com/memorial/91252712/chauncey-hobart.

16. GWR Journal, 49.

17. Hobart, *History of Methodism in Minnesota,* 372.

CHAPTER 9

Note to epigraph: Traditional African American blues lyrics, most famously recorded in 1949 by Mahalia Jackson (1911–1972). For a slightly different version, see Cone, *The Cross and the Lynching Tree,* 143.

1. GWR Journal, 50. GWR Draft, 31.

2. GWR Journal, 50–69.

3. GWR Journal, 54.

4. GWR Journal, 56.

5. GWR Journal, 56.

6. GWR Journal, 57.

7. CAR Diary, 18a

8. GWR Journal, 58.

9. GWR Journal, 59.

10. GWR Journal, 60.

11. McPherson, *Battle Cry of Freedom,* 189–92.

12. GWR Journal, 61.

13. The poem by Caroline Richardson was written in May 16, 1861, in a letter from Caroline Richardson to George Richardson. See also CAR Diary, 19a.

14. GWR Journal, 62–63.

15. GWR Journal, 67. George recalled in the journal that it was a Thanksgiving Day feast, but the year was 1858 before Abraham Lincoln declared Thanksgiving as a national holiday in 1863. Thanksgiving was celebrated in some states before 1863, and George's birthday and Thanksgiving Day are close to the same date and often coincide.

CHAPTER 10

Note to epigraph: Letter from Abraham Lincoln (1809–1865), sixteenth president of the United States, to James C. Conkling (1816–1899) of Springfield, Illinois, Aug. 26, 1863. Lincoln had been invited by his close friend, Conkling, to speak at a pro-Union rally in Springfield but could not attend. Instead, he wrote this letter answering white objections to African Americans joining the federal Army. Lincoln's advice to

Conkling: "Read it very slowly." Kearns Goodwin, *Team of Rivals,* 553–55. Text of the letter can be found at: http://www.abrahamlincolnonline.org/lincoln/speeches /conkling.htm.

1. "The Civil War 1861–*1865*," Minnesota Historical Society, 2008, accessed Nov. 19, 2021, http://www.historicfortsnelling.org/history/military-history/civil-war.

2. "The Civil War 1861–*1865*," Minnesota Historical Society, 2008, accessed Nov. 19, 2021: http://www.historicfortsnelling.org/history/military-history/civil-war.

3. Alexander Stephens quoted in Wilkerson, *Caste,* 335.

4. Stevens, *A Compendious History of American Methodism,* 522–28.

5. Frederick V. Mills, "James Osgood Andrew 1794-187," New Georgia Encyclopedia, Sept. 15, 2014, https://www.georgiaencyclopedia.org/articles/arts-culture /james-osgood-andrew-1794-1871/.

6. Stevens, 526.

7. Hobart, *Recollections,* 272–73, 276–79.

8. Hobart, *Recollections,* 312–13.

9. GWR Journal, 70.

10. GWR Journal, 71.

11. "Family of God," GWR Sermon Notebook, 136.

12. GOR Memoir, 15–16.

13. GWR Journal, 71–72.

14. Hampton Smith, "First Minnesota Volunteer Infantry Regiment," Minnesota Encyclopedia, March 13, 2012, http://www.mnopedia.org/group/first-minnesota -volunteer-infantry-regiment.

15. Hobart, *Recollections,* 313–14.

16. GWR Journal, 72.

17. GWR Journal, 73–74.

18. GWR Journal, 78.

19. GWR Journal, 78.

20. Letter from George Richardson to Caroline Richardson, April 5, 1865, Leonard H. Axe Library Archive, Professor Dudley Cornish Collection, Folder 110, PSU.

21. GWR Journal, 78.

22. GWR Journal, 78.

23. GWR Journal, 78.

24. Hobart, *Recollections,* 320–33.

25. GWR Journal, 80.

26. McPherson, *Battle Cry of Freedom,* 582.

27. GWR Journal, 83.

28. GWR, 83. He named the guide, Chaplain Patterson, in his draft: GWR Draft, 62.

29. Hobart, *Recollections,* 329; GWR Journal, 80.

30. GWR Journal, 80.

31. GWR Journal, 84.

32. GWR Journal, 85.

33. GWR Journal, 86.

34. GWR Journal, 86.

35. GWR Journal, 87.

36. GWR Journal, 87.

37. Glatthaar, *Forged in Battle,* 3–10, 35–36; Cornish, *The Sable Arm,* ix.

38. GWR Journal, 89.

39. Glatthaar, *Forged in Battle,* 35–36.

40. GWR Journal, 90.

41. Glatthaar, *Forged in Battle,* 15–16.

42. Glatthaar, *Forged in Battle,* 39

43. Glatthaar, *Forged in Battle,* 36–45.

44. GOR Memoir, 26–27.

45. Letter from George Richardson to Caroline Richardson, May 18, 1864, Cornish Collection, Folder 107, PSU.

46. Letter from George Richardson to "Home," June 12, 1864, Cornish Collection, Folder 108, PSU.

47. Notes in my personal journal, June 30, 1998, July 2, 1998.

CHAPTER II

Note to epigraph: Gen. Ulysses S. Grant (1822–1885) dispatch to Gen. William T. Sherman (1820–1891) following the massacre of Black soldiers at Fort Pillow, Tennessee, April 12, 1864. Chernow, *Grant,* 373.

1. GWR Journal, 91.

2. Cimprich, *Fort Pillow,* 3–13.

3. Ward, *River Run Red,* 2; Fuchs, *An Unerring Fire,* 14.

4. McPherson, *Battle Cry of Freedom,* 748.

5. Forrest quoted in Grant, *Personal of Memoirs U.S. Grant,* 138.

6. Chernow, *Grant,* 373.

7. Cornish, *The Sable Arm,* 175.

8. Cimprich, *Fort Pillow,* 85, 129–31.

9. Cimprich, *Fort Pillow,* 68.

10. Cimprich, *Fort Pillow,* 94.

11. "The Fort Pillow Barbarity," *New York Spectator,* May 9, 1864, 1.

12. Letter from August Chetlain to Hon. E. B. Washburne, April 14, 1864, Fuchs, *Unerring Fire,* 85.

13. Cimprich, *Fort Pillow,* 106; McPherson, *The Negro's Civil War,* 225–26; Cornish, *The Sable Arm,* 175–76.

14. Ward, *River Run Red,* 309.

15. Cimprich, *Fort Pillow,* 105.

16. Ward, *River Run Red,* 288; Cimprich, *Fort Pillow,* 101–3; Chernow, *Grant,* 373.

17. "Touching Scene in Fort Pickering—Thrilling speech by Mrs. Booth," Author unknown, *New York Spectator,* May 9, 1864; speech by Lizzie Booth in Ward, *River Run Red,* 343; Cimprich, *Fort Pillow,* 85, 105.

CHAPTER 12

Note to epigraph: *Hark! from the Tombs a Doleful Sound,* by Isaac Watts (1674–1748), was sung by Black soldiers of the Seventh US Colored Heavy Artillery Regiment with the second verse changed to "rebel head" (GWR Journal, 96). The original version of the Watts hymn was sung at the funeral of George Washington in December 1799.

1. GWR Journal, 92–93.

2. Letter from George Richardson to Caroline Richardson, May 25, 1864, Cornish Collection, Folder 107, PSU.

3. Certificate endorsed by Chetlain, May 25, 1864, commissioning George Richardson as Chaplain to the Seventh US Colored Heavy Artillery Regiment, found with original letters George Richardson wrote during the war. The certificate was also signed by Col. Turner on June 22, 1864. GWR's commission was endorsed by Chauncey Hobart on March 10, 1864, Cornish Collection, Folder 106, PSU.

4. Letter from George Richardson to Caroline Richardson, May 29, 1864, Cornish Collection, Folder 107, PSU.

5. Letter from George Richardson to Caroline Richardson, May 25, 1864, Folder 107, PSU.

6. Ward, *River Run Red,* 166–67, 198, 218, 225, 249; George Richardson also told the story of Epeneter's journey to Charleston and being used as human shield and escape: see GWR Journal, 110–14;

7. Cimprich, *Fort Pillow,* 88.

8. Letter George Richardson to Caroline Richardson, April 28, 1865, Cornish Collection, Folder 110, PSU.

9. Letter from George Richardson to Caroline Richardson, May 25, 1864, Cornish Collection, Folder 107, PSU.

10. Letter from George Richardson to Caroline Richardson, May 27, 1864, Cornish Collection, Folder 107, PSU.

11. Letter from George Richardson to Caroline Richardson, Aug. 19, 1864, Cornish Collection, Folder 109, PSU.

12. GWR Journal, 91–118.

13. Letter from George Richardson to Caroline Richardson, undated, Cornish Collection, Folder 107, PSU.

14. Letter from George Richardson to Caroline Richardson, May 25, 1864, Cornish Collection, Folder 107, PSU.

15. Letter George Richardson to Caroline Richardson, May 29, 1864, Cornish Collection, Folder 107, PSU.

16. Letter May 26, 1864, letter from George Richardson to Caroline Richardson, Cornish Collection, Folder 107, PSU.

17. GWR Journal, 93.

18. Letter from George Richardson to Caroline Richardson, May 26, 1864, Cornish Collection, Folder 107, PSU.

19. GWR Journal, 94.

20. Letter from George Richardson to Caroline Richardson, May 26, 1864, Cornish Collection, Folder 107, PSU.

21. GWR Journal, 94.

22. GWR Journal, 94-96.

23. GWR Journal, 96.

24. Letter from George Richardson to Caroline Richardson, undated, Cornish Collection, Folder 107, PSU.

25. Letter from George Richardson to Caroline Richardson, Aug. 6, 1864, Cornish Collection, Folder 109, PSU.

26. Letter from George Richardson to Caroline Richardson, June 1, 1864, Cornish Collection, Folder 108, PSU.

27. Letter from George Richardson to Caroline Richardson, June 12, 1864, Cornish Collection, Folder 108, PSU.

28. Letter from George Richardson to Caroline Richardson, June 1, 1864, Folder 108, 1864, PSU.

29. "Sick list" letter, May 26, 1865; "Snuff" letter, June 1, 1865; "Bugs" letter, Aug. 2, 1864; "the darkies," letter June 25, 1865, Letters of Humphrey Hood (1823–1903), Box 1, Abraham Lincoln Presidential Library, Springfield, Illinois.

30. Hood refers to Chaplain Taylor only by his last name. Chauncey P. Taylor, Chaplain, is listed on a roster maintained by the National Park Service with the names

of the men of the Third US Colored Heavy Artillery Regiment (along with Humphrey Hood). US National Park Service Soldiers and Sailors Database, accessed Nov. 25, 2021, https://www.nps.gov/civilwar/search-soldiers.htm#sort=score+desc&q =Chauncey+Taylor.

31. GWR's Civil War soldier portrait cards are contained in a photo album with other photos and mementos from that era, in Author's Collection. For the popularity of such cards, see Andrea L. Volpe, "The Cartes de Visite Craze," *The New York Times*, Aug. 6, 2013.

32. The photograph of a Black pastor was taken at the R. Poole photo studio in Nashville, which did not open until the 1870s, after the Civil War. The photograph was removed from GWR's photo album and placed in an envelope with no identifying information. Of the three Black pastors with whom GWR was close, the most likely in the photograph is Charles Madison who is the only one from Tennessee, born in 1847, and died in Luling, Texas, in 1900. He is buried in Austin.

33. GWR's prosthetic eating utensils are in the Author's Collection.

34. Letter from George Richardson to Caroline Richardson, June 1, 1864, Cornish Collection, Folder 108, PSU.

CHAPTER 13

1. George Richardson letters to Caroline Richardson, Aug. 1 and 3, 1864, Folder 109, Cornish Collection, PSU; letter George Richardson to Caroline Richardson, Aug. 30, 1864, Cornish Collection, Folder 109, PSU.

2. GWR Journal, 97–99.

3. Letters from George Richardson to Caroline Richardson, Aug. 6, 1864, and Aug. 9, 1864, Cornish Collection, Folder 109, PSU. GWR Journal, 97.

4. Letter from George Richardson to Caroline Richardson, Aug. 9, 1864, Cornish Collection, Folder 109, PSU.

5. George Richardson letter to Chauncey Hobart, April 8, 1888, copied into CAR Diary, 65a–69a.

6. GWR Journal, 98.

7. Trips by the author to Mississippi May 2007 and April 2013.

CHAPTER 14

Note to epigraph: Nathan Bedford Forrest (1821–1877) was a slave trader, cotton plantation owner, and gambler. As a Confederate general, he led the raiders who massacred Black Union soldiers at Fort Pillow, Tennessee. After the war, Forrest was the first "grand wizard" of the Ku Klux Klan. The quote comes from a story of how he recruited rebel raiders in 1862 and is recounted in Foote, *The Civil War*, Vol. 1, 570.

1. Lytle, *Bedford Forrest and His Critter Company*, 323.

2. Paynter, *Phoenix from the Fire*, 10; White, *American Ulysses*, 141, 259, 293.

3. Lytle, *Bedford Forrest and His Critter Company*, 323–26. See also Foote, *The Civil War*, Vol. 3, 516–18.

4. GWR Journal, 99–101.

5. Letter from George Richardson to Caroline Richardson, Aug. 21, 1864, Cornish Collection, Folder 109, PSU.

6. Letter from George Richardson to Caroline Richardson, Aug. 21, 1864, Cornish Collection, Folder 109, PSU.

7. Letter from George Richardson to Caroline Richardson, Aug. 23, 1864, Cornish Collection, Folder 109, PSU.

8. Lytle, *Bedford Forrest and His Critter Company*, 326. The quote is slightly different with other details on Hurlbut in Foote, *The Civil War*, Vol. 3, 517.

9. GWR Journal, 101–2.

10. Letter from George Richardson to Caroline Richardson, Aug. 9, 1864, Cornish Collection, Folder 109, PSU.

11. Letter from George Richardson to Caroline Richardson, Aug. 14, 1864, Cornish Collection, Folder 109, PSU.

12. Taylor, *The Internal Enemy*, 55–50

13. GWR Journal, 103–4

14. Letter from George Richardson to Caroline Richardson, July 27, 1864, Cornish Collection, Folder 108, PSU.

15. GWR Journal, 103.

16. Letter from George Richardson to Caroline Richardson, July 27, 1864, Cornish Collection, Folder 108, PSU.

17. GWR Journal, 103.

18. GWR Sermon Notebook, 41–61a.

19. GWR Journal, 104.

20. Cimprich, *Fort Pillow*, 104.

CHAPTER 15

Note to epigraph: Frederick Douglass (1817–1895) escaped slavery in Maryland and became an orator, writer, newspaper publisher, outspoken abolitionist, and the most prominent voice of Black Americans in the nineteenth century. He wrote three autobiographies that were bestsellers. The quote is from Douglass's speech on Sept. 29, 1865, at the dedication of the Douglass Institute in Baltimore, the city from where he had escaped slavery. Blight, *Frederick Douglass,* 470.

1. GWR Journal, 104.

2. Letter George Richardson to Caroline Richardson, April 5, 1865, Cornish Collection, Folder 110, PSU.

3. Letter George Richardson to Caroline Richardson, May 29, 1864, Cornish Collection, Folder 107, PSU.

4. GWR Journal, 106.

5. GWR Journal, 106–7.

6. Letter from GWR to CAR, April 12, 1865, Cornish Collection, Folder 110, PSU.

7. GWR Journal, 108. The sentence about "four and a half million of men, women and children of African dissent [*sic*]" was added in the final version GWR Journal, 108, but was not included in GWR Draft.

8. Letter from George Richardson to Caroline Richardson, April 16, 1865, Cornish Collection, Folder 110, PSU.

9. Letter from George Richardson to Caroline Richardson, April 16, 1865, Cornish Collection, Folder 110, PSU.

10. Letter from George Richardson to Caroline Richardson, April 12, 1865, Cornish Collection, Folder 110, PSU.

11. GWR Journal, 108–9.

12. GWR Journal, 109.

13. GWR Journal, 110.

14. Letter from George Richardson to Caroline Richardson, May 2, 1865, Cornish Collection, Folder 111, PSU.

15. GWR Journal, 110–14; Letter George Richardson to Caroline Richardson, April 28, 1865, Cornish Collection, Folder 110, PSU.

16. GWR Journal, 115–16. Letter George Richardson to Caroline Richardson, April 28, 1865, Cornish Collection, Folder 110, PSU.

17. GWR Journal, 115.

18. GWR Journal, 116.

19. GWR Journal, 116.

20. GWR Journal, 117.

21. GWR Journal, 117–18.

22. Letter by Humphrey Hood, June 25, 1865, Humphrey H. Hood Papers, Abraham Lincoln Presidential Library and Museum, Springfield, Illinois.

23. GWR Journal, 119–42.

24. GWR Journal, 138–39.

25. GWR Journal, 123

26. GWR Journal, 124.

27. GWR Journal, 129–30

28. GWR Journal, 133–36.

29. GWR Journal, 134.

30. GWR Journal, 139.

31. GWR Journal, 139–40.

32. GWR Journal, 141–42.

33. GWR Journal, 143.

34. GWR Journal, 143.

35. Letter from George Richardson to Caroline Richardson, April 11, 1865, Cornish Collection, Folder 110, PSU.

36. Letter from George Richardson to Caroline Richardson, April 12, 1865, Cornish Collection, Folder 110, PSU.

37. GWR's discharge papers were found among the original letters he wrote during the Civil War, Author's Collection; photocopies from the Cornish Collection, Folder 106, PSU. GWR Journal, 143–46.

38. GWR Journal, 143–45.

39. GWR Journal, 145–46.

40. GWR Journal, 144.

41. GWR Journal, 146.

CHAPTER 16

Note to epigraph: Ida B. Wells (1862–1931), journalist, pamphleteer, and civil rights activist; she sometimes wrote under the pen name "Lola." In 1893, Wells toured Great Britain when Frederick Douglass asked her to speak in his place because of his declining health. In this speech, she was critical of Dwight Moody, the most prominent white evangelical Christian leader of the time, because he held segregated religious revival meetings. Wells was also famously in conflict with white women suffragettes for spurning Black voting rights. Wells, *Crusade for Justice*, 137.

1. United States Congress, House Select Committee on the Memphis Riots, *Memphis Riots and Massacres*. The House Select Committee, 1866. Also see White, *American Ulysses*, 432–34 and Chernow, *Grant*, 571–72.

2. House Select Committee, *Memphis Riots and Massacres*, 5.

3. Christopher Caplinger, "Yellow Fever Epidemics," Tennessee Encyclopedia, October 8, 2017, https://tennesseeencyclopedia.net/entries/yellow-fever-epidemics/. See also *The Sisters of St. Mary at Memphis*.

4. "Our History," Collins Chapel C.M.E. Church, accessed Dec. 2, 2021, https://collinschapelmemphis.org/history/.

5. Cone, *The Cross and the Lynching Tree,* 126. Also, Blum, "O God of A Godless Land," 101–3. Wells recounts the destruction of her newspaper in her pamphlet, *Southern Horrors.*

6. Ida B. Wells-Barnett, "Southern Horrors: Lynch Law in All Its Phases." *The New York Age,* Oct. 5, 1892. Digital copy Carrie Chapman Catt Center for Women and Politics, University of Iowa, Ames, Iowa, accessed Nov. 20, 2021, https://awpc.cattcenter.iastate.edu/2020/09/21/southern-horrors-lynch-law-in-all-its-phases-oct-5-1892/. The article was reprinted as a pamphlet and can be viewed here: https://www.gutenberg.org/files/14975/14975-h/14975-h.htm. Accessed Nov. 20, 2021.

7. "Memphis Sanitation Workers' Strike," The Martin Luther King Jr. Research and Education Institute, Stanford University, accessed Nov. 25, 2021, https://kinginstitute.stanford.edu/encyclopedia/memphis-sanitation-workers-strike.

8. Trips by the author to Memphis April 2004 and May 2013.

9. Samuel Hardiman, "Here's where Nathan Bedford Forrest and his wife's remains will go when they leave Memphis," *Memphis Commercial Appeal,* Nov. 20, 2020, https://www.commercialappeal.com/story/news/2020/11/20/heres-where-nathan-bedford-forrest-remains-end-up/3753334001/.

10. Robbie Brown, "Memphis Drops Confederate Names from Parks, Sowing New Battles," *The New York Times,* March 28, 2013, http://www.nytimes.com/2013/03/29/us/memphis-drops-confederate-names-from-parks-sowing-new-battles.html?_r=0.

CHAPTER 17

1. GWR Journal, 147.

2. GWR Journal, 148.

3. GWR Journal, 158.

4. GWR Journal, 159.

5. GWR Journal, 160.

6. GWR Journal, 161.

7. GOR Memoir, 37.

8. GWR Journal, 161.

9. GWR Journal, 162.

10. GWR Journal, 163

11. GWR Journal, 163.

12. GOR Memoir, 37–38.

13. GOR Memoir, 39; GWR Journal, 164.

14. GWR Journal, 164.

15. Trip to Minnesota and meeting with Richardson cousins, summer 2013.

CHAPTER 18

Note to epigraph: James W. Truitt (1845–1922), Texas state legislator, lawyer, owned a lumber business and served four years in the Confederate Army. He made this observation about East Texas in a letter to his wife after touring the region and noting the high ratio of Blacks. Rice, *The Negro in Texas,* 158.

1. The author wrote extensively about the racial history of East Texas in *Willie Brown: A Biography,* chapters 1–4 and the history of East Texas generally pages 4–8. See also Rice, *The Negro in Texas,* 13–15.

2. Jackie McElhaney and Michael V. Hazel. "Dallas TX." Handbook of Texas, Texas Historical Society, https://www.tshaonline.org/handbook/online/articles/hdd01. Updated June 28, 2021. Accessed Nov. 25, 2021.

3. GWR Journal, 165–86.

4. GOR Memoir, 42–43.

5. GOR Memoir, 43–45.

6. GOR Memoir, 45.

7. GWR Journal, 165.

8. Daniels, *History of Methodism,* 714–15.

9. McConnell, *Edward Gayer Andrews,* 84.

10. McConnell, *Edward Gayer Andrews,* 27.

11. GWR Journal, 166.

12. GWR Journal, 166.

13. GWR Journal, 168.

14. GWR Journal, 167–68. Details on Larkin Carper from historical marker in San Antonio, Historical Marker Database, https://www.hmdb.org/m.asp?m=163381.

15. GWR Journal, 170

16. GWR Journal, 170.

17. GWR Journal, 170.

18. GWR Journal, 171. Also see the obituary for Jeremiah Webster, which mentions his service with the Twenty-Fifth US Colored Infantry Regiment, in *Memoirs West Texas Conference Journal 1877,* 21.

19. GWR Journal, 171.

20. GWR Journal, 171.

21. GWR Journal, 172–75. Letter from Caroline Richardson to George Richardson, April 30, 1876 postmarked May 2, 1876, Author's Collection. The journal did not men-

tion the date of the fire, but on the envelope of Caroline's letter, George Richardson wrote "Letter from Wife—after Burning of School Building at Dallas Texas April 22, 1876,"

22. "The Fire." Author unknown, *The Dallas Daily Herald,* April 23, 1876.

23. Letter from Caroline Richardson to George Richardson, April 30, 1876 postmarked May 2, 1876, Author's Collection.

24. Letter from Caroline Richardson to George Richardson, dated April 30, 1876, postmarked May 2, 1876. Author's Collection.

CHAPTER 19

Note to epigraph: From Frederick Douglass's speech in Philadelphia following a segregated religious revival by Dwight Moody in 1885, quoted in Blum, "O God of A Godless Land," 101.

1. GWR Journal, 174–86.

2. GWR Journal, 174.

3. GWR Journal, 175.

4. GWR Journal, 176.

5. The handwritten ledger has no title page, and is referred to here as "Andrews School Ledger." A notation on the first page is signed by George's second son, David Richardson in Minnesota, April 17, 1874. The ledger contains data about the Dallas school including the names of pupils, grades, tuition paid, subjects taught. The ledger was donated by the author in October 2015 to Huston-Tillotson University and is now in the university's archives. Author's Collection contains a photocopy. Names of pupils recorded, 29–33.

6. Andrews School Ledger, 28. Downes-Jones Library, University Archives, Huston-Tillotson University, Austin. Copy also in Author's Collection.

7. GWR Journal, 178.

8. GWR Journal, 179–81. GWR was not a member of the conference until a year later and did not vote: see GOR Memoir, 49.

9. Rice describes the split between Black and white Texas churches in the Reconstruction era in *The Negro in Texas,* 271–74. According to Rice, "German ministers of the Methodist Episcopal Church found it disagreeable to be associated with Negro ministers and successfully agitated for separate conferences for Negro Methodists," (273).

10. GWR Journal, 180.

11. GWR Journal, 180.

12. GWR Journal, 182.

13. GWR Journal, 182.

14. Long, *Pictures of Slavery,* 90–91.

15. Richardson, *Willie Brown,* 6–7. See also Rice, *The Negro in Texas,* 95, 133–39.

16. GWR Journal, 196–98.

17. GWR Journal, 197.

18. GWR Journal, 183.

19. GWR Journal, 183.

20. GWR Journal, 184.

21. Andrews School Ledger, 73. Downes-Jones Library, University Archives, Huston-Tillotson University. Undated handwritten tribute to Emma also recorded in Andrews School Ledger, 73. The tribute is not signed but matches George Richardson's handwriting.

22. GWR Journal, 185–86.

23. GWR Journal, 189.

24. "About Us," St. Paul United Methodist Church, accessed April 1, 2021, https://www.stpaulumcdallas.com/about-us/.

CHAPTER 20

Note to epigraph: George Richardson heard this spiritual sung in a Black Methodist church in San Antonio in 1876. He did not much care for it, but he recorded it in his journal. GWR Journal, 201.

1. "Population Statistics," Austin Public Library, Austin History Center, accessed Nov. 20, 2021, https://library.austintexas.gov/ahc/everything-austin-population-statistics. Also see "History of Austin Texas," Wikipedia, accessed Nov. 20, 2021, https://en.wikipedia.org/wiki/History_of_Austin,_Texas.

2. Hardy, "A Brief Memoir of the Reverend Charles Gillette." For a complete compilation of the correspondence between Gillette and his bishop, see *A Few Historical Records of the Church in the Diocese of Texas* and Brown, *Episcopal Church in Texas,* 119–21.

3. Rice, *The Negro in Texas,* 232.

4. GWR Journal, 187–88; Owen's version differs: see GOR Memoir, 50–52.

5. GOR Memoir, 54–56. CAR Diary, Oct. 5, 1885, 41a.

6. Brawley, *Two Centuries of Methodist Concern,* 353.

7. GWR Journal, 190.

8. GWR Journal, 198–207.

9. Letter from George Richardson to Clara Milne Richardson, March 13, 1883, Author's Collection.

10. GWR Journal, 190.

11. GWR Journal, 191.

12. GWR Journal, 192.

13. GWR Journal, 192.

14. GWR Journal, 193.

15. GWR Journal, 195.

16. GWR Journal, 194.

17. GOR Memoir, 59–60.

18. GWR Journal, 199–201.

19. GWR Journal, 187.

20. GWR Journal, 191.

21. GWR Journal, 201.

22. GWR Journal, 200–201

23. GWR Journal, 201.

24. GOR Memoir, 59–61.

25. W. Michael Born, "Richard S. Rust, a minister with a mission," Worldwide Faith News Archive, Oct. 3, 2000, http://archive.wfn.org/2000/10/msg00018.html.

26. Rice, *The Negro in Texas*, 230–31, 235.

27. GWR Journal, 210–12.

28. GOR Memoir, 61.

29. GOR Memoir, 61.

30. GWR Journal, 208.

CHAPTER 21

Note to epigraph: John Mason Brewer (1896–1975), scholar of African American folklore, poet, and a professor at Samuel Huston College. This verse is quoted in Brewer, *Echoes of Thought*, 33.

1. GWR Journal, 189–212; GOR 59–64.

2. GWR Journal, 215; Hardy, "Brief Memoir of the Reverend Charles Gillette," and Brown, *Episcopal Church in Texas*, 119–21. See also *A Few Historical Records of the Church in the Diocese of Texas*.

3. GWR Journal, 215.

4. GOR Memoir, 62; Letter from George Richardson to Owen Richardson, July 30, 1883; Letter from George Richardson to Clara Milne Richardson, Aug. 14, 1883; Author's Collection.

5. GWR Journal, 213–14.

6. GWR Journal, 214–15; GOR Memoir, 87–88.

7. Letter from Caroline Richardson to George Richardson, May 16, 1880, Author's Collection.

8. GWR Journal, 214.

9. GWR Journal, 214–15; GOR Memoir, 63–64; Rice, *The Negro in Texas*, 234–35. Rice puts the Huston estate donation at $9,000. George Richardson wrote in the journal (214) that the amount was $10,000 but then recorded in the back pages of Caroline's diary that the donation was $12,000, CAR Diary, 149. The differing accounts and faded memories of the amount probably due to the long delay in settling the estate and the delivery of the check.

10. GWR Journal, 218–19; GOR Memoir, 67–72.

11. GWR Journal, 218.

12. GWR Journal, 218.

13. GOR Memoir, 67.

14. "Presidents of Huston-Tillotson University," Huston-Tillotson University, accessed Nov. 28, 2021, https://htu.edu/offices/office-of-the-president/past-presidents. He is listed as "1876–1882 Dr. George O. Richardson." The designation of "Dr." is common among Protestant pastors, though he never earned a doctorate. The designation includes his years of service leading the school in Dallas.

15. GOR Mcmoir, 72.

16. GWR Journal, 219; GOR Memoir, 73–74.

17. GOR Memoir, 73–74.

CHAPTER 22

1. GWR Journal, 213, 224–25.

2. GWR Journal, 213

3. GWR Journal, 225.

4. Letter from George Richardson to Owen Richardson, May 18, 1883, Author's Collection.

5. GWR Journal, 225–30; CAR Diary, 163–65. The version Caroline wrote in her diary is in much the same detail as George's, probably drawn from a letter he wrote while in hiding in November 1883 addressed to "My dear wife." The original letter is in Author's Collection.

6. Rice, *The Negro in Texas*, 205.

7. GWR Journal, 225.

8. GWR Journal, 226.

9. GWR Journal, 225-230; see also Caroline's version, CAR Dairy, 163–65.

10. Letter from George Richardson to Clara Milne Richardson, Oct. 31, 1883,

Author's Collection.

11. GWR Journal, 227.

12. Letter from George Richardson to Caroline Richardson, Nov. 2, 1883, Author's Collection.

13. *King James Bible*, Psalm 17: 8–9.

14. GWR Journal, 231, 232.

15. Author's travels through the Texas Hill Country near Austin, June 2004.

16. Letter from George Richardson to Clara Milne Richardson, Feb. 25, 1884, Author's Collection.

17. GWR Journal, 240.

18. Letter from George Richardson to Chauncey Hobart, April 8, 1886, copied by George into CAR Diary, 65a–69a.

CHAPTER 23

Note to epigraph: James D. Houston (1933–2009), in his novel *Bird of Another Heaven*, writes about a central character who in middle age meets his grandmother for the first time and learns the hidden family story of being descended from Hawai'ians and indigenous Californians. Houston, *Bird of Another Heaven*, 65. Lori and I had the pleasure of meeting Houston and his wife, author Jeanne Wakatsuki, at Asilomar in 2008.

1. Birthday entry for 1883, CAR Diary, 39a–40a. She began the entry on 40a and completed it on the left page opposite, 39a.

2. CAR Diary, 40a.

3. CAR Diary, 40a.

4. CAR Diary, 39a.

5. CAR Diary, 141.

6. CAR Diary, 142.

7. CAR Diary, 163–65.

8. CAR Diary, 2a.

9. CAR Diary, 4a.

10. CAR Diary, 4a.

11. CAR Diary, 22a–23a

12. CAR Diary, 3a.

13. CAR Diary, 7a–8a. Charles Wesley, "Come, Let Us Anew, Our Journey Pursue" *Hymns for New Years Day*, 1750.

14. Above the title "A Prayer," she wrote: "Written when Andy Johnson was President of the United States." CAR Diary, 31a–32a.

15. CAR Diary, 28a–29a.

16. CAR, 49a–53a.

17. Rice, *The Negro in Texas,* 215–16.

18. CAR Diary, 52a–53a.

19. GWR, Journal 219–22.

20. GWR Journal, 219.

21. GWR Journal, 220.

22. CAR Diary, 42a–43a.

23. GOR Memoir, 73–79; GWR Journal, 224.

24. GWR Journal, 224.

25. GWR Journal, 223.

26. From her essay "Kind of Work and Remarkable Protection," CAR Diary, 151–54, 163–65.

27. GWR Journal, 217.

28. Among those who excelled in the East Texas moonshine business in the 1930s: the uncles of Willie Brown, who became the most powerful politician in California in the 1980–1990s. See Richardson, *Willie Brown,* 11–14.

29. GWR Journal, 232–35.

30. GWR Journal, 231–32.

31. Letter from George Richardson to Clara Milne Richardson, April 23, 1883, Author's Collection.

32. Letter from George Richardson to Owen Richardson, Feb. 4, 1884, Author's Collection.

33. GWR Journal, 234–35.

34. GWR Journal, 241–44.

35. GWR Journal, 244.

36. GWR Journal, 235–36.

37. GWR Journal, 241–44.

38. GWR Journal, 242.

39. CAR Diary, 43a–45a.

40. CAR Diary, 45a–46b.

41. GWR Journal, 244.

42. GWR Journal, 245.

CHAPTER 24

Note to epigraph: Howard Thurman (1899–1981) was a theologian, educator, and civil rights leader as well as a mentor to Martin Luther King Jr. His book, *Jesus and the Disinherited*, remains influential. In 1974, Thurman was named an honorary canon of the Episcopal Church at the Cathedral of St. John the Divine in New York City.

1. Stowell, *Methodist Adventures in Negro Education*, 104–9; Michele Valerie Ronnick, "Lovinggood, Reuben Shannon." Rutgers University School of Arts and Sciences, Database of Classical Scholars, 2021, https://dbcs.rutgers.edu/all-scholars /9302-lovinggood-reuben-shannon. Brawley, *Two Centuries of Methodist Concern*, 360-371.

2. Stowell, *Methodist Adventures in Negro Education*, 101–5. The book made no mention of the Richardsons' contribution, which apparently incensed Emma Richardson; she wrote a letter to Samuel Huston College to set the record straight and kept a copy with the amount of the donation erased: Letter from Emma Richardson to Stanley E. Grannum, March 15, 1943, Author's Collection.

3. Trowbridge, David J. "How Austin Became Segregated: The City Plan of 1928," Clio: Your Guide to History, June 21, 2014, accessed Nov. 22, 2021, https://theclio.com /entry/5517. Also Alberta Phillips, "Proof of Austin's Past Is Right There—In Black and White," *American-Statesman*, November 22, 2009.

4. Author interview with descendants of Wesley Church members, June 2004.

5. Author's visits to Austin and Huston-Tillotson University June 2004, May 2005, October 2015, and July 2018.

6. GWR Journal, 236.

7. Fluker, *The Papers of Howard Thurman*, vol. 3, 270–71; Thurman, *Jesus and the Disinherited*, 1949, xx, 1, 79; Foreword, Thurman, *Jesus and the Disinherited* (1996 edition), xii; see also Gates, *The Black Church*, 133–34.

8. The Thurman lectures at Samuel Huston College were endowed by Roy Lemon Smith (1887–1963), who was editor of the *Christian Advocate*, the official publication of the Methodist Church, with the goal of highlighting the work of Black pastors. Smith dedicated the talks as the Mary L. Smith Memorial Lectures in memory of his mother. Fluker, *The Papers of Howard Thurman*, vol. 3, 272.

9. Thurman, *Jesus and the Disinherited*, 88.

10. "Our Identity," St. James Episcopal Church, 2019, https://stjamesaustin.org/who -we-are/.

11. Letter from Richard S. Rust to George W. Richardson, May 9, 1882, donated by the author to University Archives, Downes-Jones Library, Huston-Tillotson University, Austin, Texas. Copy also in Author's Collection.

CHAPTER 25

Note to epigraph: Inscription on Caroline A. Richardson's tombstone in Northfield, Minnesota, seen by the author during a visit in May 2013.

1. GWR Journal, 239. He resumed writing in the "Recollections of My Lifework" in 1906, drawing from his first draft that had been inserted into CAR Diary. He also copied into Caroline's diary her obituary on the last pages in that book. The final page in her diary notebook, unnumbered, is a list George made of Christmas presents he gave to relatives in 1899, including toy soldiers, candy and bibles.

2. Obituary of Caroline Richardson, CAR Diary, 166. George Richardson's first draft of his "Recollections" ends at the death of his mother in 1872, GWR Draft, 148. He inserted various other hand-copied letters and documents into blank pages of Caroline's diary from his Texas years.

3. GWR Journal, 244–47.

4. GWR Journal, 244; GOR Memoir, 80. Owen wrote that his mother's cause of death was "Dengue Fever," a mosquito-borne virus with symptoms of fever, muscle pain, and a skin rash—symptoms not described by George. No death certificate can be found for Caroline, and medicine at the time was not much concerned with recording the cause of death, especially on the frontier where death was all too common. George's description should be taken as more reliable given that he was there, and Owen was not.

5. GWR Journal, 246.

6. GWR Journal, 246.

7. GWR Journal, 247.

8. Hobart burial plot, Oakwood Cemetery, Red Wing, Minnesota. "Chauncey Hobart," Find A Grave, June 2, 2012, https://www.findagrave.com/memorial/91252712/chauncey-hobart.

9. Letter from GWR to his children, March 3, 1891, from Dunsmuir, California, Author's Collection.

10. CAR Diary, 166. Whether the obituary was published is unknown.

11. GWR Journal, 247.

12. GWR Journal, 250–51.

13. GOR Memoir, 80, 88.

14. GWR Journal, 252–62

15. GOR Memoir, 79, 81; GWR Journal, 258.

16. GOR Memoir, 82–83.

17. GOR Memoir, 87.

18. GOR Memoir, 88.

19. GWR Journal, 261.

20. GWR Journal, 261; Nickname "Lily" mentioned by George in a letter to his family from Yellowstone, Aug. 9, 1896, copied into CAR Diary, 58a.

21. GOR Memoir, 34–36.

22. GWR Journal, 306.

CHAPTER 26

Note to epigraph: "Wild Geese," letter from George Richardson to his children, March 3, 1891, from Dunsmuir, California, Author's Collection.

1. GWR Journal, 262–65.

2. Letter from George Richardson to his children, March 3, 1891, Author's Collection. The letter appears to be a circular letter in a packet of "round robin" letters each of his children enclosed. He noted that the packet contained letters from Clara (Owen's wife), Emma, David, Frank and Mercein.

3. GWR Journal, 265–71.

4. GWR Journal, 268.

5. GWR Journal, 270.

6. CAR Diary, entry by George for Nov. 25, 1893, 54a.

7. GWR Journal, 271.

8. GWR Journal, 272–74. GOR Memoir, 99.

9. GWR Journal, 282; Yellowstone letters, copied in CAR Diary, 55a–64a.

10. Yellowstone letters, July 27–August 10, 1896, Authors Collection,

11. "Yellowstone Up Close and Personal: Yellowstone National Park Visitors Statistics," Yellowstone, accessed Nov. 20, 2021, http://www.yellowstone.co/stats.htm.

12. GOR Memoir, 110, 116–20.

13. GWR Journal, 281–85.

14. GWR Journal, 285–88.

15. GWR Journal, 290.

CHAPTER 27

1. Letter from Emma Richardson to David Fay Richardson and Clementine Richardson, Sept. 15, 1918, Author's Collection.

2. "Hamline History: The Foundation of Minnesota's First University, 1854-1869: A Red Wing Start," Hamline University, accessed Nov. 20, 2021, http://www.hamline.edu/about/history.html.

3. Emma's earlier experience teaching at Andrews Normal School, Dallas, undated

tribute to Emma recorded Andrews School Ledger, 73. University Archives, Huston-Tillotson University.

4. Hamline University transcript for Emma Richardson, September 1883 to 1888, issued on Oct. 27, 1923, shows her courses and grades (Author's Collection). University of California "Certificate of Record," 1921, Author's Collection.

5. GOR Memoir, 76. Owen graduated from Northwestern University on June 16, 1888 (GOR Memoir, 79). Owen mentions his own graduation but not that of his sister. Emma graduated June 7, 1888, confirmed by University Archives, Bush Memorial Library, Hamline University, St. Paul, Minnesota.

6. GOR Memoir, unnumbered page, "Emma and Johnie." Johnie was her dog. Photograph from 1888 graduation, Author's Collection.

7. Portrait of Hamline University's Class of 1888, "Class of 1888 Hamline University, St. Paul, Minnesota," Minnesota Digital Library, accessed Nov. 22, 2021, https://collection.mndigital.org/catalog/hmu:225#/image/0.

8. Photograph in Author's Collection.

9. Handwritten description of Emma Richardson, Alumni Records 1888, stamped with page 79 and pasted into "Alumni Record Book," 24. University Archives, Bush Memorial Library, Hamline University, St. Paul, Minnesota.

10. Street, "Reminiscences of the Family," 7, 37–38; Smith, "A Memory Book," diary entry Jan. 1, 1907.

11. Street, "Reminiscences of the Family," 7, 37–38.

12. Letter from Emma Richardson to Florence Street, May 30, 1939, Author's Collection.

13. The Hamline University records contain brief biographies of each member of the 1888 class, including Emma. It notes that she returned to Texas after graduation to teach college in Fort Worth and studied at the University of California in 1921 and 1923. "Alumni Record of Hamline University, 1924," pp.1888–89, University Archives, Bush Memorial Library, Hamline University, St. Paul, Minnesota.

14. Hamline University Alumni Association questionnaire, March 30, 1896, Alumni Association Record Book, 88, University Archives, Bush Memorial Library, Hamline University, St. Paul, Minnesota.

15. GWR Journal, 310–20.

16. Letter from Emma to Hamline Alumni Association, April 21, 1897, noting her teaching physics at South Side High School. Alumni Association Record Book, 121, University Archives, Bush Memorial Library, Hamline University, St. Paul, Minnesota.

17. Letter from George Richardson to his children, July 4, 1904, Author's Collection.

18. Life in Denver GWR Journal, 289–308.

19. GWR Journal, 307.

20. GWR Journal, 295–98; Letter from George Richardson to family, July 4, 1904, Author' Collection.

21. Letter from George Richardson to family, July 4, 1904, Author' Collection.

22. Letter from George Richardson to family, July 4, 1904, Author's Collection.

23. GWR Journal, 299.

24. Letter from Mercein Richardson to George Richardson, GWR Journal, 302.

25. GWR Journal, 303–5.

26. GWR Journal 307a; copy of Lily's obituary, GWR Journal, 307c.

27. GWR Journal, 307b.

28. GWR Journal, 310–20.

29. Lily Silver Richardson's will, "No Chance for Family to Rumpus," *Lincoln Star Journal,* Lincoln, Nebraska, Aug. 24, 1907.

30. Letter from Emma Richardson to Russell Richardson, April 18, 1907, reprinted in Street, "Reminiscences of the Family," 49.

31. GWR Journal, 311.

32. Street, "Reminiscences of the Family," 76–78.

33. GWR Journal, 312.

34. GOR Memoir, 120–22.

35. GWR Journal, 312–20.

36. Letter from Emma Richardson to Florence Street, May 30, 1939, Author's Collection.

37. Hymn by John Keith, "How Firm a Foundation," 1787.

38. Sermon No. 22, "Sanctification," in GWR Sermon Notebook, 106–7.

39. Kirk of the Highland homepage (unnamed). https://www.thekirkofhighland.com/ Accessed Dec. 10, 2021. Also see: "The Kirk of Highland 3011 Vallejo Street." https://denverarchitecture.org/site/kirk-of-highland/ Accessed Dec. 11, 2021. The Denver architecture website notes that the building was designed by architect Henry Hobson Richardson in 1894. The style became known as "Richardsonian." The architect has no known relationship to the author's family.

CHAPTER 28

1. Letter from Emma Richardson to David Fay Richardson and Clementine Richardson, Sept. 15, 1918, Author's Collection.

2. GOR Memoir, 120–22.

3. GWR Journal, 322, 331–33.

4. Letter from Emma Richardson to Stanley E. Grannum, handwritten, March 15, 1943, Author's Collection.

5. Letter from Owen Richardson to David F. Richardson, Dec. 21, 1937, Author's Collection.

6. "There was a constant undercurrent of strife between my parents over the spending of money," Street, "Reminiscences of the Family," 4.

7. Letter from George Richardson to Caroline Richardson, Aug. 9, 1864, Folder 109, Cornish Collection, PSU. Letter from George Richardson to Caroline Richardson, Oct. 19, 1865, Folder 112, Cornish Collection, PSU. The letter included a pencil sketch on gray paper of an eclipse on that same date. The sketch was not included in the PSU archive but is included with the original letter in the Author's Collection. Another sketch of a solar eclipse is in GWR Sermon Notebook, 152–53.

8. Sermon No. 42, "Power of the Gospel," GWR Sermon Notebook, 137.

9. Sermon No. 26, "We are all journeying," GWR Sermon Notebook, 113. He gave the sermon at Mount Pleasant, Minnesota, Nov. 23, 1862, GWR Sermon Notebook, 26.

10. Sermon 18, "The Harvest," GWR Sermon Notebook, 101.

CHAPTER 29

Note to second epigraph: Martin Luther King Jr. (1929–1968), Baptist pastor and the most influential civil rights leader of our time, wrote this in *Where Do We Go From Here: Chaos or Community?*, 5.

1. James Richardson, "Papers on the Ku Klux Klan in Southern California, 1975-1985." Collection number 1818, UCLA Charles E. Young Research Library, Department of Special Collections, Los Angeles. Articles from 1980: Box 4, Folder 10.

2. Tom Metzger died of natural causes in November 2020. After his forays into electoral politics, he slid further into white supremacist causes and was dogged by lawsuits. Metzger lost a $12 million civil judgment for supporting the murder of an Ethiopian man.

3. This account of the August 2017 events in Charlottesville is adapted from a commentary written by the author for *The Sacramento Bee*, "When the Nazis came to Charlottesville, ordinary people deployed their secret weapon," Aug. 17, 2017, https://www.sacbee.com/article167804257.html. Also see: Rosie Gray, "Trump Defends White-Nationalist Protestors: 'Some Very Fine People on Both Sides.'" *The Atlantic*, Aug. 15, 2017, https://www.theatlantic.com/politics/archive/2017/08/trump-defends -white-nationalist-protesters-some-very-fine-people-on-both-sides/537012/.

4. "Charlottesville's Statue of Robert E. Lee Will Be Melted Down." Eduardo Medina, *The New York Times*, Dec. 7, 2021.

5. "Klan Bust at Tennessee Capitol Removed," *The New York Times*, July 25, 2021, 16.

CHAPTER 30

Note to second epigraph: Oluwatomisin Oredein is an assistant professor of Black Religious Studies, Constructive Theology and Ethics at Brite Divinity School in Fort Worth, Texas and a Ruling Elder in the Presbyterian Church. Quote from Oredein, "We need to talk about white belief," *Faith and Leadership* (blog), Feb. 23, 2021, https:// faithandleadership.com/oluwatomisin-oredein-we-need-talk-about-white -belief?utm_source=newsletter&utm_medium=email&utm_content=feature%20story &utm_campaign=ni_newsletter.

1. Kruse, *One Nation Under God,* 252–53.

2. Michael Eric Dyson, Sermon, Jan. 27, 2021, Washington National Cathedral, https://cathedral.org/sermons/sermon-the-rev-dr-michael-eric-dyson/. Michael Eric Dyson (1958–present) is a theologian, pastor, and professor at the Divinity School at Vanderbilt University in Nashville, Tennessee.

3. "Dylann Roof is Sentenced to Death in Charleston Church Massacre," *The New York Times,* Jan. 10, 2017.

4. James Richardson, Sermon, June 21, 2015, St. Paul's Memorial Church, Charlottesville. Text in Author's Collection.

5. Former police officer Derek Chauvin was convicted April 20, 2021, of murdering George Floyd. Tim Arango, Shaila Dewan, Nicholas Bogel-Burroughs, "Derek Chauvin is found guilty of murdering George Floyd." *The New York Times,* April 20, 2021, https://www.nytimes.com/2021/04/20/us/chauvin-guilty-murder -george-floyd.html.

6. George Richardson, Sermon, May 21, 1899, Northfield Methodist Church, GWR Sermon Notebook, 165–66.

7. Genesis 32:22–32.

BIBLIOGRAPHY

ABBREVIATIONS FOR PRIMARY SOURCES

CAR Diary: Caroline Fay Richardson, diary and poetry notebook, 1851–1887. Author's Collection. This notebook contains Caroline's diary entries, poems, essays, copies of letters and newspaper clippings. After her death, George Richardson filled blank pages in her notebook with a first draft of his journal (see below) and he also inserted hand copies of letters and other documents. The page numbers present navigational challenges for the reader. Caroline and George numbered their pages separately, thus page numbers do not always appear sequentially. Adding to the challenge, both occasionally repeated page numbers, adding a letter or a number to the page number, for example pages 39a and 39b in Caroline's writing, or 70 and 70 (2) in George's. Caroline sometimes finished an entry on a facing page and then numbered the pages backwards.

DCR Autobiography: David C. Richardson, "Autobiography." Danville, CA: unpublished, 1988. Author's Collection.

GOR Memoir: George Owen Richardson, Denver, typed by his sister, Emma Richardson, on blank pages in a Samuel Huston College catalog, "Autobiography of George O. Richardson," 1937. Author's Collection. Only one copy is known to exist. On the inside front page facing the cover is a list of twelve people to whom the book was to have been mailed "and please do not keep it longer than two weeks." Only four were noted as having read and returned it.

GWR Draft: George Richardson used blank pages in Caroline's diary to write the first draft of his life story. He titled the draft "Journal and Recollections of my life" and wrote "Journal" at the top of each page. The draft ends with the death of his mother in 1872. Author's Collection.

GWR Journal: George Warren Richardson, "Recollections of My Lifework," title page 1905, but other entries include his death in 1911, recorded by his daughter, Emma Richardson. At the end of the book are records of births, marriages, and deaths of his descendants. The last entry was made in 1984 by my mother. Author's Collection.

GWR Sermon Notebook: No title page. The notebook contains sermon outlines, marriage records, and various notes and sketches, Aug. 23, 1857, to July 28, 1901. Author's Collection.

PSU: University Archives, Leonard H. Axe Library, Professor Dudley Cornish Collection, Pittsburg State University, Kansas. Dudley Taylor Cornish, a history

professor and expert on Black troops in the Civil War, had access to George
Richardson's Civil War letters likely because he was colleagues at Pittsburg State
with Claude Street, who was a professor in the psychology department. Street was
married to Florence Richardson, and inherited the letters and other possessions from
her aunt Emma Richardson in 1943, including these letters. Cornish transcribed and
typed copies of the letters. Cornish wrote *The Sable Arm: Black Troops in the Union
Army, 1861–1865* (see reference below), considered a standard work on this topic.
Cornish wrote his book in 1956, but made no mention of George Richardson or his
regiment, presumably because he did not yet have access to these letters.

SECONDARY SOURCES

Allegheny College. *Catalogue of the Allegheny College, Meadville, PA., for the Academical
Year, 1848–9.* Pittsburgh: Geo. Parking & Co., 1849.

American Bible Society. *The New Testament of our Lord and Saviour Jesus Christ.* New
York, 1840.

Authorized Version (King James). *The Holy Bible.* Cleveland and New York: The
World Publishing Co., undated.

Baldwin, James. *The Fire Next Time.* New York: Vintage Books, 1963. Reprint
published by Dial Press, New York, 1993.

Blight, David W. *Frederick Douglass: Prophet of Freedom.* New York: Simon & Schuster,
2018.

Blum, Edward J., and W. Scott Poole. *Vale of Tears: New Essays on Religion and
Reconstruction.* Macon, GA: Mercer University Press, 2005.

Brands, H. W. *The Zealot and the Emancipator: John Brown, Abraham Lincoln, and the
Struggle for American Freedom.* New York: Doubleday, 2020.

Brawley, James P. *Two Centuries of Methodist Concern: Bondage, Freedom and Education
of Black People.* New York: Vantage Press, 1974.

Brewer, John Mason. *Echoes of Thought.* Fort Worth, TX: Progressive Printing, 1922.

———. *Negrito: Negro Dialect Poems of the Southwest.* New York: The Black Heritage
Library Collection, 1972. First published 1933.

Broussard, Albert S. *Black San Francisco: The Struggle for Racial Equality in the West,
1900–1954.* Lawrence: University Press of Kansas, 1993.

Brown, Lawrence L. *The Episcopal Church in Texas, 1838–1874: From It Foundation to the
Division of the Diocese.* Austin: The Church Historical Society, 1963.

Chernow, Ron. *Grant.* New York: Penguin Press, 2017.

Cimprich, John. *Fort Pillow: A Civil War Massacre and Public Memory.* Baton Rouge:
Louisiana State University Press, 2005.

Cone, James H. *The Cross and the Lynching Tree*. New York: Orbis Books, 2013.

Cornish, Dudley Taylor. *The Sable Arm: Black Troops in the Union Army, 1861–1865*. Lawrence: University Press of Kansas, 1956.

Daniels, W. H. *The Illustrated History of Methodism in Great Britain and America from the Days of Wesley to the Present Time*. New York: Phillips & Hunt, 1880.

Davis, David Brion. *The Problem of Slavery in the Age of Emancipation*. New York: Alfred A. Knopf, 2014.

Du Bois, W. E. B. *Darkwater: Voices from Within the Veil*. 1920. First Schoken Edition, 1969.

The Episcopal Church. *The Hymnal 1982: According to Use of The Episcopal Church*. New York: The Church Hymnal Corp., 1985.

The Episcopal Church. *The Book of Common Prayer*. New York: The Church Hymnal Corp., 1979.

Federal Writers' Project. *Galena Guide*. Illinois: Works Progress Administration, 1937.

A Few Historical Records of the Church in the Diocese of Texas, During the Rebellion. Together with a correspondence between the Right Rev. Alexander Gregg, D.D., and the Rev. Charles Gillette, Rector of St. David's Austin. New York: John A. Gray & Green Printers, 1865.

Fluker, Walter Earl, Peter Eisenstadt, Silvia P. Glick, Luther E. Smith Jr., Quinton H. Dixie, Kai Jackson Issa, eds. *The Papers of Howard Thurman*. Vol. 3: *The Bold Adventure September 1943–May 1949*. Columbia: University of South Carolina Press, 2015.

Foote, Shelby. *The Civil War: A Narrative, Fort Sumter to Perryville*. Vol. 1. New York: Random House, 1974.

———. *The Civil War: A Narrative, Red River to Appomattox*. Vol. 3. New York: Random House, 1974.

Fuchs, Richard. *An Unerring Fire: The Massacre at Fort Pillow*. Mechanicsburg, PA: Stackpole Books, 2002.

The Galena City Directory. Galena: H. H. Houghton & Co., 1854

Gates Jr., Henry Louis. *The Black Church: This Is Our Story, This Is Our Song*. New York: Penguin Press, 2021.

Glatthaar, Joseph T. *Forged in Battle: The Civil War Alliance of Black Soldiers and White Officers*. New York: The Free Press, 1990.

Grant, Ulysses S. *Personal of Memoirs U.S. Grant*. Vol. 2. New York: Charles L. Webster & Co., 1886.

Hardy, Ruth Gillette. "A Brief Memoir of the Reverend Charles Gillette, Prepared by Ruth Gillette Hardy." Brooklyn, NY: unpublished paper, Dec. 1, 1941. Found in the archive at St. David's Episcopal Church, Austin.

Hobart, Chauncey. *Recollections of My Life: Fifty Years of Itinerancy in the Northwest.* Red Wing, MN: Red Wing Printing Co., 1885.

———. *History of Methodism in Minnesota.* Red Wing, MN: Red Wing Printing Co., 1918.

Houston, James D. *Bird of Another Heaven.* New York: Alfred A. Knopf, 2007

Kearns Goodwin, Doris. *Team of Rivals: The Political Genius of Abraham Lincoln.* New York: Simon & Schuster, 2005.

King, Jr., Martin Luther. *Strength to Love.* New York: Harper & Row, 1963.

———. *Why We Can't Wait.* New York: Harper & Row, 1964.

———. *Where Do We Go From Here: Chaos or Community?* New York: Harper & Row, 1968.

Kruse, Kevin M. *One Nation Under God: How Corporate America Invented Christian America.* New York: Basic Books, 2015.

Lewis, John. *Across That Bridge.* New York: Hyperion, 2012.

Lincoln, C. Eric, and Lawrence H. Mamiya. *The Black Church in the African American Experience.* Durham, NC: Duke University Press, 1990.

Long, John Dixon. *Pictures of Slavery in Church and State.* Philadelphia: Auburn Press, 1859.

Lytle, Andrew Nelson. *Bedford Forrest and His Critter Company.* Nashville: J. S. Sanders & Co., 1992. Originally published in 1931 by G. P. Putnam's Sons, New York.

MacCulloch, Diarmaid. *Christianity: The First Three Thousand Years.* New York: Penguin Books, 2009.

McConnell, Francis J. *Edward Gayer Andrews: A Bishop of the Methodist Episcopal Church.* New York: Eaton & Mains, 1909.

McPherson, James M. *Battle Cry of Freedom: The Civil War Era.* New York: Oxford University Press, 1988.

———. *The Negro's Civil War.* New York: Vintage Books, 1965. Reprinted in 1993.

Metzger, Bruce M., and Roland E. Murphy, eds. New Revised Standard Version. *The New Oxford Annotated Bible.* New York: Oxford University Press, 1994.

Murray, Pauli. *Dark Testament and Other Poems.* New York: W. W. Norton, 2018.

Newson, T. M. *Pen Pictures of St. Paul, Minnesota and Biographical Sketches of Old Settlers.* St. Paul, MN: Brown, Treacy & Co. Printers, 1886.

Paynter, Mary. *Phoenix from the Fire: A History of Edgewood College.* Madison, WI: Edgewood College, 2002.

Price, Sally, and Richard Price. *Romare Bearden: The Caribbean Dimension.* Philadelphia: University of Pennsylvania Press, 2006.

Quarles, Benjamin. *The Negro in the Civil War.* Boston: Little, Brown and Co., 1953. Reprinted by De Capo Press, 1989.

————. *Allies for Freedom & Blacks on John Brown.* New York: Oxford University Press, 1974. Reprinted by De Capo Press, 2001.

Rice, Lawrence D. *The Negro in Texas: 1874–1900.* Baton Rouge: Louisiana State University, 1971.

Richardson, James. *Willie Brown: A Biography.* Berkeley: University of California Press, 1996.

Simpson, Matthew, ed. *Cyclopædia of Methodism: Embracing Sketches of Its Rise, Progress, and Present Condition.* Philadelphia: Everts & Stewart, 1878.

The Sisters of St. Mary at Memphis: With the Acts and Sufferings of the Priests and Others Who Were There with Them during the Yellow Fever Season of 1878. Printed but not published, 1879. Transcribed by Elizabeth Boggs and Richard Mammana, 2000–2001.

Smith, Ruth Richardson. "A Memory Book," edited by Madge Richardson Walsh. Redding, CA: unpublished, 1991. Originally written 1907–1909 (Northfield, MI).

Stevens, Abel. *A Compendious History of American Methodism, Abridged from the Author's "History of the Methodist Episcopal Church."* New York: Eaton & Mains, 1867.

Stowell, Jay S. *Methodist Adventures in Negro Education.* New York: The Methodist Book Concern, 1922.

Street, Florence Richardson. "Reminiscences of the Family," edited by Madge Richardson Walsh. Portland, OR: unpublished, 1983. Originally written in 1943.

Taylor, Alan. *The Internal Enemy: Slavery and War in Virginia, 1772–1832.* New York: W. W. Norton & Co., 2013.

Thurman, Howard. *Jesus and the Disinherited.* Nashville: Abingdon Press, 1949. Reprinted by Beacon Press, 1996.

United States Congress, House Select Committee on the Memphis Riots. *Memphis Riots and Massacres,* July 25, 1866. Washington, DC: Government Printing Office.

United States War Department. *The War of the Rebellion: A compilation of the official records of the Union and Confederate armies.* Washington, DC: Government Printing Office, 1880–1901.

Ward, Andrew. *River Run Red: The Fort Pillow Massacre in the American Civil War.* New York: Viking, Penguin Press, 2005.

Wells, Ida B. *Crusade for Justice: The Autobiography of Ida B. Wells.* Chicago: University of Chicago Press, 2020. Originally published 1970.

Wesley, Charles. *Hymns for the New-Year's Day* 1750.

White, Ronald C. *American Ulysses: A Life of Ulysses S. Grant.* New York: Random House, 2016.

Wilkerson, Isabel. *Caste: The Origins of Our Discontents.* New York: Random House, 2020.

INDEX

Photographs are indicated by figure number.